THE CIVIL WAR BATTLES OF MACON

THE CIVIL WAR BATTLES OF MACON

Niels Eichhorn, PhD

The History Press

Published by The History Press
Charleston, SC
www.historypress.com

First published 2021

Manufactured in the United States

ISBN 9781467146944

Library of Congress Control Number: 2020945747

To Judy Gentry.

Content

Preface

Having written two books before, this was an extremely different book for me to write. I am a big-picture historian who likes to think about the impact of the United States on the world and vice versa. This was far from my usual line of work, doing a narrow-focused community study. Furthermore, usually people will tell you in the acknowledgements about the years of work, research, and writing. This book came about in the spur of the moment. I was and am still working on a larger study on mid-nineteenth-century diplomatic relations to finally contextualize transatlantic relations, but I needed a break from reading all those handwritten letters.

Having done tours for my own students as well as my wife's high schoolers related to Macon during the War of the Rebellion era, I had heard many times the sentence "I did not know..." regarding the battles that took place around the city, its industrial capacity and the sheer importance of the town to the Rebel war effort. During some downtime at the Southern Historical Association Meeting in Louisville, I cracked open the *Official Records of the War of the Rebellion* and started writing. I quickly developed the story lines for the individual battles but realized that I had to provide the reader some background as well.

What struck me immediately were the events in July 1864, when George Stoneman's U.S. cavalry appeared before Macon. I had attended the reenactment event hosted by Ocmulgee National Historical Park in 2014 to commemorate the sesquicentennial events and contributed a paper in November to its small conference. At the time, I had not thought much about writing a book on the topic. However, as I embraced more of a memory focus in my teaching, I heard more from my students about the lack of remembrance of these events around Macon.

My students had done a few projects in the past about local history sites that had piqued my interest: the "cannonball"-struck Asa Holt House in downtown Macon, with one student suggesting that the proper term should be the "Hotchkiss Shell House." As I looked into the story, I was first surprised that public memory has completely forgotten the Rebel shell that hit the Dunlap Farm House and forced the widow to evacuate her home. At the same time, there were some uncertainties with regard to the range of the artillery pieces on Dunlap ridge. I greatly appreciate the help from Chattanooga and Chickamauga National Military Park's park historian, James Ogden. He is an invaluable resource for anything in the Tennessee and Georgia region.

As I tried to establish the story and realized that my initial research had not uncovered any mention in the local paper about the shot, I returned for more work at Washington Memorial Library in Macon. I found Reference Assistant Cynthia Blunt's help in locating some additional information about the Asa Holt House incredibly valuable.

Furthermore, the addition of a chapter on the memorial landscape in Macon was greatly enhanced by the brief exchanges I had with Angela Bates at Ocmulgee National Historical Park and Judd Smith, the parks historian of the Georgia Parks, Recreation and Historic Sites Division.

Of course, friends and family were invaluable in making this project a reality. I want to thank John Legg and David Schieffler for their helpful comments and conversations. Furthermore, my wonderful wife read the entire manuscript, despite her passionate dislike of military history. Even more, Stephanie and our three quadrupeds were a welcome break from the writing process as we chased the legacies of Sherman around Middle Georgia on our weekly hiking adventures.

I am dedicating this book to my friend and mentor Judy Gentry. Judy was an invaluable force directing me in my early days as an undergraduate at the University of Louisiana at Lafayette. She guided my interests in the diplomatic relations of the War of the Rebellion era with her keen eye for interpretation and unfailingly harsh ability to foster writing excellence. Her guidance and mentorship are still a significant part of who I am today as a scholar. It was a great shock when she revealed to me at the Southern in Little Rock that she had been diagnosed with a condition that would make it increasingly impossible to vocalize her thoughts. She had much more to say.

Introduction

Located on the banks of the Ocmulgee, right at the fall line of the river, the lush floodplains, elevated plateau and hilly surroundings of what eventually became the city of Macon had drawn people for millennia. The industrial, agricultural transportation hub that was Macon drew people and, in the course of the rebellion, enemy forces. When the cannons and small arms fire interrupted the hot and humid July day in 1864, Macon's perception of safety shattered. For the next year, Maconites were left to worry about the possibility of U.S. forces attacking and destroying the city. Its crossroads character underwrote Macon's success but also made the city a target in 1864 and 1865.

In ancient times, the Mississippian culture had recognized the benefits of this location and had established a vast town with mounds, funeral grounds, ceremonial sites and agricultural fields. As Mississippians gave way to Muscogees and eventually European settlers, the location remained attractive as a crossroad for trade and transport. Macon's place as a railroad hub, river port and industrial center made the city ideal for the Rebel government to move its armory and arsenal to the town. However, those facilities made Macon a target once U.S. forces opened the gates to Georgia in late 1863 at Chattanooga.

Established in 1823, the city of Macon was a frontier outpost on the edge of white settlement but was also located along the cotton borderline, which pushed westward with it plantations and enslaved people. From its start, Macon symbolized the nineteenth-century South and the deep ties between slavery and agriculture.

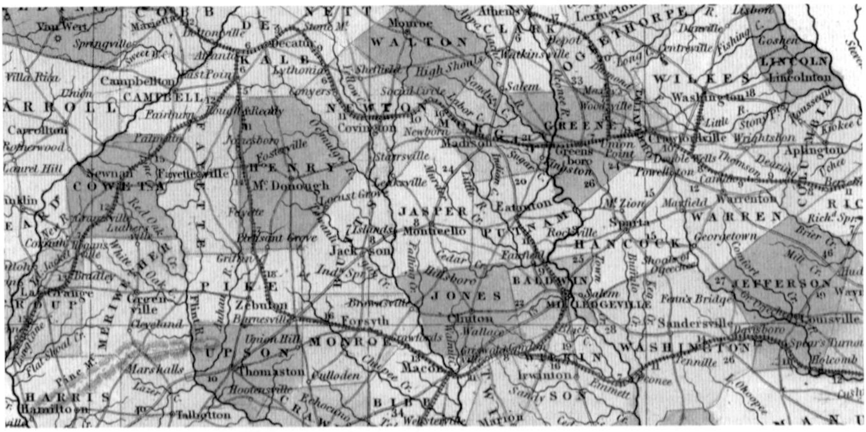

A New Map of Georgia, Philadelphia, Pennsylvania, Thomas Cowperthwait, circa 1854. *Hargrett Rare Book and Manuscript Library, University of Georgia Libraries.*

However, its river location made the city able to dominate its surrounding hinterland by drawing the products of the region to this inland port. From Macon's river landings, cotton and other agricultural products made their way down the Ocmulgee and Oconee Rivers to Darien, Georgia, on the Atlantic coast. While steamships plied the river, a new innovation placed boilers on wheels and tracks.

The arrival of the Central of Georgia Railroad altered Macon, transforming it from a dead-end port at the river fall line into a railroad hub. Not dependent on water levels or shut down during flooding, railroads were all-weather modes of transportation. The iron needs of railroads and plantations brought foundries to the city. By 1860, the city and county's more than sixteen thousand residents, free and enslaved, represented the South with its industry, agriculture, trade and modern transport system. However, the Macon South did not exist everywhere in the region and was still a rare South.

The outbreak of the rebellion, with South Carolina's secession and the firing on Fort Sumter, did not immediately alter Macon's role as a center of commerce. However, the fall of Fort Pulaski at the entrance of the Savannah River placed Savannah in danger, removing industrial facilities to Macon. The arrival of the arsenal—with the takeover of the Findlay Iron Works, the construction of the armory building on the edge of town and the Confederate laboratory in the Vineville suburb of Macon—converted the city into a major cog in the Rebel war machine. Therefore, Macon, besides Augusta and Columbus, was an essential location to materially support the war effort. Once William Tecumseh Sherman's armies advanced on Atlanta in May 1864, Macon increasingly realized the threat the advancing U.S. Army posed to the city.

This work is about the threats posed to Macon in the last year of the rebellion by U.S. cavalry generals George Stoneman, Judson Kilpatrick and James Wilson. It tells the story of the four engagements that occurred in the Macon area in June 1864, November 1864 and April 1865. Today, these events are largely forgotten, and Macon's landscape shows few visible reminders of these four battles.

Furthermore, previous studies about the battles at Macon have been rather one-sided. Despite using the vast trove of U.S. military documents, the narratives are usually slanted toward the Rebel defenders of the city. For example, works like William H. Bragg's *Griswoldville* and Richard W. Iobst's *Civil War Macon* presented a decidedly pro-Confederate view of the events on the battlefield. Moreover, their works are weak on military and battlefield tactical details. This study will go into greater detail of what took place on the battlefield and try to paint a vivid picture of the unfolding battles.

Furthermore, the military events around Macon have never been put into one study together. While Iobst described the two engagements at Walnut Creek in July and November 1864 and the occupation by General Wilson,

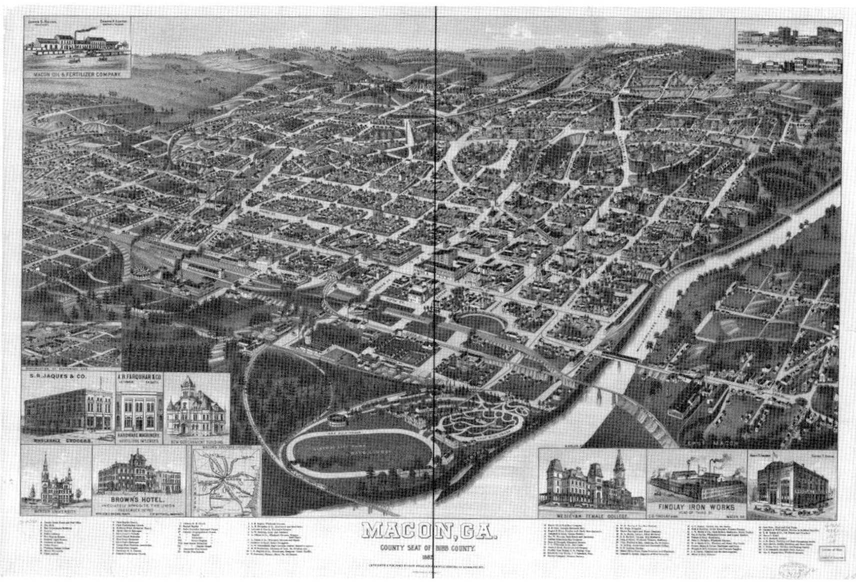

Macon, Georgia county seat of Bibb County. Henry Wellge, Adam Beck and Clemens J. Pauli, Printers. Henry Wellge & Company, Milwaukee, 1887. *Library of Congress.*

his work ignores the events of Griswoldville. Similarly, works on Wilson's raid unfortunately conclude with the capture of Columbus and not his follow-up work in Macon and the arrest of Jefferson Davis. This book, for the first time, groups all four military engagements together, allowing readers to see the threats Macon faced from U.S. cavalry forces.

The battles around Macon only involved a few hundred men and never reached the level of destruction and human death that the more familiar engagements at Chickamauga, Shiloh or Gettysburg caused; nevertheless, the battles of Macon are a good reminder that every community in the Southern states was liable to suffer as a result of the rebellion. Macon's industrial capacity made the city a target, and despite many threats, it never suffered occupation until the surrenders of Generals Lee and Johnston had technically put an end to the rebellion. Similarly, large battles were not the normal experience for soldiers in either army. They were far more likely to face boredom, drill and the more frequent small skirmishes that occurred around Macon. Macon's story is one of the many that challenge us to rethink the war beyond the stereotypes of an industrial North versus an agrarian South or that Sherman brought wholesale destruction to all of Georgia.

Chapter 1

Macon's Creation

With its lush vegetation, the broad Ocmulgee River and its floodplain provided a perfect environment for agricultural pursuits. The fertile area's agricultural benefits provided a suitable home for vast civilizations. Since ancient times, people had realized the benefits of the location along the river and used the rivers and paths in different directions for trade. What native peoples started on foot or in canoe, Europeans replaced with steamboats and the railroad. By 1860, Macon had become a transportation hub carrying the slave-produced agricultural products of the region to the world market.

Settled as early as seventeen thousand years ago by hunters and gathers, the Macon plateau eventually became home of the moundbuilding Mississippians. Their town—with its large temple mounds, earth lodge, residences and vast fields—became a trade center. Frequent floods ensured the fertility of the fields and prosperity of this hierarchical civilization. The decline of the Mississippian culture, European arrivals and the emergence of the Muscogee people meant that human civilization continued relatively uninterrupted on the banks of the Ocmulgee even as the faces and identities of the people changed.[1]

One of the earliest Europeans to write about the Macon plateau was the naturalist William Bartram, who had come up from the Atlantic coast. He reached the "Oakmulge," where the river and the trading path from Augusta intersected. Here, he came upon the fields and crops of the Muscogee people. He reported his observation that the trade path "runs nearly two miles through ancient Indian fields, which are called the Oakmulge fields: they are the rich low lands of the river." As he looked around, he saw the evidence of the old Mississippian town, with its "artificial mounts or terraces, squares and banks, encircling considerable areas."[2] Bartram most likely realized the importance of the location for a future inland town.

Obtaining the land on the banks of the Ocmulgee from its native occupants was a long process. The U.S. government and the Muscogee people signed a series of treaties in the first quarter of the nineteenth century as the native people surrendered more and more of their land to the white invaders. As the European settlement frontier encroached on more and more of their land and treaties got broken, the Muscogees slowly ceded the land east of the Chattahoochee River to the United States and the State of Georgia. Bibb County came into existence by an act of the state assembly in 1822, named after William Wyatt Bibb, Alabama's first governor and a former Georgia senator.[3]

Following the decision to create Bibb County, the state incorporated the city of Macon in 1823. The state outlined how the new city's government would operate. Governing the town were elected city commissioners, who faced the voters annually. In addition, the city and county had a judicial system with the creation of the inferior court and justices of the peace.

In order to turn the abstract Macon into a reality, the state authorized the commission to prepare the town's layout and start selling plots of land—"the commissioners of appointed to lay out the town of Macon are hereby authorized and required, within three months from the passage of this act, to sell not exceeding forty half acre lots adjoining those already sold in said town of Macon." However, the act prohibited the sale of lots on the river.[4] Macon's location was well selected, situated at the fall line of the Ocmulgee River. The unobstructed flow of the river to the ocean allowed Macon to become an important inland port.[5]

Once the state had incorporated Macon as a city, the new town had to provide its residents some basic essentials, such as a cemetery and banking institutions. To locate a suitable place for the city's cemetery, the state selected a four-acre plot of land near Fort Hawkins, where two burial grounds already existed. In addition, the state ordered the Bank of Darien to open a branch in Macon, close its branch in Marion and transfer all funds from Marion to Macon.[6] The small town of Macon made its appearance on the map, and soon visitors started to appear.

On March 29, 1825, only two years after the city's incorporation, Gilbert du Motier, Marquis de La Fayette (Anglicized to Lafayette) and his entourage visited this small frontier outpost. They arrived from Milledgeville. The citizen of Macon welcomed the famous French guest and former revolutionary leader with great enthusiasm. The city hosted a dinner in his honor.

With the city having only recently come into existence, Auguste Levasseur recorded, "Macon, which is a small and handsome village, tolerably populous, did not exist eighteen months since; it has risen from midst of the forests as if by enchantment. It is a civilized speck lost in the yet immense domain of the original children of the soil." The group realized that within only a short distance the land was untamed, "virgin forests." The forests were old and had not yet made way for the growing agricultural empire of the Southeast.[7]

As the city matured over the next few years, its spiritual needs required attention. In the age of the Second Great Awakening, people sought spiritual guidance, and revival meetings were common. To satisfy the religious needs of people, the state incorporated Presbyterian, Episcopalian, Methodist and Baptist churches for the city.[8]

In addition, as the city continued to grow, the city commissioners had to satisfy the land hunger among interested parties, but they could only sell up to forty plots per year. At the same time, the state worried about the preservation of the timber supply in the city's immediate surroundings. Some land on the southwestern side of the city, the state suggested, should not be sold and instead remain a timber reserve. The state legislated that anybody who cut down a tree wider than two inches and two feet above the ground, except for a pine tree, would be liable for "malicious mischief."[9] These odd policies by the state ensured the existence of sufficient building material as the city continued to grow.

By 1829, the city had reached a level where the state had to seriously investigate infrastructure needs and work on Macon's connectivity with the rest of the state, laying the foundation for Macon's future as a transport hub. In order to facilitate an easy crossing of the Ocmulgee River, the state allocated $25,000 for the construction of a bridge. The city had to allot land for the "butment" on each side of the river. The road across the new bridge was supposed to enter the city at Fifth Street.[10] Importantly, this bridge eventually connected Macon with the state capital of Milledgeville.

However, before construction could start, a survey was necessary to ensure the correct placement of the bridge along the banks. Aware that the bridge would contribute to the city's prosperity and likely see a significant amount of traffic, the state implemented safety measures. The state required that if anybody raised doubts about the bridge's safety, the justices of the inferior

"Market Scene in Macon, Georgia." 1867. Wood engraving of sketch by A.R. Waud. *Harper's Weekly*, July 13, 1867. *Library of Congress.*

court should immediately proceed to the bridge and make a survey assessing its condition. The city was responsible for the repairs and its costs. During the closure of the bridge, the city had to implement a ferry service to connect the eastern and western banks of the Ocmulgee. The rope ferry originated at Sixth Street and charge the same as the bridge toll.[11] As a result, Macon improved its connectivity with the rest of the state.

The connection between the two banks of the river contributed to the growth of the town on both banks. However, the homes on the eastern bank were not part of Macon. Even as transportation across the river remained a handicap, ever more people settled on the eastern bank of the Ocmulgee, creating the municipality of East Macon. In 1829, the state determined to extend Macon's municipal boundaries to that side of the river and integrate the homes and residents of East Macon into Macon.[12] As a result of the need for a better organization of the city government, the state divided the city into four wards.[13] With the incorporation of East Macon, Macon officially occupied both banks of the river.

Macon attracted not only more residents but also workshops, raising the specter of an industrial society akin to British society. As a result, the state permitted the creation of the Mechanic Society of Macon, a trade union.

The law required that the organization "be not repugnant to the constitution and laws of this state." [14] The appearance of a trade union signaled the arrival of industry in Macon.

In addition to permitting the creation of a trade union, the state also incorporated the Monroe Rail Road Company in 1833. The new company was permitted to provide service between Macon and Forsyth. With this railroad, Macon laid a foundation that eventually turned the city into a railroad hub. Soon after, the state also incorporated the new Central Rail Road and Canal Company of Georgia, which was supposed to provide service between Savannah and Macon.[15] These two lines provided the backbone of the emerging railroad network in the state and ensured Macon's future as a transport center.

In addition to the Monroe Railroad to Forsyth and Central Railroad to Savannah, there was also a proposal for the Western Railroad Company that appeared in 1835. The Western Railroad Company stood in competition to the Monroe Railroad. The two companies ran parallel between Macon and Forsyth, but the Western intended to continue onward to West Point (Troup County) or somewhere in the vicinity of the town. The state left it open to the company whether to continue construction to the Alabama and Tennessee state lines, as well as whether to build a spur line to Milledgeville, should the company decide to construct a network on the eastern shore of the Ocmulgee River.[16]

Since railroads were costly enterprises, charters for new railroad companies often included banking to allow the company to raise enough funding for the construction of tracks, purchase of rolling stock and other necessary equipment.

After numerous attempts, in 1836, the state once more authorized a bank for Macon, the Ocmulgee Bank of the State of Georgia. The starting capital of the new financial institution was set at $500,000, "divided into five thousand shares of one hundred dollars each." Subscription for stock was possible in Macon, Forsyth, Thomaston, Perry, Clinton, Hawkinsville, Marion and Monticello.[17] With railroads and banking, Macon continued its rise as a trade hub.

Furthermore, a growing city with wooden structures faced a constant fire danger; as a result, more than a decade after its creation, the state authorized Macon to create two fire companies. Each company included between thirty and fifty persons, who elected their four officers. Once the two companies had presented themselves to the mayor, they had the right to use Macon's fire engines. Like in other states, members of fire companies were exempt from militia service.[18] However, they were not excluded from the military draft instituted by the Rebel government in the course of the 1860s.

Despite the emergence of the railroad as a new means of transportation, the slow pace of construction offered steamship companies opportunities to continue to move vast quantities of cotton down the rivers. However, obstacles in the river hampered the voyage. In 1835, the state provided $10,000 for the improvement of the navigation on the Ocmulgee between Macon and the Oconee River. The plan did not call for a widening or deepening of the river, but simply the removal of debris.[19] Furthermore, in 1838, the state incorporated the Washington Steam Boat Company in Macon, making sure that the river traffic continued unabated.[20] River transport remained an important aspect of Macon's existence as a transport hub.

Therefore, the state frequently suggested making improvements to the Ocmulgee to make the trip for steam vessels easier and safer by deepening and widening the river, as well as clearing more dangerous debris. The first steamship to reach Macon was the *North Carolina* on January 13, 1829. Eventually, companies even built steamboats in Macon, stretching the vessels as large as the river could accommodate to maximize the haul of cotton taken to the coast. Some vessels carried more than seven hundred bales. By 1842, there were eight steamers operating on the river between Macon and Darien.[21] Inevitably, railroads took over much of the steamboat traffic.

Before any construction or even grading work could start, much less the laying of track, the railroad companies had to survey possible routes to locate the most suitable land for construction along the entire length of the proposed line. As early as 1834, "an experimental survey" had confirmed that construction along the "Northern Route," north of the Oconee and Ocmulgee Rivers, was the best option. After the incorporation of the Central of Georgia, the company undertook another survey in 1836, which started in Macon, specifically at the courthouse, measuring an elevation of "386 feet above Tide water." The survey sketched out the topographic difficulties and challenges as well as solutions of the surroundings of Macon and how the railroad might make its final approach into the city without too much excavation and cost incurred.[22] The city was ready to embrace the new age of transportation.

By 1839, the city looked vastly different from what La Fayette had seen. In March, the former British Member of Parliament James Silk Buckingham visited Macon. Buckingham approached Macon like La Fayette had, from Augusta and Milledgeville. He was already cross that he could not locate a daytime conveyance between the state capital of Milledgeville and Macon; however, three nighttime coaches existed. The coach departed Milledgeville at 9:00 p.m. and had completed the thirty miles to Macon by 4:00 a.m. Buckingham noted, "The wretched state of the ordinary roads thus operates as an additional stimulus to the construction of railroads."[23]

Upon his arrival, Buckingham settled into the Central Hotel for a week, impressed by the town's prosperity. He delivered lectures at the recently constructed Presbyterian church. In fifteen years, Macon had grown to about eight thousand residents, about three thousand of whom were enslaved, with a prospering cotton economy built on the latter's backs and labor.[24]

Macon sat in prime agricultural land with thousands of bales of cotton leaving the city every year. Apprehensively, Buckingham wrote, "The labourers employed are wholly negro slaves," mixing two distinctive and contradictory labor systems together. He noted that cotton slavery was not as brutal as rice and sugar growing. Nevertheless, enslaved people "are in the same dark, degraded, and hopeless state as the African race generally throughout the Southern States." At the same time, field slaves as "instruments of production, are maintained with as little cost as possible."[25] Despite some terminology issues, Buckingham provided an eloquent description of the town and its enslaved population.

For his British readers, Buckingham also provided a vivid description of the layout of Macon as a typical southern town:

> *The plan of Macon, like that of nearly all the towns in the United States is remarkably regular; the streets run at right angles with each other, and are from 100 to 120 feet in breadth. The houses are mostly of wood; many of these are spacious and elegant; and some of the private dwellings are of brick, well built and in good taste. The public offices are large, well proportioned, and indicative of a rising and prosperous city. The City Hall is among the most prominent of these; it stands in a fine open space at the end of one of the principle streets, which displays it to great advantage.*[26]

Furthermore, Macon already had suburban extensions for the rich. The valley on the westside of town contained a "cluster of villas and cottages, to which the wealthy inhabitants retire in the hot season." The hill separating Macon from the valley of wealth contained additional private mansions and the unfinished building of the women's college, which eventually became Wesleyan College. Buckingham assumed that the school had room for 200 boarders and another 200 day-scholars. Even before its completion, 150 young ladies had already enrolled at the school, which Buckingham equated to other female academies in the country.[27]

Highlighting how Macon dominated its hinterland, Buckingham noted that the city had three newspapers: *Telegraph*, *Messenger* and *Southern Post*. All three papers were weekly and aligned with political organization and southern ideologies.[28] In addition, the city had five churches: Episcopalian, Presbyterian, Methodist, Baptist and Universalist. He was surprised to find "Hardshelled Baptists" in the city, a group he was unfamiliar with.[29] Finally, Buckingham pointed to the importance of the two fire brigades since twice in the past year alone, arson incidents had threatened the city.[30] The Macon Buckingham saw was not the small frontier enclave La Fayette had stayed in—it was a vibrant economic center.

As pointed out by Buckingham, the road network around Macon was dismal, and the city's future and well-being required more new roads and the repair of old ones. The state legislature required that the county's inferior court appoint commissioners to oversee these activities. All men in the county, even the enslaved, had to provide labor for road projects and bring their own tools. Similar to militia service, men were only required to do twelve days per year and no more than three days in a row.[31]

Since this was rather cumbersome work, the city eventually decided to contract out such construction and repair work. As a result, the Tobesoufsky Causeway in 1834 was a private project by Robert Collins and John Bailey, who operated the road and collected a toll from all users, helping to repay their initial construction investment.[32] Despite improvements in the roads around town, the future remained with the Central of Georgia.

The Central of Georgia Railroad had initially only included the line from Savannah to Macon. From Macon, there were other lines to Columbus, Atlanta and Milledgeville, but these were constructed and operated by individual small companies. Just like Macon desired the opportunity to be a transport hub, Savannah's desire to remain competitive with Charleston had sparked the construction of the Central of Georgia Railroad. When Charleston's business interests started work on the railroad connection with Hamburg, which would open the Savannah River hinterland and Augusta region, Savannah's merchant community had to act.[33]

After putting in place the initial charter and raising the necessary money for construction, the Central of Georgia Railroad and Banking Company formally began operations in January 1836. By May 1838, the company's first engines were running on the first twenty-six miles of track out of Savannah; another sixty-seven miles were ready for track laying. Even by November 1840, the tracks were still seventy miles from Macon. On October 13, 1843, the Central of Georgia officially opened the final stretch into Macon.[34] Maconites celebrated the opening of the line and their new role as a transport center.

The seven years of construction were costly for the Central of Georgia Railroad. The 190 miles came to $2.5 million or $13,000 per mile. Despite running about $200,000 over budget, the costs were only half per miles what other routes in the country paid for construction, which later historians attributed to "the level character of the country, the lightness of the rail, and to the excellence and economy of administration." Potentially the use of slave labor contributed to the lower costs as well. The huge debt burden was a problem for the company, as cotton prices remained depressed in the 1840s, meaning low earnings on freight. Adding to its woes was the bankruptcy of the Monroe Railroad in 1845, cutting earning in half briefly.[35] Macon's success was closely tied to that of the Central of Georgia, and there was some worry.

Like Atlanta to the north, Macon became a hub for the emerging railroad network in the state. Besides the Central of Georgia, Macon was the terminus of the Macon and Western Company (the former Monroe Railroad), which by 1853 "had a good and thoroughly equipped road, with a small debt, and under a fairly sound administration." The company provided easy service into Atlanta 103 miles distant. In addition, there was the "petty line" of the Thomaston and Barnesville Railroad, only 16 miles long, a branch off from the Macon and Western constructed between 1843 and 1847. Sold at auction after bankruptcy, the Central of Georgia absorbed this feeder line.[36] Many other feeder lines tried to raise adequate capital; some made it, but many did not.

Since the Central of Georgia faced stiff competition from steamships during the high-water months, the railroad reduced rates for cargo to draw traffic from the river. At the same time, "Rates on goods hauled for planters remained low at all times," supporting the cash crop production in the Middle Georgia region. However, Macon's city leaders were not happy when they realized that the rate policies of the Central of Georgia seemed disadvantageous to the area's planters. The city threatened a lawsuit to force the railroad company to change rates. The cause of disagreement was that Griffin shippers paid only thirty-one cents for every one hundred pounds of cargo in contrast to Macon's forty-five cents for the same amount and a shorter distance.[37] Despite embracing the railroad hub nature of their city, Maconites also quickly realized the issues railroads brought with them.

As the railroad network around Macon grew in size and scope, there were calls to construct a railroad bridge across the Ocmulgee into Macon for the Central of Georgia. However, there was opposition; city leaders worried that Macon might deteriorate from being the terminus of the Central of Georgia to becoming a mere stopping point along the route. Such a change could dramatically alter the economic impact of the railroad.[38] With the railroad bridge constructed over the Ocmulgee, Macon was a leading railroad center in Georgia.

From its humble beginning as a frontier town on the Ocmulgee in the 1820s, Macon grew in the three decades before the secession winter of 1860 into a trade and transportation hub. Like native people, white Europeans selected the Macon plateau on purpose to use the Ocmulgee River to ship agricultural products, grow crops on the fertile floodplains around the city and benefit from a global demand for cotton. The arrival of the Central of Georgia and other railroad companies added to Macon's connectivity and reach. By 1860, Macon had connections to virtually all parts of the state and as a transportation hub provided essential service to the state and its people.

Chapter 2

Macon in the Civil War

The secession of eleven Southern states following the constitutional election of Republican presidential candidate Abraham Lincoln and the outbreak of violent rebellion with the firing on Fort Sumter in Charleston Harbor had a dramatic impact on Macon. The city's location in the heart of Georgia meant long distances to the front lines, a protected and sheltered location and a refuge for people.

By the 1850s, Macon had not only dominated its hinterland with the river and railroad network radiating out, but the city also provided its surroundings with tools and equipment. As a result, a series of iron foundries emerged in the city to support the agricultural and railroad sectors. These ironworks provided the backbone on which the Confederate military-industrial complex turned the city into a vital supply center for the war effort. However, those very industrial capacities were also what made Macon a target for William Tecumseh Sherman and George H. Thomas's cavalry forces in the last year of the war.

When on December 20, 1860, South Carolina used the recent election of Abraham Lincoln and the fear of what he would do to the institution of slavery to trigger secession, a mild euphoria swept through the Southern states, but support was not universal. In Georgia, Governor Joseph Brown ignored the popular will of the people for delay until Lincoln's inaugural and pushed the state out of the United States and into alliance with its neighbors. Georgia became a founding member of the Confederate States of America, but its commitment was reluctant at best.[39]

By the time of the secession winter in 1860, Macon had a population of 16,289 residents. There were 6,790 enslaved people toiling on the plantations around Macon. Of the county's large planters, 26 had five hundred acres of land, compared to the 196 farms with fewer than 100 acres. One person in the county owned 100 slaves, and 222 residents owned between 10 and 100 slaves. In addition, there were 41 free people of color living in the county, about half in the city and the other half in the surrounding county.[40] Macon was a relatively typical southern urban environment, with its enslaved urban population and the enslaved on the plantation estates in the surrounding county.

However, Macon was not typical and does not fit the stereotypes some have of the South. Macon and its surroundings were not solely an agricultural society. Georgia in particular had made great strides in the prior thirty years to embrace industry. For a while, Athens was the largest industrial center in the state.[41] However, by the 1850s, other cities had also embraced industrial development, turning the states that eventually constituted the Confederacy in 1860 into one of the top five most industrialized regions in the world. Macon contributed greatly to the strength of Confederate industry.

Macon was a town with significant economic diversity. T. Addison Richard provided a snapshot of Macon in 1860 for the Appletons' travel guide. The city had a population of about nine thousand residents, but Richard did not break down the number between free and enslaved people. Guests could reach the city from various directions. "From Augusta, by the Augusta and Waynesboro, 53 miles, to Millen," Richard reported, "on the Central Railway, thence, 112, by the Central road from Savannah." Milledgeville had a direct line to Macon. The Georgia Railway connected Macon with Atlanta; meanwhile, the South Western Railways connected Macon with Columbus, Americus, Muscogee and Fort Valley. For those having arrived in Macon, the only accommodation available was the Lanier House Hotel. Tourist-minded guests could visit Georgia Female College, Rose Hill Cemetery, the fancy homes on "Lamar's Mound" and the "pleasant suburban village of Vineville."[42] The guidebook made no reference to the native mounds on the east bank of the Ocmulgee; however, Richard did not mention Macon's industrial capabilities either.

By that April, when the rebellion turned violent, Macon had developed into a small industrial center in central Georgia. Among the leaders of this process of industrialization was the Findlay Iron Works. Born in Scotland, Robert Findlay had come to the United States in 1828. A decade later, he came to Georgia, delivering a locomotive to the Monroe

Railroad. He and his cargo traveled up the Altamaha and Ocmulgee Rivers, as the only proper means of conveying such a heavy item was by riverboat. Upon reaching Macon, Findlay had to construct a temporary track from the river to the track already laid by the Monroe Railroad farther inland. By November 22, Findlay was ready to test the engine. In mid-December, the track from Macon to Forsyth was complete, and Findlay's engine and passenger cars were making the short journey between the two cities.[43] Realizing the future of Macon as a transport hub and the need for iron products, Findlay perceived that the city offered him many professional opportunities.

Findlay determined to remain in Macon after he completed his delivery to the Monroe Railroad. He purchased a plot of land on the Columbus Road for ten dollars at a sheriff sale. In October 1839, he invested in the Macon Brass and Iron Works, owned by Nathaniel Smith and William John McElroy. Soon the company enhanced its profile to include larger products up to steam engines. Problems between the partners ended with Smith selling his stake to his partners, and in 1841, Findlay bought out McElroy. However, McElroy retained ownership of the brass works, separate from the ironworks.[44] The Macon Brass and Iron Works was reconstituted as the Findlay Iron Works.

By 1847, Findlay had expanded his operation, purchasing adjoining properties. As a major producer and employer in the city, including enslaved people, Findlay received many special favors from the city council, such as a twenty-dollar-per-year fee for unlimited use of the Ocmulgee toll bridge by one horse-drawn wagon and one dray. He also got permission to build a railroad spur to his factory, but only if the cars were horse-drawn. Findlay, by selling his products throughout the Deep South, helped put Macon on the map industrially. His product line of iron-made commodities for textile factories allowed Findlay to benefit from the massive cotton growing operations in the region.[45] Besides supporting the cash crop agricultural business, Findlay branched out into other areas.

By November 1853, Findlay was advertising his services in the local newspapers: "Steam Engines and Boilers of any required form and size; Circular, Single and Gangsaw Mills, on the most approved plan, by steam or water power. Machinery for Flouring and Grist Mills, Sugar Mills, Syrup Boilers, Bullock's Cotton Press, Gin Gearing, Bark Mills, Car Wheels, Iron Castings, Hodgkiss Water Wheels, French Burr, Esopus and Cologne Mill Stones, Brass Castings, Parker's Water Wheels." Findlay prided himself on offering work "equal to that of the first class establishments at the North" at similar prices.[46] By the mid-1850s, the Findlay Iron Works was offering a diverse and multifaceted product portfolio on par with other industrial centers in the country.

The arrival of the Central of Georgia Railroad and the expensive rail network around the state allowed Findlay to increase his operations. As an iron foundry, Findlay directly catered to the needs of the new transport system. His success and the ease of communicating along rail lines allowed the foundry to expand geographically. In 1849, he opened an iron foundry in Griffin, a town created by the Monroe Railroad. Only an economic downturn in 1857 prevented a similar development with a Findlay-purchased property in Albany, Georgia.[47] Findlay was an expansion-minded industrialist.

In April 1851, Findlay revealed his plans for an expansion of his Macon foundry to encompass a full city block along Oglethorpe and Third Street on the southern side of Macon. At the cost of $20,000, Findlay constructed a two-and-a-half-story building with a width of 50 feet and length of 312 feet. Findlay installed 130 windows for natural light and ventilators to ensure air circulation. He even laid tracks to transport heavier products around the factory. The building was stuffed with a machine shops, finishing rooms, a smithy, foundry rooms and casting and woodworking machinery. Findlay's factory included other buildings with forges, office buildings and more. To produce the items sought around town, Findlay invested heavily in tools to make patterns for repetitive processes.[48] Findlay worked hard to maintain his ironwork's competitive advantage.

Despite Findlay's financial and industrial successes, planters were reluctant to patronize and invest in the foundry or industrial enterprises in general. At least Findlay and other industrialists could tap into the wealth of planters by borrowing money from them to expand their operations and help diversify the southern economy.[49] Dying on November 25, 1859, Findlay never witnessed what his company would eventually do for the Rebel war effort. Upon his death, his sons, James Nelson and Christopher DeSwan Findlay, took over and continued the profitable path set by their father.[50]

The Findlay Iron Works drew attention as the most important of Macon's industrial facilities. In February 1860, the *Weekly Georgia Telegraph* covered the imminent delivery of a stationery steam engine to Greenville, Alabama. The machine, No. 121, had twenty horsepower with "a cylinder of 12 inch bore…a stroke of eighteen inches and intended for 110 revolutions per minute." The success of the ironworks, with eight additional engines on order, forced the Findlays to hire more workers, as turnover at the factory

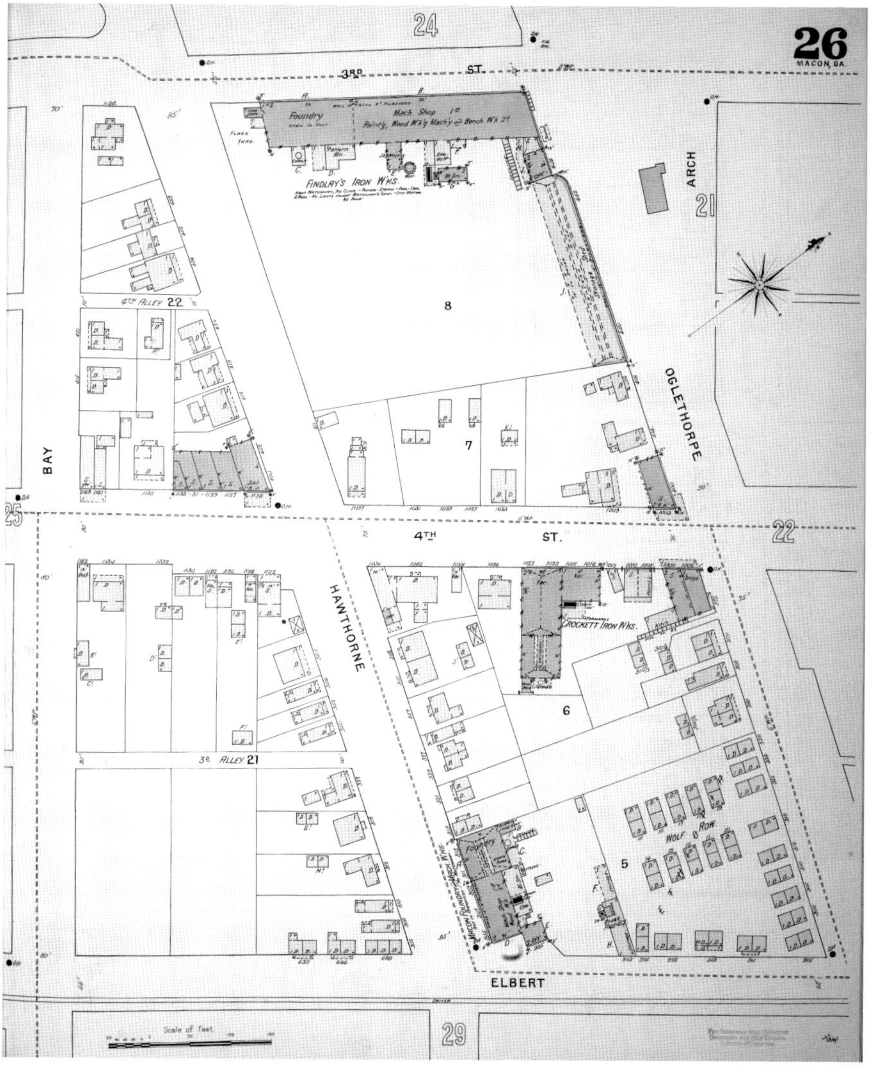

Page 26 of the 1895 Sanborn Map of Macon shows the location of the Findlay Iron Works building, which was the Confederate arsenal during the war. Not all buildings are visible and existing anymore. Sanborn Fire Insurance Map from Macon, Bibb and Jones County, Georgia. Sanborn Map Company, 1895. *Library of Congress.*

remained high. "Up to a little while ago," the reporter wrote, "they had 70 hands—now they have 50, and need an increase."[51] But the Findlay Iron Works was not alone.

In 1860, Macon had five foundries with 184 workers, a larger operation than the four foundries in Atlanta.[52] Besides Findlay, there was also the

Nisbet and Levy Iron Works. In 1855, T.C. Nisbet announced that he had bought out his partner, C.P. Levy. Nisbet continued the production of iron material at the foundry. Like Findlay, Nisbet produced, "STEAM ENGINES and BOILERS, SAW MILLS, UPRIGHT and CIRCULAR, BARK and SUGAR MILLS, GIN and MILL GEARING, WATER WHEELS, and CASTINGS, and MACHINERY IN GENERAL." Nisbet claimed that he employed in his company the "best Mechanics in the Southern country," promising satisfactory work and on-time delivery of orders. Furthermore, he had also reduced the prices for iron products to four cents per pound.[53] Nisbet tried to increase his operation and increase his market share versus Findlay.

In contrast to the Findlay Iron Works, the Nisbet and Levy Iron Works had a number of firsts to its record, including assembling the first steam engine in Macon. By mid-1855, the company was boasting about the assembly of one hundred such engines. Under Nisbet's leadership, the ironworks expanded into rice and sugar processing machinery.[54] While not as large as Findlay, Nisbet had a respectable operation, adding to Macon's status as an industrial center.

By the end of the 1850s, Findlay and Nisbet had gotten additional competition. John and Joshua Schofield had opened their own foundry and offered local residents "Steam Engines, Circular Saw Mills, Mill and Gin Gearing, Sugar Mills, Brass and Iron Castings, of every description." They even offered to beautify homes with iron railings. Like their competitors the Schofield brothers claimed that they offered "the most complete assortment of Iron Railings in the State." For those interested in sampling the work of the Schofield Iron Work, the advertisement pointed likely customers to Rose Hill Cemetery and private residences around the city.[55] Like Findlay, the Schofields were British immigrants.

John Shepley Schofield had arrived in Georgia from his native England in 1844. After initially working as a locomotive engineer, he started a small six-man operation in a log shed, his first foundry. The Schofield foundry initially split its work between producing directly for customers and producing for competitors like Findlay. As a machine tool maker, Schofield was in high demand. Apparently, nobody in the South had the ability to produce machine tools; in 1862, Schofield "added such machines to his product line."[56] Schofield brought a unique set of experiences to the Macon foundry scene.

In April 1862, Macon's industrial fate turned. The city previously had attracted the Confederate government's attention with its industrial facilities, but the interest in the protected city grew due to events along the coast.

On April 10, U.S. gunners on Tybee Island opened fire on Fort Pulaski, located on Cockspur Island in the Savannah River. U.S. General Quincy Gilmore had prepared to turn Fort Pulaski into a test case of the superiority of rifled artillery over masonry coastal forts. After more than thirty hours of unrelenting firing, U.S. gunners had opened a hole in the wall and threatened to hit the fort's powder magazine. The fort's commander surrendered.[57] As a result, Savannah was under threat of a U.S. occupation.

With the fall of Fort Pulaski, Confederate industrial activities in Savannah were no longer safe. Therefore, Richard Matthaei Cuyler had to locate a new site for Savannah's industrial capacity. Cuyler and the Findlays worked out an agreement where the government leased the ironworks for $25,200 per year. Cuyler hired Findlay's workers, rented the twelve largest warehouses in town, signed a contract with the Schofield Iron Works and turned the facility into a new arsenal to support the rebellion's military needs.[58] Cuyler quickly realized that Findlay's facility was insufficient for the new country's needs.

As a result, Cuyler added to the industrial campus of the Macon Arsenal. Since the Findlay furnaces were too small, the resulting cannons could rupture during firing and injure their crews; therefore, Cuyler built larger furnaces to cast cannons. He added a carpentry shop, a wheelwright shop, a mechanical hammer shop and even worker housing. However, besides the Findlays disagreeing with these additions to their ironworks, which they would eventually have to pay for, there were more fundamental problems, with money shortages affecting workers' pay and a lack of qualified workers.[59] The Confederate Arsenal suffered from the very problems the state faced.

With its staff of up to five hundred workers, dramatically larger than Findlay's Iron Works ever was, the Macon Arsenal produced shots, shells, pistols, rifles, ammunition and entire artillery batteries. Per day, the facility had an output of 125 artillery shells and 10,000 rounds of small arms ammunition. The arsenal produced some 80 cannons (twelve-pound Napoleons and ten- and thirty-pound Parrott guns), some of them used and captured by U.S. forces during the Battle of Chattanooga in late November 1863.[60]

Besides the Confederate Arsenal, the evacuation from Savannah also included the Confederate States Central Laboratory. The project to build a laboratory got underway in the fall of 1862 after the Rebel government purchased more than one hundred acres of land along the Macon and Western Railroad in the Vineville area. The decision to not build in Macon was largely due to the explosive risks that laboratories posed to

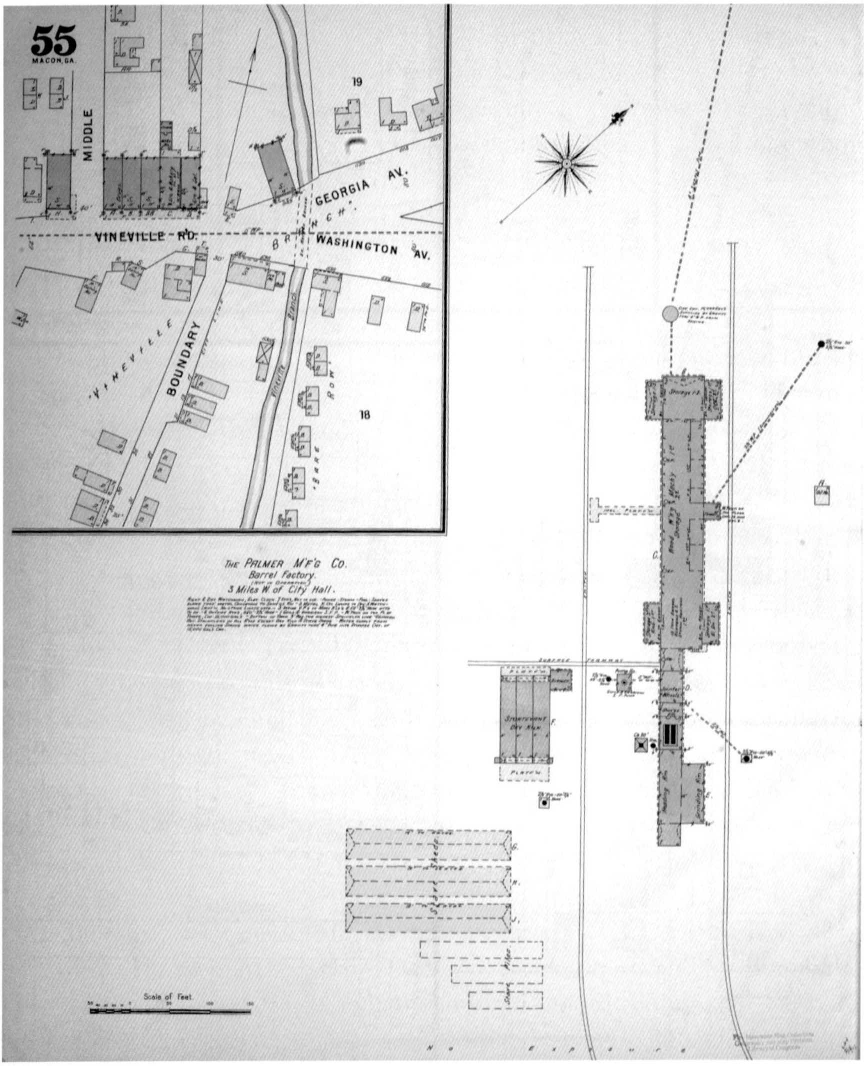

Page 55 of the 1895 Sanborn Map of Macon shows the location of what started as the Confederate Central Laboratory Building on Vineville Avenue. Sanborn Fire Insurance Map from Macon, Bibb and Jones County, Georgia. Sanborn Map Company, 1895. *Library of Congress.*

their surroundings. A number of accidents at other sites justified locating the laboratory in Vineville instead of Macon itself. The authorities rented enslaved people from the surrounding plantations to construct the building. However, delays plagued the progress to finish the permanent laboratory building. As a result, the rebellion ended before enslaved people completed the main structure. Nevertheless, T.C. Downie, the official in charge of the laboratory, did produce some molds for smoothbore muskets. He also ordered large amounts of supplies in England such as chemicals, twine and equipment.[61] The Confederate laboratory never reached the success of the arsenal.

In addition to arsenal and laboratory, Macon also gained a Confederate armory to produce weapons. The city had provided the central government an area west of the City Bridge. The land already contained several usable structures. In addition, the authorities worked out an agreement to use the old Macon and Western Depot. Besides the construction of buildings, James H. Burton also had to train people in the operation of machinery and toolmaking. Eventually, Burton obtained another forty-three-acre plot of land bordered by the Macon and Western Railroad, Calhoun, Hazel and Lamar Streets. Located on the edge of town, the site was perfectly suited for Burton's needs.[62]

Burton's workers at the armory were primarily responsible for weapon manufacturing and repair. Their first tasks were to repair two thousand gunstocks. With work steadily increasing, Burton had 136 workers in the armory by January 1863. He also rented enslaved people from slave owners around the region. Just like their colleagues at the arsenal, the armory staff faced constant shortages, especially in trained machinists and blacksmiths. Furthermore, like at the arsenal, the armory suffered an exodus of workers due to low or unpaid wages.[63] The military-industrial institutions at Macon were a microcosm for the rebellion itself, with its many problems.

Since its inception, southern industry was torn between using paid wage labor and renting or purchasing enslave African Americans. In *Civil War Macon*, Richard Iobst confusingly noted that the Rebel authorities at the armory had a difficult time locating "black laborers." This statement implies that Burton sought free people of color to work in the weapons industry. Iobst even wrote that Burton offered "salaries" of ten dollars per month plus food and clothing. Only then did Iobst confess that these "laborer" were enslaved people whom their masters rented out to the armory, pocketing the ten dollars for themselves. These were not "laborers"—these were enslaved men rented out by their masters to engage in more profitable business ventures than, for example, cotton planting.[64] This was similar to other southern industrial projects where slave and free labor uneasily coexisted. Furthermore, in Macon existed an uneasy balance between industry of destruction and caring for wounded.

Confederate artillery captured at Missionary Ridge at headquarters, Army of the Cumberland. Some of the straight muzzles, which indicate a Confederate make, had "A," "M" or "C" on the barrel, indicating their origins (Augusta, Macon or Columbus). *Library of Congress.*

Early in the conflict, nobody expected the war to last long and inflict heavy casualties. Once the first battles had shattered some of these perceptions, city leaders in Macon realized that they might soon have to care for wounded troops. After the first major, deadly engagement in the Western Theater at Shiloh Church, Rebel military authorities started to ship casualties to cities in the adjoining states. The Floyd House became the first hospital in Macon, housing some 200 to 250 wounded soldiers and assisting them in their recovery. One of the next major crises for the city's hospital system came in September 1863 after the Battle of Chickamauga (September 19–20, 1863). With Atlanta hospitals at capacity, Macon started to receive its first wounded on September 24. Even city hall served as a hospital in the immediate days after the battle.[65] Macon was then a hospital center as well as an industrial one.

In addition to Floyd House and city hall, Confederate authorities used the Academy of the Blind on Orange and College Streets as a hospital. In early 1864, it was reconstituted as the Ocmulgee Hospital; however, there apparently were several hospitals by that name. As the need for hospital

Confederate artillery captured at Missouri (i.e., Missionary) Ridge headquarters, Army of the Cumberland. Some of the carriages in this image have "Macon Arsenal" stenciled on them. *Library of Congress.*

facilities increased, authorities increased the size of the Ocmulgee Hospital. By the time of the Atlanta Campaign, starting in May 1864, Macon's various hospitals could accommodate about eight hundred patients. By the summer of 1864, the Ocmulgee Hospital then located on Walnut Street was providing care for hundreds of wounded soldiers.[66] The city was ready to receive casualties as General William T. Sherman and Joseph E. Johnston slugged it out north of Atlanta.

With Atlanta threatened by Sherman's army, its hospital facilities needed relocation. Medical Director S.H. Stout informed Maconites that the evacuation of sick and wounded from Atlanta, as well as the cutting of the Georgia and West Point Railroad, had forced the Army of Tennessee to send its wounded in the direction of Macon. Stout outlined the needs: "Labor, material of all sorts (lumber, straw, &c, &c.) wagon and ambulance transportation are much needed. Good and suitable houses for hospital purposes are in demand." He appealed to the patriotism of the city residents, hoping that such an appeal would yield positive results.[67]

The editors of the local newspaper added their own pleas for refreshments and support. Residents at Vineville especially could help transport wounded from the station to the nearby hospital. In addition, Stout had inquired whether planters could send enslaved people to help. The newspaper cautiously only referred to "negroes" putting up additional tents, avoiding the terminology of slavery.[68] Macon's status as a hospital town added to its importance for the war effort.

With the growing importance of Macon came also an increased need to provide for its defense. In the summer of 1864, the Confederate authorities recruited additional forces in and around the city under the promise that these troops would remain in the city. On July 14, 1864, M.H. Freeman posted in the *Daily Telegraph* a notice that he sought recruits for Findlay's Battalion. He explained that the secretary of war had promised that the soldiers "will not be removed from Macon, but kept here for…defense and guard duty." As much as this was an offer, there was a threat that if men did not enlist in the unit, they would soon face the draft.[69]

As the hazards of war drew closer to Macon, the authorities were anxious to enlist all the available men they could and threaten those who might try to evade military service. Major General G.W. Smith posted in the *Daily Telegraph* on July 20 that men should come forward and enlist in his company. He promised them that they would remain in the county for another ten days if they enlisted by the evening of the publication and would be employed to "assist in arresting and sending to the front, all who remained at home after the 20th, who are made subject to military service by the Governor's proclamation of the 9th last."[70] Apparently, few responded, as the call reappeared in the paper. The military situation in the rebellious states grew increasingly desperate as the calls for more recruits certainly indicates.

Recruiting men into military service had the unfortunate side effect of taking them out of the essential factories in the Macon area, which provided the armies in the field with critical war material. Macon was an essential cog in the machinery of the Rebel war effort. Besides providing shelter to wounded soldiers and nursing them back to health and fighting ability, the arsenal, armory and laboratory made Macon crucial to the success of the rebellion. However, the major military facilities in the city also meant that Macon had a large target painted on itself, inviting the enemy to attack.

Chapter 3

Atlanta Campaign, Stoneman's Raid and Dunlap Farm

On May 7, William Tecumseh Sherman set in motion the U.S. Armies of the Tennessee, Cumberland and Ohio. In the course of the next two and a half months, Sherman's forces advanced to the gates of Atlanta, one of the major industrial and transportation centers in Georgia. As the Siege of Atlanta became protracted, Sherman sought different ways to break the stalemate with sorties against the enemy supply lines and other industrial centers around the state. The first threat to Macon emerged from Major General George Stoneman's cavalry division, part of the Army of the Ohio, in July 1864. Macon repulsed the attack with ease, but the arrival of U.S. forces was a reminder of Macon's importance and vulnerability.

With Sherman surrounding Atlanta, Maconites feared for their city's well-being. The *Daily Telegraph* on July 26, a day before Stoneman set out on his raid, pointed to a number of cavalry raids in the environs of Atlanta. U.S. forces harassed Rebel supply lines and bases with relative impunity. Resistance was minimal. Cavalry units had struck out to Covington and destroyed railroad tracks and bridges. There were fears that Macon, Milledgeville and Eatonton might be targets as well. In addition, Conyers's depot had fallen victim to the raiding parties, as had the railroad lines toward Alabama.[71] Sherman's men tried to isolate the besieged John Bell Hood and his army in Atlanta by cutting all lines of supply and communication.

Faced with such an omnipresent threat all around the state, Major General Howell Cobb, commanding the Georgia Reserves, issued a reminder on July

"Major General Howell Cobb, Portrait, head and shoulders, facing left." Photograph, dated between 1861 and 1868. *Library of Congress.*

23 to the people regarding their duty to serve in the Confederate or Georgia military. Like the rebellion in general, Georgia also exempted any person who owned fifteen or more "able-bodied field hands" (slaves). Cobb noted that enrolling officers would continue to do their work and enlist new soldiers. With the threat of Sherman's army, the state needed to tap into all possible manpower resources.[72]

On July 27, at 3:00 a.m., Stoneman and his 1,800 cavalrymen set off from Decatur. The raid got off to a bad start from the very first moment. Stoneman marched his force past the "romantic 'Stone mountain,' standing as a lone sentinel keeping watch over a surrounding lovely country." As the men headed south to Covington, Mechanicsburg and Monticello, Stoneman discovered that he had false intelligence regarding crossing points over the Ocmulgee River. Instead of the supposed three bridges above Macon, there was none at all. As a result, Stoneman changed direction, heading south, directly toward Macon. He was going to wreak havoc on the Central of Georgia Railroad.[73]

As the officers debated their next move and approached Macon, Stoneman dispatched Colonel Adams to Mechanicsville to monitor enemy

Portrait of Major General George Stoneman, officer of the Federal army, image dated between 1860 and 1865. Brady's National Photographic Portrait Galleries. *Library of Congress.*

activities on the other side of the Ocmulgee. His orders called for Adams to "gain definite information as to crossings between the mouth of Yellow river and Macon, and to oppose any movement of the enemy on his flank." Waiting for a report from Adams, Stoneman halted his force for hours in Monticello.[74] Stoneman had made a grave error.

Unfortunately, "No communication from Colonel Adams at 12 o'clock (midnight); [Stoneman] became impatient; sent party to communicate, and ordered his command to join main column on the road to Macon."[75] The surprising lack of bridges and delay due to Adams's lack of communication hindered Stoneman's advance and allowed the enemy to prepare for his arrival.

As news of Stoneman's departure reached John Bell Hood in besieged Atlanta, he wired Secretary of War James Seddon in Richmond about the planned attack on the Central of Georgia Railroad. Hood explained that he had dispatched his cavalry in pursuit of the U.S. cavalry forces. In addition, he sent warnings to Macon and to the commander of Camp Sumter at Andersonville about the approaching threat.[76] As Stoneman's men trotted south, Cobb's men prepared to defend the city.

After Monticello, Stoneman took the road to Hillsboro and divided his small force. Major Davidson's 14th Illinois Cavalry, about 125 men, struck out toward Gordon to destroy the track of the Central of Georgia Railroad in the vicinity of that village and gallop on toward the Oconee River to destroy the railroad bridge over the river. His instructions were to "do all the damage he could, and bring his command out safely."[77] The Macon newspaper claimed that Davidson's command had orders to "destroy all the stations and water tanks from Gordon to the Oconee."[78] A small group of twelve men reached the Oconee bridge at Emmet and destroyed it.[79] Davidson's raid was an embarrassment for the Rebel authorities in Middle Georgia.

The *Telegraph* reported, "On arrival in sight of Gordon, they discovered that a train full of militia was on the way to Millegeville [*sic*], followed by a passenger train, and deeming it imprudent to attempt their capture, the raiders concealed themselves on the left of the railroad and allowed both trains to pass unmolested. As soon as they were out of sight they dashed into the town and proceeded in their work of destruction." The small group destroyed foodstuffs and "furniture, belonging to refugees." The "vandal" set ablaze more than 150 rolling stock. The citizenry, the paper reported, prevented much fire damage, and only forty cars suffered irreparable damage. Closing the account, the *Telegraph* pointed out that the raiders robbed the postmaster of Gordon of $11,000 in Confederate currency and a gold watch. While the paper lauded the efforts of the residents of Gordon in putting out the fires, the paper also scolded them for being unarmed and not having acted in defense of their town.[80] The arrival of U.S. forces in the region illustrated the lack of preparation and division on how to best deal with the enemy forces.

Further infuriating Macon's patriotic newspaper editor, the raiders had filled one engine's furnace with pine wood and set the engine at full throttle down the tracks to Griswoldville, where it hit a passenger car, "splitting it in two and throwing the two portions on both sides of the track." The engine quickly ran out of steam and did only little additional damage.[81] While the paper portrayed such actions as barbaric and unacceptable, at the same time, the paper cheered atrocities done in other parts of the country by individuals like Quantrill. As the surrounding suffered, Macon faced its own potential demise.

While Davidson caused havoc and Colonel Horace Capron's men advanced toward Macon, "Colonel Adams' brigade moved on right hand from Clinton to Macon, Colonel James Biddle's brigade on left-hand road, and Colonel Capron's brigade on the left to strike railroad." On July 30, the three wings charged forward toward Macon, brushing aside any resistance they faced. The advance was successful and got the U.S. troops to within one mile of the city.[82]

The main body of troops advancing on Macon were from Colonel Horace Capron's brigade. The brigade consisted of the 14th Illinois Cavalry, 8th Michigan Cavalry and McLaughlin's Ohio Squadron. The men had advanced down the country road from Hillsboro on July 29 until they were about four miles from Clinton (modern-day Gray). After passing through Clinton, Capron's men camped along the road about ten miles from Macon.[83]

On Friday, July 29, news had arrived in Macon by couriers that a large force of U.S. cavalry was on the way to the city. As a result, the authorities ordered all troops in the vicinity of the city to get ready for a potential battle, including the militia.[84] Howell Cobb determined to get as much advance notice as he could and sent Major W.S. Wallace with fifty-two cavalrymen in the direction of Clinton. The men departed at around 5:00 p.m. At the split of River Road and Clinton Road, Wallace ordered four men up the River Road to see if any enemy advanced from that direction. A few miles from Clinton, Wallace and his men encountered and engaged the enemy. Scattered by U.S. cavalry, Wallace eventually rallied fourteen men, but as they only had six muskets between then, he determined that the wisest thing to do was to withdraw to Macon.[85]

By noon, July 30, Confederate scouts had reported to Cobb that the enemy was about twelve miles from the city, yet the size of the enemy contingent remained unknown.[86] As a result, Macon's defenders started to cross the river and assume a defensive position on the high ground overlooking Walnut Creek and at the heights around the ruins of Fort Hawkins. Among the troops deployed to defend Macon was Findlay's Battalion, recruited among the ironworkers.[87]

As Macon's male population picked up arms to defend their home against U.S. forces, Macon certainly had an overabundance of commanders, especially a large set of high-ranking officers. As the fighting got underway, Howell Cobb and Joseph E. Johnston, the recently dismissed commander of the Army of Tennessee, arrived on the battlefield. Cobb asked Johnston to assume command. He refused but provided helpful suggestions.[88] This was likely for the better considering Johnston's military record over the previous three years. Macon was ready for the oncoming battle.

Cobb's work was complicated by the lack of crossing points over the Ocmulgee. On July 27 and 28, Cobb had struggled to ferry pickets across the river, despite appeals to the mayor of Macon, Stephen Collins, to provide better services during this emergency.[89] On Saturday, July 30, at 7:00 a.m., "several thousand" men took up a battle formation on the banks of Walnut Creek, awaiting the enemy. Among Macon's defenders were six hundred Tennesseans under Major John W. Nisbet, another one thousand militiamen and five hundred Macon Home Guard forces.[90] The *Macon Daily Telegraph* assumed that "the Federals moved up the river evidently disappointed at meeting so large a force to dispute his passage to Macon." Nevertheless, the U.S. troops were to destroy the bridge over Walnut Creek and a smaller trestle about one mile down the line. The paper claimed that only a small section of the railroad got damaged in the raid. Even more, blaming the inexperienced troops, the paper noted, "The bridge across Walnut Creek could have been saved had a proper degree of vigilance been exercised."[91]

While Rebel defenders prepared for their arrival, Stoneman's forces advanced toward the city from Clinton. As the cavalrymen of Colonel Biddle's brigade engaged the enemy, Capron's men received orders to destroy as much of the Central of Georgia Railroad as possible. Capron reported his men's work: "I divided my command into detachments, striking the railroad at different points from six and a half to three miles from the city, burned and destroyed 5 miles of track, 2 passenger trains, and 1 stock train loaded with hogs and horses, also destroyed 3 locomotives and burned 1 large machine-shop, within three miles of the city." In addition, Capron and Biddle's men burned the railroad trestle over Walnut Creek.[92] Major Haviland Tompkins confirmed that the assault resulted in the destruction of two burned bridges and the destruction of three cargo trains.[93] The raiders left a mark on the transport network. However, the fighting was not over.

Having been heavily involved in the course of the brief engagement, the 14th Illinois devoted some space in its regimental history to the fighting. The book reported, "Within four miles of Macon we met the enemy in force and pressed forward, driving him rapidly before us. Capron's brigade moved on the railroad fighting back the enemy." There even were opportunities for heroism. Lieutenant Albert B. Capron, Company A, 14th Illinois, observed a train approaching the area where the men destroyed the tracks. He "sprang upon an engine, standing on the track all fired up, and uncoupling it from its train, he seized the lever, opened the valve, and sent the engine with terrible speed to meet the incoming Johnnies; there was a terrible crash, but the amount of damage inflicted we never knew, as

Roughly the location where the U.S. cannons were during the first battle of Macon in July 1864, with the Dunlap House to the side. *Author's collection.*

we moved with alacrity from that position."[94] The Rebels certainly would not have viewed this as a heroic act, but keeping enemy forces away from battle maintained a balance on the battlefield.

Meanwhile, the fighting on the west bank of Walnut Creek continued. Capron's men had pushed the enemy back toward Fort Hawkins, "an old U.S. fort standing on the east side of the Ocmulgee River on a hill commanding both the bridge crossing and the city." The Rebel forces had fortified the hill around the fort, including the construction of abatis.[95]

Unfortunately, the attack was unable to proceed beyond Fort Hawkins. U.S. cavalry forces had hoped that Colonel Adams's command would arrive along the River Road from the northwest and open a second front against the defenders. The regimental history of the 14th Illinois noted that "after several hours of anxious waiting no attack was made by Adams, and it was presumed that he had met with opposition."[96] Adams never showed. Left alone, Stoneman's other two brigades had no choice.

As U.S. forces had reached the high ground beyond Walnut Creek, they positioned their artillery pieces and opened fire on the surroundings. After the attack, the *Daily Telegraph* called out the "brutality" of shelling the "eastern portion of the city." Thankfully, no civilian suffered injury. As the battle unfolded, Rebel gunners drove the U.S. artillery from Dunlap Hill. The infantry acted with "gallantry" in the course of the battle.[97]

Nevertheless, enough damage was done that a few homes were hit by cannon shells, and a building was "perforated with bullets." Located on the top of Dunlap ridge was the home of Mrs. Dunlap, which suffered some damage, including the destruction of stables, for the creation of an entrenched position. Unfortunately, one of the Confederate shells hit the Dunlap house, forcing the Dunlaps to leave their sheltered home. After some derogatory statement about U.S. leadership's intentions, the paper pointed out that "the Yankees took away all of the negroes belonging to this lady."[98] The paper did not elaborate on any other damaged property in the city.

People around Macon were anxious to join the fighting and show their manliness. "We could hear the cannonading distinctly," reported J. William Blackshear, a worker in the ironworks. "I hurried down town as soon as possible, and together with John Stubbs, shouldered my musket and fell in with a company of veteran troops from the west. Marching over to East Macon a Battalion of 4 companies was formed and march[ed] to Fort Hawkins thence to the hill on the left where we lay the balance of the day waiting for the Yankees, thinking they might try to flank us and cross the river above Macon. Our cannon was playing on the enemy from old Fort hill and by 8 o'clock had retreated two or three miles out men following."[99] The euphoria to join the fight suffered some disappointment when the men did not get to fight.

At the same time, the editors of the *Daily Telegraph* were not surprised by the outcome of Stoneman's assault on Macon. The paper reported, after the battle had ended, that Stoneman had brought thirteen regiments from Kentucky, Indiana and Illinois to the fight. However, his failure was unsurprising since Stoneman was "a Yankee who figured somewhat conspicuously in Virginia for his repeated failures on expeditions of a similar nature."[100] Despite Macon suffering no significant damage, the threat of Stoneman remained.

At 3:00 p.m., Stoneman ordered his forces to withdraw from Macon. Faced with the unyielding nature of the troops in his front and news of Wheeler's ten thousand cavalrymen closing in on his back, Stoneman had little choice.[101] During their return to Clinton, Capron's men ran into Rebel pickets. After a swift skirmish, they drove away the pickets and liberated thirty-three prisoners. In one of the few acts of vengeance, the command burned the jail.[102] Having withdrawn from Macon to Clinton, Stoneman had to decide where he would take his command next. He tried to escape back to the U.S. forces around Atlanta. His escape was not to be.

As the *Daily Telegraph* reported the details of the battle on Dunlap and Fort Hawkins hills, the paper could also report that Brigadier General Alfred Iverson had caught up with Stoneman and taken the general and five hundred of his men captive following a brief engagement at Sunshine Church.[103] On the evening of August 1, Stoneman with his staff arrived in Macon under escort of Confederate forces. He was situated in Camp Oglethorpe, the prison he had intended to liberate. The writer of the *Daily Telegraph* gloated, "He will be able to reflect, for a few days, on the vicissitudes of fortune, and to regret that he was mad enough to go so far from home." The newspaper hoped that the prisoners were searched so that any stolen items could be returned to their owners. Furthermore, the *Daily Telegraph* suggested, "We think that if the raiders are treated as prisoners of war they should be compelled to restore all their plunder they have taken from the citizens, and made to repair the railroad they have damaged."[104] Maconites were glad to have escaped danger and sought revenge.

Those men of Stoneman's command who had escaped Sunshine Church slowly made their way back to the lines around Atlanta. By August 4, there were reports of some eight hundred raiders making an appearance in the Eatonton area.[105] Some of the men took weeks before they returned to the U.S. lines around Atlanta.

In his official report, George Stoneman explained himself and placed blame. He regretted, "Before I had completed what I desired to accomplish I learned that force of the enemy's cavalry was close upon my rear, and the only course for me to pursue to get out was to turn upon and, if possible, whip this force." Stoneman failed to do so in the battle of Sunshine Church on July 31, 1864.[106] He corrected any false assumption "that I had surrendered the whole command, and that the order was given for every one to save himself. I have not heard from the Kentucky brigade since it left. Capron's brigade I learn was considerably cut up, and several hundred of it captured. I feel better satisfied with myself to be prisoner of war, much as I hate it, than to be amongst those who owe their escape to considerations of self-preservation."[107] Stoneman sought to justify his action, protecting his men from fighting a futile engagement.

With the crisis averted, Maconites turned inward. The *Daily Telegraph* and spiritual leaders of the city reminded their flock of the importance of giving thanks in prayer. With "such imminent danger," the people should remember the importance of prayer, a person identified as "Believer" wrote to the *Daily Telegraph*. People should give thanks to god for their deliverance and to maintain "Divine favor."[108]

On August 3, the *Daily Telegraph* announced that Christ Church would hold a "special thanksgiving service" the next morning, a Thursday, at 10:30 a.m. to give thanks for "our deliverance, of our city from the great and apparent danger wherewith it was compassed, the whole glory whereof belongeth to Him who is the giver of all victory."[109] The perception of a god-ordained cause and the need to maintain divine favor shone through in these requests to visit the local churches for thanksgiving services.

As the communities along Stoneman's route recovered, stories, true and false, emerged about the supposed atrocities committed by the U.S. cavalrymen. A letter to the editors of the *Daily Telegraph* spoke with disgust about the damages done to R.W. Bonner's property in Clinton. Bonner lived in Samuel Griswold's former home with Griswold's daughter, Ellen, Bonner's wife;[110] this likely made his house a target. Stipulating that he had not been at home, though his "two small sons" were, he explained the damages and theft committed by the raiders, including the removal of "all of my silver ware, table cutlery, bed-cloth of all kinds, all of my wearing apparel, notes, title deeds, money, shoes, hats, double barreled gun and pistol; took the most of my bacon, and every horse and mule I had." He noted that his "servants" tried to stop some of the plundering.[111] Stoneman and the raiders were an evil force of vandals and barbarians to the Rebels, who had suffered material damage.

In contrast, as the paper lambasted in vile language the work of Stoneman's raiders, it republished approvingly a piece on W.C. Quantrill from the *Houston Telegraph*. The paper presented Quantrill as "never cruel, never ostentatious, or boastful, never boisterous or common-place, but always shows the polished, educated gentleman." Even more, Quantrill had good etiquette, descending from an aristocratic family, and illustrated the benefits of "good breeding." He was a hero who still "sleeps as quietly and smiles as sweetly as though he had never slain a Yankee."[112] While U.S. raiders were vandals, Rebel murderers were heroic individuals.

The damages by Stoneman's men to the Central of Georgia were limited. Well over a week after the raid, the Central of Georgia was partially back in operation. The *Daily Telegraph* reported, "The damage to the tressel [*sic*] on this side of the river has been repaired, and they are now at work on the other side." The Walnut Creek bridge remained out of operation for a while longer.[113] While the physical damage was minor, there was significant psychological damage, putting fear into the minds of Macon residents.

As an important railroad hub, communication center, industrial supplier of the Confederate armies, hospital town and location of a prisoner of war camp, Macon quickly attracted U.S. military attention during Sherman's Atlanta campaign. As the city on the Chattahoochee came under siege, Sherman's cavalry struck out against outlying cities and supply bases. Macon was one such target. Faulty intelligence and reluctance for decisive action doomed Stoneman's operation from the start. Nevertheless, U.S. forces arrived on July 30 and suffered defeat against the city's defenders. Macon had survived the first challenge, but peace returned only for a short time.

Chapter 4

March to the Sea and Walnut Creek

Macon had escaped damage in July 1864, but the fall of Atlanta raised new concerns about William Tecumseh Sherman's intentions and his next target. After Stoneman's raid caught them off guard, Maconites did not take their security for granted and prepared better defenses around the city for a potential next attack. In November, as Sherman set his army in motion to Savannah, Macon faced the specter of occupation for a second time.

As Sherman prepared his army for the advance on Savannah, he gave clear instruction about the purpose of the expedition and what was permissible and what was not: "The army will forage liberally on the country during the march. To this end, each brigade commander will organize a good and sufficient foraging party, under the command of one or more discreet officers, who will gather, near the route traveled, corn or forage of any kind, meat of any kind, vegetables, corn-meal, or whatever is needed by the command, aiming at all times to keep in the wagons at least ten days' provisions for the command and three days' forage."[114] Like in previous campaigns, the country passed through would provide for the army.

On November 9, 1864, with Special Field Orders No. 120, Major General William T. Sherman opened the March to the Sea. He had divided his army into two wings. Major General Oliver O. Howard was in command of the Right Wing, or the Army of the Tennessee, which contained Major General Peter J. Osterhaus's 15th Corps and Major General Frank Blair Jr.'s 17th Corps. Major General Henry W. Slocum took charge of the Left Wing, or the Army of Georgia, which included Brigadier General Jefferson C. Davis's 14th Corps and Brigadier General Alpheus S. Williams's 20th Corps. In addition, marching parallel to the infantry was a cavalry brigade under the command of Brigadier General Judson Kilpatrick. Kilpatrick and Howard's wing posed the greatest danger to Macon as the U.S. Army nearest the city on the Ocmulgee.[115]

When Sherman set out on November 15, he left the enemy uncertain about the target of his army. The confusion left Macon, Augusta and even Columbus struggling whether to prepare for a fight and forced the few remaining forces in the state to divide. All three of these cities were industrial centers and therefore attracted U.S. military attention to bring the rebellion to a swift close. On November 15 at 7:00 a.m., as ordered, the lead elements of Sherman's force set out for Savannah, the real target of the March to the Sea.

Sherman had ordered his troops to forage freely but also to respect the privacy of people and their property. He instructed, "Soldiers must not enter the dwellings of the inhabitants, or commit any trespass, but during a half or a camp they may be permitted to" forage for food near their camp. Most importantly, to cripple the Rebel ability to produce food, cash

Image of the Confederate earthwork in the foreground and the Dunlap House in the background at Ocmulgee National Historical Park. *Author's collection.*

crops or industrial products, Sherman ordered to "destroy mills, houses, cotton-gins, &c."[116]

Even more, Sherman ordered restraint, aware that this campaign was just as much about psychological warfare as it was about doing battle. In case guerrillas caused problems and destroyed bridges or obstructed roads, he permitted his troops to "enforce a devastation more or less relentless according to the measure of such hostility." Sherman was not going to tolerate irregular warfare against his troops. If Rebel forces decided to engage in such barbaric tactics, the civilian population would suffer. At the same time, Sherman noted that "cavalry and artillery may appropriate freely and without limited, discriminating, however, between the rich, who are usually hostile, and the poor or industrious, usually neutral or friendly."[117] He hoped that his campaign could further undermine support for the war among the lower classes, bringing the rebellion to a conclusion.

Finally, in enforcing Lincoln's Emancipation Proclamation, Sherman suggested that his commanders use their best judgment when encountering runaway slaves. He urged them to take along slaves who could provide useful services but also to keep an eye on the supply situation of the army.[118] Sherman's psychological warfare to undermine support for the rebellion was multilayered and ready to kick into high gear.

In the aftermath of the assault on Macon in July, local military leaders determined that there was a need for better defensive preparation. General M.L. Smith, the chief engineer of the army, and Captain Edward Winston placed works all around the city that by mid-November were in a "forward state of completion." The *Daily Chattanooga Rebel* reported, "These defenses consist of a series of lunettes or small forts, three or four hundred yards distant from each other, capable of holding two or three hundred men each, and connected with each other by covered ways and rifle-pits....The forts are near enough together to enable their defenders to command the intermediate space with musketry, while the connecting rifle-pits would shower destruction, which, with the cross-fire from the forts, no moral force could stand." The hope was that even a small force could hold these defenses and protect the city.[119]

However, construction progress was slow. Captain M.B. Grant oversaw the digging that would provide Macon with defenses to prevent a repetition of Stoneman's raid. Grant impressed labor from the enslaved population to construct the new fortifications. The medical officials in the city provided care for these "workers," and the chief of staff allowed the tools to remain at the construction sites until the work was finished. However, Cobb and Grant did not have sufficient manpower to complete work and lacked the necessary tools and equipment to provide Macon with a proper defensive line. With the labor requirement, Cobb could not even provide burial squads, leaving the sheriff to impress additional enslaved people for that task.[120] Despite the urgency of the matter, the failures of the Confederate states were on full display, as progress on the fortification was slow.

As Sherman prepared to leave Atlanta, Macon heard about these preparations. A person who had recently been in Stone Mountain reported that "on Wednesday morning at day break terrific explosions were heard in the direction of Atlanta." Reports indicated that only eight thousand U.S. troops were in the city, but there were clear arrangements for a departure with prisoners and contraband being sent up the railroad.[121] Maconites and Rebel authorities remained in the dark about Sherman's intentions.

News soon arrived that the enemy was in motion. Maconites worried if the fate they had avoided in July was headed their way. By November 18, news had arrived of enemy forces in the Griffin area. As a result of the emergency situation, Howell Cobb once more called on "every man capable of bearing arms…[to join] the defense of the city." At the same time, there was hope that the military authorities could stop the enemy advance before reaching Macon. Besides the reports of infantry in Griffin, there was also news that placed U.S. cavalry just eight miles from Forsyth. However, Rebel forces had burned all the bridges between Forsyth and Indian Springs to slow the advance of U.S. cavalry.[122] As the enemy continued to draw closer, rumors circulated that Sherman's troops had burned Monticello and Hillsboro.[123]

With all this uncertainty and confusion, as well as to slow Sherman's anticipated push into the middle of the state, John Bell Hood ordered the railroad companies to remove their own tracks to prevent them from falling into enemy hands or being used as an invasion and supply route. Sherman did not have to do damage—the railroads did it for him. The Macon and Western Railroad henceforth stopped in Barnesville; all tracks beyond the city were built back.[124]

Nevertheless, confusion abounded about Sherman's true intentions. The assumption that Sherman only feinted toward Macon to strike against Augusta and Savannah remained alive for a long time. Drawing forces to Macon and protecting the Central of Georgia Railroad would leave the other two cities undefended. Aware that Sherman had crossed the Ocmulgee River near Indian Springs, authorities still assumed that Sherman was headed to and prepared to strike Augusta.[125]

The forces in Macon heard about the advancing enemy from a wide variety of sources, Judge C.B. Cole's son-in-law telegraphed from Forsyth that he had been within enemy lines for two days in the Indian Springs area gathering valuable intelligence and hoping to meet with Cobb.[126] Other reports indicated that Sherman was quickly advancing toward Griswoldville and the Central of Georgia.[127] Even then, city residents continued to hope that Sherman would bypass the city entirely. Nevertheless, additional forces had arrived in Macon to defend the city, raising the confidence that the city "can be held against any force Sherman can bring against it."[128] Left in this limbo about their safety, Maconites prepared for the worst.

As fears increase and Sherman drew closer, the *Macon Daily Telegraph and Confederate* highlighted the danger faced, calling Sherman's advance "a crisis which they had not anticipated until recently." It was important to bring awareness to the coming danger since people needed time to prepare for the possible fighting. Aware that the state had insufficient manpower to defeat

General Judson Kilpatrick, seated by tent, September 1863. Timothy H. O'Sullivan, Warrenton, Virginia. *Library of Congress.*

the enemy, the paper hoped that people would at least do their best. In the end, "when our homes are threatened we should not stop to inquire whether they are safely defended by others, but it is our solemn and imperitive duty to assist in their defence." Assuming that Sherman would put Macon under siege, the paper's editors hoped the city's residents would excel just like the residents of Richmond and Petersburg. In biblical language, the paper closed, "If the people of Georgia refuse to rally to the defence of their State, then wo be unto them, for the day is near at hand in which the sceptre will depart from Judah and they and their possession be left to the mercy of an unsparing foe."[129] Seemingly, Macon's newspaper was not fully convinced about the residents' patriotism, feeling the need to urge them on.

Macon's elite and the newspaper's editors were concerned about how few men stood between their safety and Sherman's army. With Hood's departure from the state, the Rebel authorities had only 2,800 infantry, three batteries of artillery and 250 cavalry left for the defense of Georgia. Most of these men lacked training, as they had avoided frontline service so far by being part of the Georgia Reserves and Georgia State Troops. In addition, Macon's defenders had only 125 rifles (insufficient for its 300 defenders), 250 cartridge boxes and 6,000 cartridges available. In addition to his 300 recruits, there were also some veteran soldiers, wounded men and industrial workers whom Cobb could call on for the defense of Macon.[130]

By November 21, 1864, Macon was ready for Sherman's arrival. Many of the male residents were under arms and ready to fill the new defensive positions around the city. There was hope that Sherman would avoid Macon altogether because of the "large force gathered here and the splendid fortifications which surround the city."[131] This hope was seriously misplaced and an overestimation of Macon's defense. Thankfully, Sherman had no intention of wasting his infantry in a direct assault on Macon.

Providing protection to Howard's wing of the army and shielding the location of the entire force, Kilpatrick's cavalry had an important duty to perform. He had concentrated his force of around 5,500 men and six pieces of artillery near Marietta and, in obedience of Sherman's orders, set out on November 14. The first target for the army was Milledgeville, the capital of Georgia. Kilpatrick had orders to "feint strongly toward Forsyth, cross the Ocmulgee, move on Macon as if to attack it, strike the Georgia Central Railroad and as near Macon as possible, then fall back toward Gordon destroying track till the arrival of the infantry."[132] Kilpatrick was not to capture Macon, but rather demonstrate against the city to distract and confuse enemy forces.

After his departure from Atlanta on November 15, Kilpatrick's two brigade passed through Jonesboro, revisiting the old battlefield from the end stage of the Atlanta Campaign. The next day, Colonel Eli H. Murray's brigade charged Joseph Wheeler's forces, who had occupied the old earthworks at Lovejoy's Station. After a brief skirmish, Wheeler withdrew to Griffin. With Wheeler no longer a threat, Kilpatrick separated his force to destroy "the greater amount of cotton, cotton gins, and other valuable property." Having demonstrated toward Forsyth, Kilpatrick crossed the Ocmulgee at Planter's Factory to reach Clinton on November 19.[133]

While Kilpatrick guarded the U.S. army's flank, the infantry of the 15th Corps made their way from Atlanta toward the Milledgeville area. The 1st Brigade of the 1st Division, under the command of Colonel Milo Smith, started its march at White Hall on November 13. From there, the six regiments took the road to East Point, Rough and Ready and McDonough to finally reach the Clinton area. The 2nd Brigade, under Brigadier General Charles C. Walcutt, followed in the 1st Brigade's footsteps, touching on McDonough, Indian Springs, Ocmulgee Mills and Hillsborough before reaching Clinton.[134]

Major Asias Willison and his 103rd Illinois Volunteer Infantry, which served in Walcutt's brigade, departed Vining's Station at 7:00 a.m. on November 13, 1864. After crossing the Chattahoochee River and passing through the city of Atlanta, the regiment bivouacked a short distance from the city before continuing the march with the rest of the brigade to Rough and Ready Station.[135]

Walcutt's command included the 46th Ohio, 97th and 100th Indiana, 6th Iowa and 40th and 103rd Illinois. By November 22, Walcutt had 1,513 men under his command: Lieutenant Colonel Isaac N. Alexander's 46th Ohio contained 218 soldiers, Major Asias Willison's 103rd Illinois contained 219 enlisted men, Lieutenant Colonel William H. Clune's 6th Iowa contained 177 men, Colonel Robert F. Catterson's 97th Indiana went into battle with 366 men, Major Ruel M. Johnson's 100th Indiana contained 327 men and Lieutenant Colonel Hiram W. Hall's 40th Illinois had 206 soldiers enlisted.[136] While Walcutt's men remained uninvolved in the Second Battle of Macon, they played a significant role during the Battle of Griswoldville (discussed in the next chapter). Kilpatrick had to guard the location of these infantry units against the prying eyes of his Rebel counterparts.

Throughout the advance toward Macon, Joseph Wheeler's cavalry shadowed the enemy and skirmished with them on a daily basis. Wheeler kept his superiors—Generals Bragg, Hood, Hardee and Taylor—as well as

Georgia governor Brown, informed about the enemy's movements. Just like when Johnson had come to town just in time for the first battle, Cobb was glad that in the morning of November 19, General Hardee arrived and assumed command of the forces in Macon. Even by this day, Cobb still believed that Sherman was only feinting toward Macon and that his real target was Augusta and its more significant industrial capacity.[137]

To help Macon's defenders, Wheeler allocated a brigade under the command of Anderson to the defense of Macon, placing the unit under the direct authority of Major General Cobb. Cobb positioned Anderson's force on the Clinton Road. As Sherman's forces drew closer to Macon, Wheeler also dispatched Colonel C.C. Crews to the city, and Cobb assigned them the road to Milledgeville.[138] That same day, Wheeler discovered that Sherman's army had crossed the Ocmulgee; therefore, Wheeler advanced to Macon himself.

Upon reaching Macon, Wheeler conferred with General Hardee, who had assumed command of the Confederate forces in the area. Hardee ordered Wheeler to advance toward Clinton and "ascertain the enemy's force and location." Wheeler quickly discovered that U.S. infantry forces from Osterhaus's Corps were in Clinton; however, dense fog obscured the movement of both forces. As a result, "Six men dashed into the town and captured General Osterhaus' servant (an enlisted man) within twenty feet of General Osterhaus' headquarter. A regiment of the enemy's cavalry charged us, making the retreat of my small escort necessary." The U.S. forces defending Osterhaus's headquarter quickly ran into reinforcements from Wheeler's command. A brief back and force between the cavalry of the two sides ensued. However, Wheeler soon heard that additional cavalry forces had made their way toward Griswoldville and that Colonel Crews had engaged those troops, leaving the Milledgeville approach to Macon undefended. Wheeler quickly withdrew his forces in the direction of that road to provide protection to Macon and give Cobb sufficient warning of an enemy approach.[139]

Having reached Clinton, Kilpatrick had to defend the infantry against the aforementioned assault by Wheeler's cavalry. On November 21, Kilpatrick send Colonel Smith D. Atkins's 2nd Brigade—which include the 92nd Illinois Mounted Infantry; 3rd Indiana Cavalry; 9th Michigan Cavalry; 5th , 9th and 10th Ohio Cavalry; and McLaughlin's Squadron—toward Macon to tear up the tracks of the Central of Georgia Railroad. As the units approached Walnut Creek, the tributary to the Ocmulgee that Stoneman's troops had crossed less than three months ago, the command set to work on the destructive task, maintaining a tight picket guard for protection. The 9th Michigan damaged the track near Griswold Station, including a train with thirteen cars. The men also destroyed the station and the "pistol, soap and candle factories" at the town.[140]

At the same time, the 3rd Kentucky, commanded by Lieutenant Colonel Robert H. King, had advanced toward Macon but remained occupied with the destruction of the Central of Georgia Railroad before falling back to Griswoldville at nightfall on November 20. It continued its destructive work the next day.[141]

After the skirmishes with Wheeler's cavalry at Clinton, Kilpatrick prepared for the demonstration against Macon. The 9th Pennsylvania Cavalry sent Captain E.A. Hancock with one hundred men toward Macon on the Clinton Road to locate the enemy and engage them in battle. Hancock eventually found two enemy regiments and skirmished with them for two days.[142]

As the noose tightened around Macon, Cobb and Hardee prepared for the defense of the city. Defending Macon along Walnut Creek were Rebel forces under the tactical command of Colonel T.M. Colmes, who was officially also in command of the 5th Tennessee. Colmes directly reported to Hardee and Cobb. Colmes faced the difficult challenge of turning his hodgepodge of forces into an effective fighting force. Colmes had available Lieutenant Colonel Brooks with the 15th Tennessee, Captain Walker of the 2nd Convalescent and some additional men on the eastern part of Dunlap ridge. There was artillery support from five different units.[143] Having sent out pickets, Colmes assumed that he would have sufficient advance notice of the approaching cavalry forces. The pickets were along each river crossing, including the railroad bridge over Walnut Creek.[144] Colmes was correct in putting pickets ahead of his force. When Kilpatrick's men arrived before Macon, these units stood ready to engage the enemy in the new fortifications.

At 3:30 p.m. on November 20, Kilpatrick's cavalry units struck the outer pickets along Walnut Creek and on the road to Cross Keys (today a neighborhood of Macon). Hearing the gunfire and thus aware of the approaching enemy, Colmes rode to the frontlines to rally his men for the impending attack. The *Macon Daily Telegraph and Confederate* observed, "The old Hero, having been in the smoke of other battles, and heard the booming of other guns and the crack of other rifles, was not alarmed though he was surprised." With the pickets pushed back, some of them rushing back to the main line, the enemy was quickly upon the Rebel forces on Dunlap ridge. As an old-school commander, Colmes sought to inspire his men from high on horse, an exposed and dangerous position, directing his men but apparently forgetting "his years, his gray hairs and white beard," not to mention the perfect target he presented to the enemy. Inspiring his men, they awaited the U.S. cavalry on horse and foot, ready to charge them.[145]

On the other side of the fighting, U.S. Lieutenant Colonel Matthew Van Buskirk's command, the 92nd Illinois Mounted Infantry, left the Clinton area at noon to advance toward Macon. After four miles on the road, the 92nd encountered barricades put up by enemy soldiers. Fighting on foot, Van Buskirk's soldiers charged the enemy position. Colonel Atkins report noted, "The charge was received and repulsed and the enemy charged in turn, when the entire brigade of the enemy cowardly ran off, scattering through the woods." Focused on their target, the soldiers continued toward Macon.[146]

The official regimental history recounted the events with more drama:

> *The Rebel pickets were soon struck, and, about three miles out, the enemy was found in considerable force, being Crews's brigade of Rebel cavalry. Captain Becker, of Company I, with a battalion, dismounted, passed through the woods to within a short distance of the enemy. The Rebels were preparing to charge, and a cavalry regiment galloped "forward into line" to meet it; but the charging column of Rebels did not come far. Starting with a yell, the Rebels rushed out of their rail barricade, and came toward Captain Becker, with his battalion of Spencers concealed in the brush, when the Captain ordered the boys to fire, and the head of the Rebel column was surprised and halted; and it was now our turn to charge, and the Tenth Ohio Cavalry started for the enemy with a shout and flashing sabers; and then the entire brigade of graycoats, like frightened birds, scattered, in confusion, through the woods and fields, in terror and dismay.*

As Crews's men scattered into the woods, the U.S. troops decided to continue to Macon and not get bogged down pursuing the scattered elements of the rebel cavalry.[147]

The 92nd Illinois next encountered the enemy along Walnut Creek. The regiment deployed along the railroad bridge, which Stoneman's men had damaged a few months earlier. The men dismounted and charged over the creek on foot. The men belonged to Captains Becker and Hawk's command. Upon arriving on the battlefield, Lieutenant Colonel Van Buskirk had divided his troops, with some tearing up track and others engaging the enemy. The attack by Becker and Hawk was to relieve pressure from the attack by the 10th Ohio along the road to the north. The charge by the two companies was successful in that Confederate forces withdrew into their entrenched

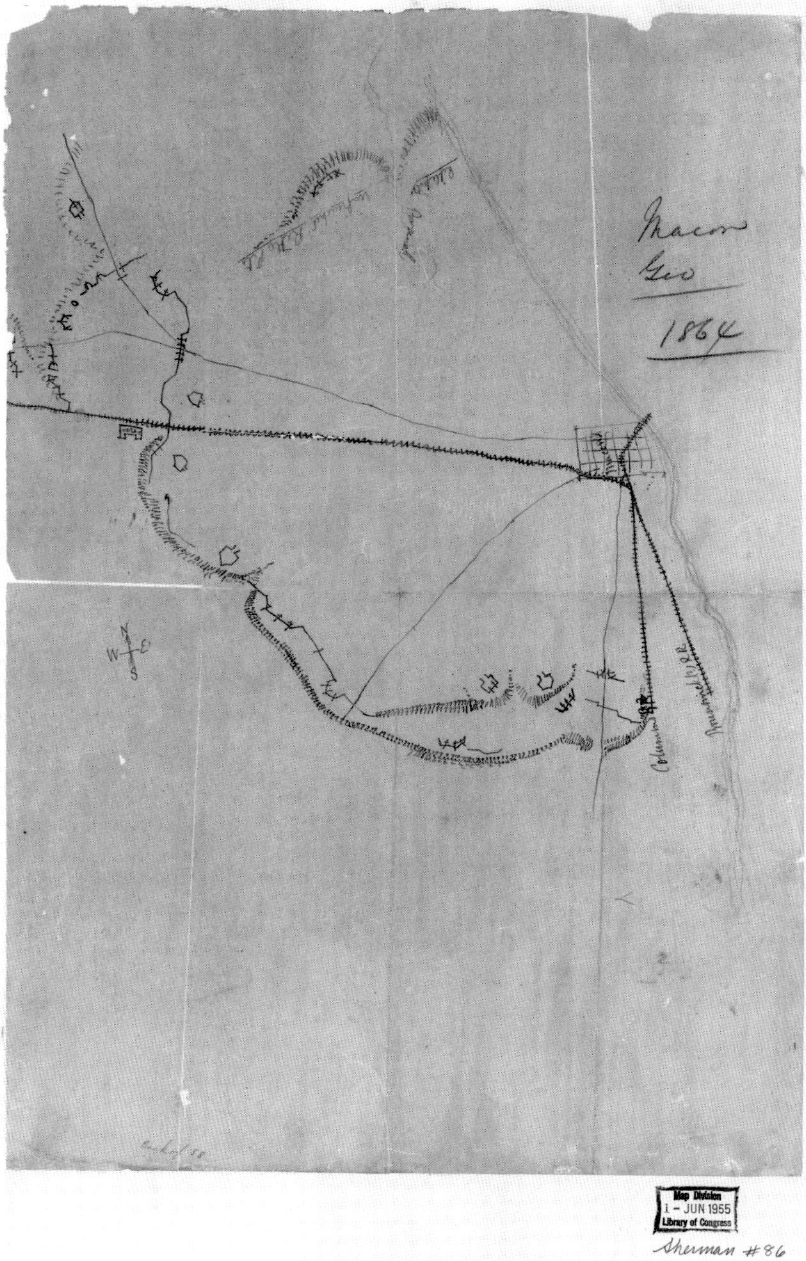

Macon, Georgia, 1864. *Library of Congress.*

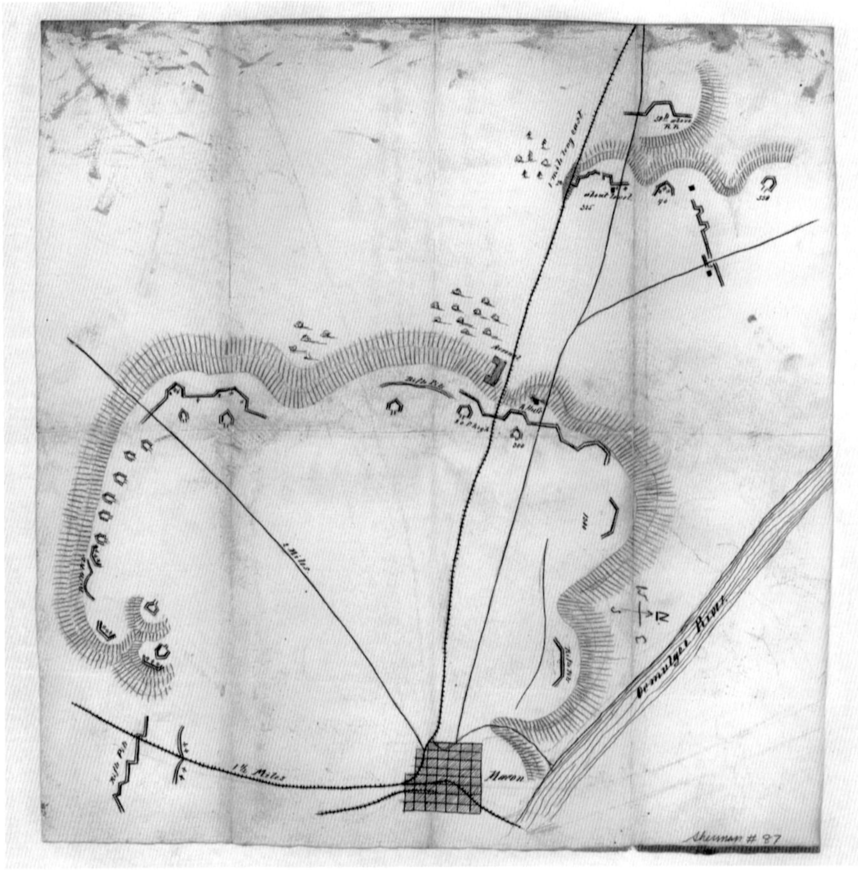

Map of Macon, Georgia, and vicinity, 1864. *Library of Congress.*

position.[148] "The Ninety-Second was dismounted, and drove the enemy from the creek, and crossed over, and up the hill, driving the enemy from the hill beyond," the regimental history recounted.[149] However, the men quickly came under artillery fire, forcing them to withdraw.[150] Without pressing their advantage, Van Buskirk ordered the men to withdraw, having accomplished their objective.[151] Kilpatrick ordered them to do damage, not get involved in a battle to capture Macon, which the men adhered to.

Defending the railroad trestle over Walnut Creek was Captain E.S. Hance of the 24th Tennessee. When the U.S. forces approached the crossing, he had taken about a dozen of his men to the bridge. After the pickets had encountered the enemy, Hance determined to defend the position. After "a few well directed volleys," the cavalrymen withdrew.[152]

Meanwhile, to silence the artillery fire, the 10th Ohio under Lieutenant Thomas W. Sanderson advanced along the Milledgeville road toward the enemy battery. Atkins reported, "They crossed the creek in a most difficult place, and charged in column of fours up the road, and were successful in gaining a momentary possession of the enemy's outer works and several pieces of artillery."[153]

The 10th Ohio had to cross about a half-mile stretch of open ground to reach the enemy pieces. Sanderson reported, "The regiment…in pursuance of orders, charged along the road, reached the enemy's guns, which were in a redoubt, completely blocking the road, there being only room for two horses to enter the works abreast." Once the men had reached the redoubt, they found the position supported by trenches and rifle pits filled with infantry. For a brief moment, the 10th Ohio had "complete possession" of the redoubt, with the enemy infantry "stampeded and panic-stricken and were rapidly falling back." The men from Ohio quickly faced the second line of infantry, a force of "older and steadier troops," as well as a force approaching them from the woods on the left, where Dunlap Farm and another redoubt was located. Therefore, the regiment withdrew in good order, covered by elements of the 92nd Illinois.[154]

Facing the charging 10th Ohio was Captain Rivers and his artillery unit. The cannons, located in a redoubt along the road, faced serious self-inflicted problems. Because of "the bad condition of his friction Primers," the guns were unable to obliterate the advancing cavalry coming toward them. With drawn sabers charging, the U.S. troopers tried to dislodge the gunners. At this point, the Rebel infantry charged the position and repulsed the cavalry forces. Meanwhile, a battery at Fort Hawkins was raining shrapnel on the enemy forces. After the failed charge, Kilpatrick's men withdrew back to Walnut Creek.[155] Rebel forces were lucky, as Kilpatrick's men did not push their advantage in the fight and took their order to demonstrate serious.

By this point, Wheeler's men had reached the Rebel line from their Clinton expedition to help connect the redoubts on the outskirts of Macon. He reported on the cavalry charge by the 10th Ohio that "four of them had attempted to capture a gun, but had been driven back, leaving an officer (whose horse was killed) in the hands of our infantry."[156] Rebel cavalry and infantry prevented a breach of the line; however, they could not do anything about the destruction behind the lines.

Colonel Smith D. Atkins had devoted two regiments to the fighting, leaving the rest of the brigade to destroy vital infrastructure. Supporting the two attacks along Walnut Creek was the 5th Ohio Volunteer Cavalry as a reserve. Meanwhile, the 9th Ohio Volunteer Cavalry and parts of the 5th and 10th Ohio "tore up the railroad track and telegraph wire for about two miles."[157] The distraction by the few dozen men charging the Rebel position allowed their comrades to bring destruction to Macon's railroad network.

At nightfall, Kilpatrick's entire command withdrew, with the 92nd Illinois Mounted Infantry performing rearguard duties on its way to Clinton, where the troops prepared for the next day's action, a strike against Griswoldville.[158] Overnight, the cavalry guarded the Clinton/Macon and Milledgeville/Macon road intersections to allow the infantry to move their supply wagons along. However, Van Buskirk reported that the enemy "had been feeling his position very strongly." Therefore, the lieutenant colonel decided to repulse the enemy before following the orders to withdraw. The enemy charged sooner than expected, forcing the pickets of Captain Lyman Preston and Captain William B. Mayers to lie flat in front of their barricaded comrades to allow them to repulse the Rebel cavalry. The attack came from three directions, with one Rebel regiment trying to get behind the 92nd. The regimental history proudly reported, "And on they came, until the Ninety-Second had their two mounted columns in good range, when the Regiment opened a cool, steady and terrible fire with their Spencer decimating Repeating Rifles. No enemy ever live long within range of those guns, in the hands of the Ninety-Second men."[159] The unit stood its ground just like its enemy had done hours earlier around Macon.

Years later, the regimental history of the 92nd concluded on the fighting, "The cavalry had demonstrated so strongly upon Macon, that the enemy was effectually deceived, and massed all his cavalry and available forces, to guard that point, and the cutting of the railroad east of Macon gave Sherman's columns an open road, uninterrupted by any of the enemy's troops, as Sherman's army swung off to the south-east toward Louisville, Georgia."[160] Its demonstration against Macon had not brought about the occupation of the city, but it achieved the goal of distracting the enemy from the true target of the raid.

After the enemy unsuccessfully struck the city's defenses and decided to withdraw about eight miles away, the local paper voiced a cautious optimism. However, only the cavalry attacked, leading the editors of the *Macon Daily Telegraph and Confederate* to assume that the infantry was still headed toward Augusta and the cavalry around Macon was simply a diversionary column.[161] There also remained uncertainty if the U.S. forces might turn to fight their way into Macon since they still hovered in the Clinton and Gordon area.[162]

Macon took a breath of relief when Kilpatrick's men withdrew, just like when Stoneman's had, but the city residents did not feel comfortable.

The fall of Atlanta had raised fears in Macon that it might be the next target to destroy the military-industrial complex in the Georgia heartland, a fear that had turned out all too real. Having already suffered one attack by Stoneman's cavalry in the summer, the city had prepared for another attack, with great success. When Kilpatrick's cavalrymen appeared before Macon, ordered to demonstrate against the city, they encountered a more heavily fortified city, but the lines of fortification were understaffed. Nevertheless, with only a few dozen men charging, the few defenders could hold the line. Kilpatrick's men never pushed their advantage. Richard Iobst eloquently summarized the Second Battle of Macon: "Sherman's men failed to capture a city which they did not really intend to take."[163] With Macon protected, the Rebel commanders decided to follow up their victory and challenge the enemy along the road to Gordon.

Chapter 5

Griswoldville

With their success around Macon, and still uncertain about where Sherman was headed, Confederate forces departed the protection of their trenches only thirty-six hours after winning in an effort to locate the enemy along the road to Gordon. Unfortunately for the soldiers, this was a terrible decision with devastating consequences.

After the fighting in Macon, Wheeler moved his forces in the direction of Griswoldville to locate the enemy.[164] Near the hamlet, the Rebel cavalrymen once more encountered their U.S. cavalry counterparts. What started as a cavalry skirmish quickly escalated into a full-fledged battle. As the Rebel infantry arrived and pushed the enemy cavalry back, they ran into U.S. infantry men from Walcott's brigade. A brief but heated engagement ensued. Despite numerically superior numbers, Rebel forces lacked the experience of veteran soldiers and were unable to capitalize on their number advantage. Defeated, they had to withdraw.

On the morning of November 22, Brigadier General Charles C. Walcutt—part of Brigadier General Charles R. Woods's 1st Division and Major General Peter J. Osterhaus's 15th Corps—advanced toward Griswoldville to dislodge enemy cavalry who had followed Kilpatrick's withdrawing forces.[165] Standing in the way of the advancing Rebel forces was the 5th Kentucky Cavalry.

On the evening of November 21 around 9:00 p.m., Wheeler's cavalry charged the 5th Kentucky Cavalry's camp without success. After some night rest, the skirmishers of the two sides encountered each other again, and Rebel forces pushed the enemy pickets aside. Four companies under Major Kimmel charged the Rebels and pushed them back across the stream, where they faced "a heavy force of cavalry under Wheeler." Kimmel had to withdraw and await the arrival of the infantry. Despite the briefness of the action, the Pennsylvanians suffered five killed, twenty-one wounded and forty-two missing, plus the loss of forty-nine horses (fourteen killed).[166] As the day went on, the infantry took over from the cavalry, and the fighting intensified.

Similar to Kilpatrick's men the day before, Walcutt's troops were instructed only to demonstrate and to avoid a major battle. Osterhaus explained that he had ordered U.S. forces to make a "demonstration" against Griswoldville. The corps commander accompanied Walcutt's forces on the march. As Walcutt's men approached the small hamlet, they linked up with Kilpatrick's cavalry. Informed that the cavalry had unsuccessfully tried to push back the advancing Rebel forces, Osterhaus ordered Walcutt to "relieve the cavalry" and assumed a defensive position.[167] What had started as two cavalry forces engaging each other escalated into a cavalry versus infantry battle and quickly turned into a full-scale infantry battle.

Taking over the line of battle, Walcutt committed the 46th Ohio, 97th and 100th Indiana, 6th Iowa and 40th and 103rd Illinois to the fight.[168] Skirmishers, two regiments of infantry and some cavalry support struck the enemy line. Having taken the Rebels by surprise, "Walcutt kept pushing forward, and his men pursued in double-quick with cheers and laughter the fleeing horsemen, waded the creek, marched through the belt of timer beyond until they reached an open prairie-like field, which was in possession of large rebel cavalry forces." Here Walcutt paused for a moment and reformed his lines. After another brief skirmish, the Rebel cavalry "fled in confusion." As Wheeler's forces withdrew in various directions, Osterhaus worried that the Confederate cavalry might swing around Walcutt's forces to attack them in the rear. Therefore, he ordered Walcutt to return to the edge of the prairie-like field and take up a defensive position.[169] U.S. forces prepared for the next assault by putting in place some basic field fortifications.

As the Rebel infantry forces came into sight, Major Asias Willison deployed Companies A and B of the 103rd Illinois as advanced skirmishers. The regiment itself had taken position between the 97th Indiana on the right and the 6th Iowa on the left; the three units were on the right of the brigade.[170] The brigade occupied a powerful position, overlooking a ravine on high ground near Duncan's Farm.[171] The position was well selected. Osterhaus explained that it was "in the edge of the timber and along a slight

Brigadier General Charles C. Walcutt, dated between 1860 and 1870. *Library of Congress.*

rise in the ground, at the base of which a kind of marshy swamp formed a natural obstruction to the approach; the right and left of the position was pretty well secured by swamps."[172] With skirmishers and a strong defensive position, Walcutt's veteran forces, many of whom had fought at Vicksburg and in Chattanooga, were ready.

On the elevated ground, Walcutt's 1,500 men awaited the arrival of the Georgia Rebel forces from Macon, which came into view at around 2:30 p.m. Willison claimed in his report that it was at 1:00 p.m. when his skirmishers first encountered enemy forces, and they slowly withdrew to the main line. He observed, "A strong line was soon seen forming on the west side of the field, and advanced." Seeing the enemy advance toward them, Willison's veterans quickly decided to prepare a solid defensive position and "awaited the approaching enemy."[173] The same was true along the rest of the line.

Colonel Robert F. Catterson had taken position with his 97th Indiana at the right edge of the line, protecting the brigade's flank. He reported, "We had scarcely taken position in the edge of timber skirting the farm on the east when our pickets were fired upon." Taking advantage of some quickly created obstructions to cover themselves, the troops awaited the enemy onslaught. Catterson continued, noting that the enemy "was soon discovered emerging from the woods about 800 yards from our position, and rapidly running across an open field toward us in three lines of battle, either of which more than covered our brigade front."[174] However, the infantry had to await their turn to engage.

As the Rebel infantry charged through the open field, both sides engaged in a sharp artillery exchange. Placed in the center of the U.S. line, the artillery pieces of Walcutt's brigade opened on the enemy infantry before coming under artillery fire from their Rebel opponent. As a result, one of the first Rebel shots hit a caisson and caused some damage.[175] The infantry men would have to rely on their own fighting ability to hold and defend the position.

As the attacking forces came within one hundred yards of the U.S. line, the men had to cross a deep ravine. The result was devastating, as the ravine slowed down the enemy, destroyed their formation and forced them to advance uphill against an entrenched enemy position with a broken line. Catterson wrote, "The fire was so terrible that ere [the Rebels] reached it many of his number were stretched upon the plain."[176] Even before reaching the ravine, Willison noted in his report, "As soon as they came within range of our muskets a most terrific fire was poured into their ranks, doing fearful execution." The ravine held the Confederates up briefly and scattered their ranks, forcing them to reform their lines "within forty-five yards of the works." The devastating fire from the U.S. line prevented the reforming of the Rebel line and forced them to withdraw.[177] The first Rebel attack had failed.

As the fighting heated up, the commander of the brigade, Brigadier General Walcutt, had to leave the battlefield. A shell fragment hit his right leg. Luckily, Walcutt's injury did not require an amputation, and he eventually returned to duty. Colonel Robert F. Catterson, the commander of the 97th Indiana and a veteran of the Vicksburg Campaign, replaced Walcutt at the head of 2nd Brigade.[178] Command shifted smoothly from one veteran to another.

Catterson surveyed the battlefield upon assuming command and realized that the enemy concentrated for another attack on the right of the line, where his former unit—the 97th Indiana, 103rd Illinois and 6th Iowa—had taken position.[179] In the middle of the line were his "two pieces of artillery."[180] With the left—containing the 40th Illinois, 100th Indiana and 46th Ohio—also under pressure, Catterson called for assistance from division command.

Besides his pressured flank, Catterson had other, more pressing problems. His thin line of troops was quickly running low on ammunition, and the nearest supplies were two miles away. He had to consider withdrawing if his supplies ran out.[181] To protect the flank, Osterhaus dispatched Major Elbert

Overview of the Griswoldville Battlefield Park. *Author's collection.*

D. Baldwin's 12th Indiana to the aid of the pressed troops on the extreme right. The regiment arrived at 4:00 p.m. to prevent "the enemy from turning that flank."[182] For the most part, the 12th Indiana was not needed, and the U.S. forces carried the day as their line held.

The engagement was over by sunset on November 22. Rebel forces withdrew from the field, leaving Walcutt/Catterson's brigade in control of the area. Catterson ordered skirmishers to advance and follow the retreating enemy for a short distance. They captured 42 enemy prisoners and an additional 150 abandoned small arms.[183] Major Willison reported that in front of his unit, there were 51 enemy killed and wounded and 83 stands of small arms.[184] He explained that the three Confederate assaults "were as often repulsed with terrible slaughter." Of the 1,300 U.S. soldiers engaged, 14 had died during the fighting and 42 were injured.[185] Division command eventually reported only 13 killed but 79 wounded and 2 missing.[186] Once the fighting had ceased, at 8:00 p.m., the brigade received orders to move off the field and join the other brigades of the division on their way to Milledgeville.[187]

The untrained local forces had suffered mightily at the hands of the veteran soldiers of Walcutt's brigade, and Maconites were well aware of the situation. The *Macon Daily Telegraph and Confederate* reported on November

24 (Thursday) that on Tuesday Rebel pickets had come upon U.S. forces near Griswoldville. When the pickets encountered the U.S. line, "Our forces immediately deployed in line of battle" and drove the enemy pickets back until running into the main line. "Our men advanced boldly to the attack and a severe and protracted flight continued until dark," the paper reported. When Rebel forces pulled back, the enemy did not pursue. The paper was glad that the militia "behaved with distinguished gallantry," advancing in perfect order. The casualty list followed the brief battlefield report.[188]

As a confrontational patriotic newspaper, the *Macon Daily Telegraph and Confederate* focused on the property damages done by U.S. forces. The paper had dispatched a reporter to cover the events following Griswoldville. He reported that "the whole country laid waste from Griswoldville to the Oconee river." The reporter claimed that large amounts of private property were destroyed in the path of the U.S. forces.[189] The reporter confirmed most of the assumptions about Sherman but did not distinguish between property useful for military purposes and private property destroyed.

Sherman had ordered his forces to destroy any property that could benefit the rebellion's war effort. Therefore, his men laid waste to the industrial landscape of the region but, as ordered, avoided the destruction of private property. Despite having to deal with daily skirmishes and the battles in Macon and Griswoldville, Kilpatrick's cavalry division could report for November 21 the destruction of "1 pistol factory, 1 soap factory, 1 candle factory, 1 foundry, in employ of rebel Government, 400 boxes of soap, destroyed at Griswold, Ga.; 12 wagon and carts, and 1 wagon load carpenters tools, Government property, destroyed at Griswold, Ga.; 1 shoe-blacking factory destroyed at Griswold, Ga."[190] Despite not taking down Macon's industrial capabilities, Kilpatrick's cavalry did significant damage to the industry in the surrounding areas.

In his report, Osterhaus cheered his men for their fighting ability at Griswoldville: "Their artillery threw a terrific fire into the frail works of Walcutt, while their columns of infantry marched in heroic style to within fifty yards of our line. It was all in vain! Walcutt and his brave brigade proved that superior skill, coolness, and valor made up for the great disparity in numbers."[191] Brigadier General Charles Wood also lauded his brigade commanders: "I cannot speak in too high terms of the coolness and gallantry of Brig. Gen. C.C. Walcutt and Col. R.F. Catterson, Ninety-seventh Indiana Infantry. The skill with which they handled the troops and the results obtained show them to be men of marked ability."[192] The commanders were satisfied with the results of the Battle of Griswoldville.

After the battle victory, General Howard congratulated the troops involved. Noting their successful and victorious efforts the previous day, Howard observed, "I am exceedingly sorry that any of our brave men should fall, and for the sufferings of those that are wounded." He hoped that Brigadier General Walcutt would make a speedy recovery and "that his wound may not disable him."[193] Considering Walcutt's brigade engaged in a defensive holding action, they had won a good victory at little cost to themselves.

The Rebel military leadership had gambled and lost; unfortunately, many Georgians had paid a high price for this miscalculation. Nevertheless, the authorities tried to put a good spin on the events. Following Griswoldville, on November 24, 1864, Governor E. Brown issued a proclamation to the state lauding the heroism of the units involved. Brown called to attention the bravery of the Georgia forces during the battle. "[O]ur noble armies are doing everything in their power to defend our homes and property, and are entitled to the lasting gratitude and active support of the people of this State," Brown wrote. He noted how these raw recruits and veterans had fought gallantly in all engagements and "constantly annoy the enemy as he passes through our State." Decrying the "predatory bands of thieves and robbers," Brown was upset that people had to rely on their own devices to defend themselves. He demanded that law enforcement officials protect the people, and in an act of defiance to the government in Richmond, he stopped all "impressment of private property" unless authorized by the War Department and signed by Major Norman W. Smith, Major General Howell Cobb or Major General Joseph Wheeler.[194] There apparently was a significant problem with Southerners looting and destroying property, not just the destruction brought by Sherman.

As Sherman's forces withdrew from the Macon area, Maconites took a collective sigh of relief again. The newspaper announced, "We are happy to announce that Macon is considered safe. The Commander of the Post has declared the city upon peace footing and the order of Major General Cobb, ordering out every man capable of bearing arms is withdrawn." The paper gloated in the success that the city was unharmed and again in a "perfectly quiet and orderly" state.[195]

Having defeated Kilpatrick's cavalry but still uncertain about the exact location and goal of Sherman's main body, Rebel leaders in Macon decided to send their inexperienced troops away from the protection of the defenses around Macon and toward Griswoldville to locate and confront the enemy. In Griswoldville, these men encountered a veteran brigade of infantry that had fought in battles like Vicksburg and Chattanooga. While the event is often presented as a slaughter of the young teenage and elderly men of Middle Georgia, Rebel authorities bear the blame for the outcome, having sent these men in search of battle. At the same time, the Battle of Griswoldville was a small engagement in the great scheme of the Civil War. The numerically superior Rebel forces could not overcome the superior firepower, experience and training of their opponents, who used the terrain to their advantage, inflicting heavy casualties. Griswoldville was an utterly futile and unnecessary engagement.

Chapter 6

Macon's Final Engagement

Having repulsed two cavalry assaults against the city and Sherman having left the area, continuing on his way to Savannah, Macon seemed safe. The city, like Augusta and Columbus, could continue to produce material for the fledging armies of the rebellion and deliver war material using the disintegrating railroad network of the Southern states. However, the peace was not to be. In the dying months of the rebellion, Macon one last time became a target, and this time there were insufficient defenders and a lack of willingness to fight. Some of the final stages of the war took place in this small community in Middle Georgia.

On March 22, Brevet Major General James H. Wilson departed with his cavalry division from northern Alabama. He intended to finally bring the war's reality to the so-far-untouched regions of Alabama and Georgia, hoping to terminate his raid in Georgia's industrial centers, maybe Columbus or Macon. Wilson took his force from northern Alabama into the depths of the state, attacking Tuscaloosa and Montgomery. Faced with Nathan Bedford Forrest's cavalry, Wilson kept a close eye on the feared and murderous cavalry commander. He dispatched forces on a number of occasions to hunt down the enemy commander when rumors placed Forrest in the vicinity.[196]

The primary goal of Wilson's cavalry was to further undermine the Confederate military-industrial complex in the region and, therefore, the ability of the Rebels to continue the war. Wilson's men destroyed industrial facilities like the Red Mountain Iron-Works, Cahawba Valley Mills, Bibb Iron-Works, Columbiana Works and many others. On March 31, the two sides met in battle near Montevallo, "enemy having made his appearance, Upton moved out and attacked, driving him in great confusion, taking nearly 100 prisoners from Roddey's command and Crossland's Kentucky brigade." The two sides continued to skirmish through the region.[197] Wilson's troops left a trail of destroyed industrial facilities in their path.

Aware of Georgia being a likely target of Wilson's cavalry, especially once he was done with Alabama, the *Macon Daily Telegraph and Confederate* paid close attention to the events in Alabama and was saddened to learn that U.S. forces had taken possession of Montgomery, the former Confederate capital. At the same time, even a week after Lee's surrender, the *Telegraph* still hoped for Lee to make a comeback and continue the rebellion successfully. The paper's evening edition announced "Lee's Army Must Be Fed."[198] There was a growing delusion among ardent Rebel supporters like the editors of this local paper.

As Wilson drew nearer to Georgia, Macon's newspaper called for the defense of Columbus, illustrating an unwavering devotion to the cause of the rebellion. With great anger, the *Macon Daily Telegraph and Confederate* noted that Montgomery had "ignominiously fallen" and that "the State of Alabama is abandoned to a small column of Yankee troops." Pointing fingers, the paper explained that the planter oligarchy of the state had refused to put the militia in the field; therefore, Alabama was "the opprobrium of Southern history."[199] From Macon's perspective, Alabama had clearly failed to defend itself against invaders. And Wilson vividly illustrated the inability of the rebellion to defend its territory.

As Wilson's forces drew closer, the hysteria increased. The *Macon Daily Telegraph and Confederate* asserted that Columbus, Eufaula and Macon were likely targets of Wilson's troops. Painting a grim picture of the future, the paper hypothesized that U.S. forces would "garrison these cities strongly, and from thence, send forth raiding parties into every county in Middle and Southwestern Georgia—free the negroes, destroy the growing crop, gather up for their own subsistence the provisions on hand, and thus reduce the people to beggary and the army to starvation." Therefore, the defense of Columbus seemed essential. The paper hoped that Governor Brown and Major General Cobb would act, and Columbus would not turn into a second Montgomery.[200]

Aware of the situation, Governor Joseph Brown issued a proclamation on April 15 informing the residents of the state that the movements of Wilson pointed to his forces making its way into Georgia. He asked, "To enable us to meet this successfully, it will require the united efforts of all who are able

Portrait of Major General James H. Wilson, officer of the Federal army, dated between 1860 and 1865. Brady's National Photographic Portrait Galleries. *Library of Congress.*

to bear arms, whether they belong to State or Confederate service."[201] Just like on previous occasions, Maconites had to prepare for another attack, but the looming end of the war created uncertainties. There remained hope that a vigilant defense could save the city one last time.

By April 16, a week after Robert E. Lee had surrender at Appomattox Court House, Wilson's men prepared their assault on Columbus. On this day, "Upton arrived in front of the defenses of Columbus." After some reconnaissance work, three hundred dismounted men of the 3rd Iowa charged the enemy position along the Salem road at 8:00 p.m. The men charged toward enemy cannons firing devastating canister shot and grapeshot. In addition, the 10th Missouri charged against the enemy position and broke the line, and two companies were able to pursue the enemy so closely that Rebel forces were unable to destroy the bridges, railroad and foot. As U.S. troops had drawn closer, they also unleashed "a withering fire from their Spencers." Wilson held the 4th Iowa in readiness in case his attacking troops needed assistance. Wilson's precaution was unnecessary; the attacking forces were successful.[202]

Columbus was a major prize, with 1,200 prisoners and fifty-two pieces of field artillery. Wilson's victory further decimated the Rebel military in the area. He had only suffered 24 casualties in the battle to capture the city. Wilson was proud that his 300 men had taken down 3,000 enemy soldiers. The next day, the destruction of the arsenal, foundry, navy yard, armory, sword and pistol factory, paper mills, cotton factories and vast quantities of rolling stock and agricultural products took place.[203] Columbus and its industrial capacity was lost to the rebellion.

The *Macon Daily Telegraph and Confederate* reported that the enemy forces appeared before Columbus from the direction of Opelika and encountered Confederate pickets at 2:00 p.m. The paper noted, "All accounts agree that the citizen soldiery of Columbus, as well as the regular troops, fought with a heroism worthy of the fame of veterans of this, or any other war." Nevertheless, concentrating later in the evening on a weak point in the Confederate line, the enemy broke through. The cavalry unit immediately took the remaining bridge to ensure a crossing point over the Chattahoochee.[204] The implications of Columbus's fall were far reaching and ominous for Macon.

With Columbus fallen and Macon the likely next target, the local authorities called for the organizing of a cavalry unit to defend the city against "Yankee vandals" and prevent the devastation of the land. Colonel J.W. Avery called out to Maconites, "Let us organize and arm to meet them!"[205] In addition, the *Macon Daily Telegraph and Confederate* demanded "Fall In!" from its readers. The paper appealed to the manhood and patriotism of its readers, suggesting, "It will be a burning shame, if some three or four thousand Yankees be permitted to capture and plunder the principal cities of Georgia." Pointing to how people had taken up arms during Stoneman's raid, the paper hoped that Maconites would do the same again.[206]

The editor of the *Macon Daily Telegraph and Confederate* continued his angry diatribe about the unnecessary surrender of Columbus, likely also thinking about the similarly shameful surrender of Montgomery. There was the increasingly familiar call on the people to take up arms, defend the city and repeal the enemy forces.[207]

Not satisfied with simply arming, there was also a call to the slaveholders in the Macon area to be patriotic and to send their chattel to Lieutenant Colonel R.W. Frobol to improve and strengthen the fortifications around Macon. The enslaved should bring tools to conduct the work. The paper estimated, "The fortifications are in a tolerable good condition, and, with a few days' labor by such a force as the city and neighborhood can send, can be put in such condition that a very few determined troops can successfully defend the city against the force which took Columbus." To boost their argument, the paper reminded its readers of the "disgraceful surrender of Montgomery."[208] In addition, all citizens could contribute to the defense of the city.

The paper advised residents to use easily accessible material to obstruct Macon's roads against enemy forces. Using the large amount of cotton stored in the city and the likelihood of its destruction, the paper suggested to haul it out to the edge of the city, where it could become a barricade. Sounding less confident, the paper wrote, "This will prove a serious barrier to his entrance to the city, and with trusty sharpshooters behind, might possibly defeat the enemy at last."[209] Despite the small size of Wilson's force, he caused far greater fear than Stoneman and Kilpatrick, likely because the city lacked defenders.

While the newspaper urged on the defensive-mindedness of the city's residents, the reality seemed to look different. There were few men working on improving the defenses, which seemed rather "poor" in style, with some dirt thrown up. It looked decidedly like Rebel authorities intended to evacuate the city and not make a stand to defend Macon. By April 18, the railroad depots in Macon had become crowded with people, some trying to take the Macon and Western Railroad to take refuge in Atlanta. The refugees never made it, as the local citizenry outside of Barnesville stopped the train, claiming the proximity of the enemy, and turned the train around back to Macon.[210] Interestingly, only the day before, Richard Cuyler had shipped two train loads of ammunition from the arsenal to the Confederate frontlines.[211] As the third attack on the city neared, the authorities seemed woefully unprepared to meet this new challenge.

Besides the miserable state of preparation, the city also seemed increasingly isolated from national events. While the Army of Northern Virginia had surrendered more than a week before, the Macon papers still lacked news from Appomattox or had not seen fit to report it. When the paper barely mentioned the apparent surrender of Robert E. Lee's army, the editors decided to dismiss the news, claiming that information from Virginia was unreliable and likely untrue.[212] Instead, the paper highlighted under a big headline, "From General Lee's Army—Glorious News: The Enemy's Loss Tremendous"—that Lee's army once more was victorious in the field.[213] Likely the *Telegraph* hoped against hope and tried to maintain Macon's fighting spirit.

Meanwhile, on April 18 in Columbus, General Wilson ordered Colonel Minty's division to advance toward Macon. Needing to cross the Flint River, Minty sent Lieutenant Colonel Pritchard with the 4th Michigan and

3rd Ohio ahead on a forced march to Double Bridges, fifty-four miles from Columbus, with order "to save them at all hazards." Pritchard did extremely well, pushing the enemy so closely that the Rebels had to abandon three pieces of artillery. In addition, Captain Hudson of the 4th Michigan led an unusual and successful sabre charge. By the evening of April 19, Minty's force was three miles east of Thomaston, where they destroyed three cotton factories. On April 20, Colonel White's 17th Indiana, Minty's lead element, encountered an advance guard of two hundred to four hundred Rebel cavalrymen on the Thomaston Road near Spring Hill, twenty-one miles from Macon. Caught by surprise by the superior-equipped U.S. veteran cavalrymen, the Rebel forces withdrew after a few charges from the U.S. forces.[214] The road to Macon lay wide open.

At the bridge over Tobesofkee Creek, Minty's men once more encountered resistance. About three hundred enemy troops had entrenched on the other side of the bridge. Especially troublesome to Minty were the enemy sharpshooters. The Rebels had taken position behind a rail barricade. There were clear signs of destruction, with planking torn up and even fire damage to the bridge. A cavalry charge across the bridge stalled when the men discovered the missing planks. Therefore, the cavalrymen "dismounted and crossed on the burning stringers in the most gallant manner, routed the enemy, and saved the bridge."[215] Having chased off the Rebel forces, Minty's men had drawn dangerously close to Macon.

Thirteen miles from the city and three miles from the Tobesofkee bridge, Colonel White encountered a flag of truce. He decided to send the dispatch down the line to Colonel Minty, halting the advance toward Macon until he had received instructions. By this point, the cavalrymen had traversed 104 miles in forty-eight hours.[216] With only a few miles to the city, the phenomenal march stalled briefly.

Minty sent the message that the flag of truce delegation delivered down the line to General Wilson. In the message, General Howell Cobb informed his U.S. counterparts that based on an armistice between Sherman and Johnston, negotiated at Bennett's Place, the war had concluded. Cobb suggested that Wilson leave Macon alone for the moment.[217] The letter read:

> *Maj. Gen. H. Cobb:*
>
> *Inform general commanding enemy's forces in your front that a truce for the purpose of a final settlement was agreed upon yesterday between Generals Johnston and Sherman, applicable to all forces under their commands. A*

> *message to that effect from General Sherman will be sent him, as soon as practicable. The contending forces are to occupy their present position, forty-eight hours' notice being given on the event of resumption of hostilities.*
>
> *G.T. Beauregard*
> *General, Second in Command*[218]

Having received this communication, Wilson personally rode to the front to instruct White to halt his advance. Wilson intended to consult with Cobb to ascertain if the armistice was real. Potentially, he needed to find a way to communicate with General Sherman to confirm the existence of the armistice. Wilson reported, "I declined without questioning the authenticity of the armistice or its applicability to my command, upon the ground that my subordinates were not authorized to act in such matters; that I had hurried to the front with all dispatch, but not in time to prevent the capture."[219] Wilson desired to rein in his troops until he had clarity, but he came too late.

As Minty and Wilson read and contemplated Cobb's message, White had resumed his dash toward Macon. Minty had ordered White to give the flag of truce party a five-minute head start and then to resume the advance and take the flag of truce party prisoner if they were on the road. Along the road to Macon, Minty's men saved another bridge before Rebel forces could burn it. Before Wilson could catch up, White had forced the city's surrender and taken its defenders captive, despite protests from Cobb. Minty reported 5 generals, 345 officers and 1,843 enlisted men prisoners, as well as sixty artillery pieces captured.[220]

As the cavalrymen had approached the city, there were some shots fired at them, but the offenders quickly dispersed into some nearby gardens. Upon reaching the outer limits of the defenses of the city, the men tore down a small palisade, crossing over the earthworks. Approaching Macon's defenders from behind, White's men told the leaderless militia men that they were surrounded and cut off. The ruse worked and the Rebels surrendered.[221] Macon had fallen without a fight, just like Montgomery had.

At 8:30 p.m., Wilson finally reached Macon and immediately sought an interview with Cobb. Wilson informed Cobb that Sherman and Johnston had likely worked out an armistice, but since Wilson was in command of the cavalry of the Military Division of the Mississippi, the armistice did not apply to his forces. Wilson had not served under Sherman since October 1864, when Wilson's cavalry became part of General George

Thomas's command. Nevertheless, Wilson telegraphed Sherman to get clarity on the subject.[222]

As Wilson settled into the occupation, Cobb complained to General Beauregard about the treatment he and his garrison had received. He wrote to Beauregard that he had informed Wilson by a flag of truce of the armistice. Cobb "informed him that I had issued orders to carry out the armistice desisting from military operations, requesting an interview." Angered, Cobb found the U.S. forces not honoring the armistice and instead demanded an unconditional surrender. Cobb "was forced to submit under protest."[223] Wilson had no interest in working with Cobb, as he had the upper hand.

Apparently, Cobb was not the only one shut down under protest. April 20 was the last issue of the *Macon Daily Telegraph and Confederates*. The paper reappeared as the *Daily Evening News* on May 4 for one day, followed by the *Macon Daily Herald* on May 8 for a handful issues and finally returning as the *Macon Daily Telegraph* on May 12. The tone of the paper remained the same: unrelenting support of the rebellion's war effort.

On April 21, a telegram arrived from General Sherman in Macon in which he confirmed the information Cobb had provided to Wilson. Sherman had indeed agreed with General Johnston on a "universal suspension of hostilities." Sherman had apparently not yet been told that he had to renegotiate his ceasefire. With the confirmation, Wilson "issued the necessary orders" and paroled his prisoners.[224]

Within days, everything changed as the government and General Grant countermanded Sherman's armistice. Once the notice reached Macon, Wilson determined to use his command to locate and arrest the fleeing Confederate president. He had "heard from citizens, however, that Davis was making his way toward the south with an escort, I directed my command to take possession of the railroads, and to send scouts in all directions in order that I might receive timely notice of the rebel movements." In addition, the voiding of the armistice meant that Wilson also moved his forces around the state to parole Rebel forces and facilitate their return home.[225]

On May 6, 1865, Wilson dispatched Lieutenant Colonel Henry Harnden with 3 officers and 150 men of the 1st Wisconsin Cavalry from Macon to Dublin. The U.S. authorities had reliable information that Jefferson Davis was in the area. At 7:00 p.m. the next day, the force reached Dublin, having left 30 men behind in Jeffersonville to scout that area. Once they reached Dublin, Harnden dispatched scouting forces to locate the fugitive Rebel leader. Interviews of white residents returned "ignorance and indifference";

however, African Americans were more forthcoming with information and told the U.S. cavalrymen that the group they searched for included Davis and his wife, as well as eight wagons and a cavalry escort.[226]

Therefore, Harnden had sufficient evidence that he was on the right track and communicated his findings to General Croxton. According to Wilson, "The trail led southward through a region of pine forests and cypress, almost uninhabited, and therefore affording no food for either men or horses." However, the swampy areas meant the pursuing cavalry lost the tracks a few times. The pursuers crossed the Ocmulgee at Brown's Ferry on May 9. The ferry operator informed Harnden that Davis and his party were only a short distance ahead and had crossed at 1:00 a.m., only a few hours before.[227]

As Harnden continued his pursuit, he encountered the advance elements of the 4th Michigan. Lieutenant Colonel B. D. Pritchard had moved his unit down from Hawkinsville. While Harnden's men continued the pursuit, their commander briefed Pritchard on the hunt. After an hour of conversation, during which Harnden informed his counterpart that his force was sufficient to deal with Davis's bodyguard, the two officers separated and continued their individual marches. However, without informing Harnden, Pritchard decided to proceed by a circuitous route to Irwinville and also try to arrest Davis. As he drew closer to the target, Pritchard told the local citizenry that he was Davis's rearguard to coax information about the fugitive Confederate leader out of them. He continued with the help of some African American guides.[228]

When Pritchard had come within half a mile of Davis's camp, he ordered Lieutenant Purinton and twenty-five men to dismount. The men were to noiselessly move to the northern side of the camp and cut off the ability to escape in that direction. Should Purinton's small group run into enemy guards, they should attack the camp, with Pritchard providing support. If everything went as planned for Purinton and they did not encounter any opposition, Pritchard's goal was to attack at daylight. The assault went off like clockwork, and within a short amount of time, Pritchard and his men had secured Davis and his group.[229]

Coincidentally, the moment Pritchard's men charged the camp, Harnden and his troops arrived, ran into the picket line of Lieutenant Purinton and exchanged fire. Since both commanders "expected desperate resistance," the collision between the two U.S. forces was fiercer than required. Unfortunately, two men died in the incident. Colonel Harnden could not have expected another U.S. unit in the area.[230] The sad encounter and unnecessary casualties caused much anger and animosity between the two commanders.

News of Davis's arrest traveled quickly. On May 13, in the evening edition, the *Daily Telegraph* in Macon had a brief statement regarding the arrest near Abbeville in Wilcox County.[231] As more information arrived, the paper could confirm that the prisoners would arrive in Macon within hours.[232]

The next morning, the *Daily Telegraph* used a bold set of headlines to tell the story of Davis's arrest: "Capture of Mr. Davis—Preparation for Flight—Desertion of His Escort—Threatened Attack of Guerrillas—Betrayal by a Ferryman—The Flight and Capture—Arrival in the City." The paper quickly located two targets for blame. In part, Davis's escort had made it known by the time they had reached Abbeville that they would not fight, likely considering the rebellion over and unwilling to risk their lives. Lauding the "six noble Kentuckians of Duke's brigade who manfully remained by him," the paper clearly was unprepared to admit defeat. Even more, the paper searched for a scapegoat, finding one in the Abbeville ferryman who helped the small party cross the Ocmulgee and who communicated this to the pursuing cavalry. The arrival of the captive in Macon drew quite a crowd, forcing the cavalrymen to draw sabers to keep the mob under control. After a brief stay, Davis and his party were on a train to Atlanta and captivity.[233]

With the departure of Jefferson Davis, the final episode of the War of the Rebellion ended in Macon. More struggles and skirmishes lay ahead for U.S. forces in the region, as they had to battle terroristic violence in the years of Reconstruction. Despite the fighting having ceased in Virginia and North Carolina, Wilson was unaware of the cessation when he departed Columbus for Macon. Having twice repulsed U.S. cavalry forces, there was some hope that Macon's defenders could repeat that feat; however, Rebel authorities were not prepared to defend the city like they had been the previous year. Wilson's cavalry easily captured Macon, acquiring the industrial center the city represented and adding Wilson's name to another final aspect of the war with the capture of Jefferson Davis. One of the concluding episodes of the rebellion transpired in Macon.

Chapter 7

Asa Holt–Cannonball House

The War of the Rebellion has spun a vast number of myths in the southern states, and Macon is no different from the rest of the region. The events in July 1864, when a shell hit a house in Macon, created one of the most persistent stories in Macon lore. Today, most Maconites know about the "War of Northern Aggression" and Sherman "atrocities" because of the "Cannonball House." The story of the home—operated by the Sidney Lanier Chapter of the United Daughters of the Confederacy—became commonly known during the period after the Second World War, turning the Asa Holts House into the "Cannonball House."

The story is often retold in the words of Howell Cobb's wife, Mary Ann Lamar Cobb. In her letter to her mother on July 31, she wrote:

> *Yesterday morning cousin Mary Ann woke me with the news that the Yankees were two or three miles from town and that Pa had gone to meet them. The fight was at Walnut bridge. We could hear the musketry and cannon and thought we could see the smoke but I believe it turned out to be the smoke from the bombs. A bomb fell behind the Ocmulgee Hospital right across the street and a ball or a bomb one or the other struck the* [page break] *in front of Mr. Holt's house and rebounded or ricocheted went through one of the posts or pillars and the window smashing the upper part of the window sash and shattering the window panes. I believe that was the only damage done in this part of the city.*[234]

View of the Asa Holt House. *Author's collection.*

The language of Cobb's letter is extremely convoluted and riddled with uncertainty. Considering Asa Holt's wife found the unexploded shell in her house and that it must have remained around the structure, Mary Ann Lamar Cobb could not identify the shell correctly as a conical Hotchkiss shell, calling it instead a ball. Similarly, did the shell rebound or ricochet?

Correspondingly, the *Daily Sun* in Columbus ran a brief note similar to the narrative in Cobb's letter: "One shell struck a bank, and rebounding passed through a column on the porch of Mr. Asa Holt's house on Mulberry street, then broke through a window of the parlor and passing through a partition wall fell on the floor of the gall. Mrs. Holt had been sitting on the exact spot not fifteen minutes before the shell fell there. Fortunately, she was visiting the hospitals at the time of the occurrence." While the article above this section noted that its information came from the Macon papers, this specific section does not indicate so.[235] Therefore, its origins are uncertain. How would a paper in Columbus have such detailed information when the *Daily Telegraph* in Macon did not cover the shell hitting the Holt House (which it did not)?

In modern times, the story of the shell hitting the Asa Holt House has received significant embellishment.[236] In some modern iterations, the cannonball supposedly rolled to the feet of Asa Holt's wife.[237] Other stories have her absent from home at the Ocmulgee Hospital. Similarly, there is the undocumented claim that the shell was supposed to hit the Hay-Johnston House, a few houses over.[238] Most likely, the shell was a miss and was supposed to hit nearer the hospital grounds.

From a military perspective, there are some issues worth considering. Stoneman's artillery chief, Captain Hardy, had three-inch ordnance rifles at his disposal.[239] These weapons had an effective range of about 1,800 to 2,000 yards, or 1,600 to 1,800 meters, at a cannon elevation of about five degrees. If the cannon had an elevation of sixteen degrees, the range could increase to as much as 4,100 yards, or 3,800 meters.[240] For the longest time, the Asa Holt House presented a round cannonball instead of the correct ordnance used by Captain Hardy, a conical Hotchkiss shell. The distance from the Dunlap Farm hill, where the artillery battery was, and the Asa Holt House is about 3,170 yards, or 2,900 meters, within range of the high cannon elevation but not the more typical five-degree elevation. Operating at such a long range, the shot hitting the Holt House was most likely a dud.

However, until the 1970s, the story remained relatively unknown, and references to a "Cannonball House" were absent from the newspapers and travel literature. Examples of the latter did not even mention the house as an attraction in Macon. A change of ownership to the Sidney Lanier Chapter brought a swift and dramatic alteration to the story of the Holt House, which became known only as the "Cannonball House."

The *Official Automobile Blue Book* of 1922 devoted a small section to Macon and its tourist offerings. Aside from its automotive connections of the Dixie and National Highways, there were steamboats to Savannah and Brunswick, as well as the Central of Georgia Railroad, with its fancy new passenger terminal (opened in 1926), supposedly the "finest south of Washington." From there, the guide listed local attractions: the Sidney Lanier House, the Academy of the Blind, Central City Park, Idle Hour Nurseries, the Ocmulgee Mounds and the city's large cotton mills. However, the guide did not list the privately owned but historically important Hay or Holt homes.[241]

The 1940 Federal Writers' Project work *Georgia: A Guide to Its Towns and Countryside* was similarly silent, but it devoted significantly more space to Macon and its history. Oddly, the guide did not mention the Stoneman or Kilpatrick raids. At the end of the Macon section came the most important part: the local points of interest, which included the Citizens and Southern National Bank, the Municipal Auditorium, Wesleyan Fine Arts Conservatory, Washington Memorial Library, Mercer University, the Sidney Lanier House, city hall, Baconsfield Park and Central City Park. The guide did mention some private homes of interest, such as the Johnston

Canning House, 854–56 Mulberry Street, Macon, Bibb County, Georgia, 1933. Historic American Buildings Survey. *Library of Congress.*

(Hay) House and Ralph Small House. The description of the Hay House was elaborate and detailed: "built about 1855, is a 24-room house in a modified Italian Renaissance style. The interior, with its frescoed ceilings and crystal chandeliers, is finished in solid mahogany and rosewood." Just like with the *Blue Book*, the Federal Writers' Project did not mention the Asa Holt House at all.[242]

Similarly, a 1939 Work Projects Administration publication about Macon and its history continued to refer to the Asa Holt House, not the "Cannonball House." Besides brief elaboration about the architecture and decoration, the booklet mentioned the "mended column and a dent in the floor of the hallway" as evidence of the "cannonball" hitting the house. In contrast to contemporary works, the WPA project mentioned that it was the "second column from the left" that suffered the hit.[243]

However, by the 1920s, the United Daughters of the Confederacy had increasingly tried to lay claim to the history of the rebellion and its stories in Macon that foster the organization's agenda. A prominent member of the organization, Mary Callaway Jones, contributed a brief article regarding the Asa Holt House to the *Macon Telegraph*.[244] Jones was part of the Sidney Lanier Chapter in Macon. In the 1950s, a fellow member of the United Daughters of the Confederacy problematically called Jones "the scholarly daughter of a distinguished Confederate family, who followed in her father's footsteps as a careful and devoted writer on Southern history."[245] Hardly an accurate description, considering the organization's history.[246]

In her article, Jones recounted the famous story of the "cannonball" hitting the "house then owned and occupied by Judge Asa Holt." She again told the story of the cannonball deflecting off the sandy sidewalk, hitting the "second column from the left, passing over a window and through an upper corner of the front parlor into the hall." Importantly, in her story the house was the Holt House, not the "Cannonball House."[247] She was refreshing the memories of the residents of the city.

Even during the 1950s, the name lingered. In a newspaper article in 1951, Gus Bernd referenced the "Asa Holt House" when talking about Stoneman's raid and the firing on Macon.[248] The local community continued to use the owner's name to describe the structure.

In the early 1960s, the Asa Holt House became the purchasing target of the United Daughters of the Confederacy's Sidney Lanier Chapter. In a newspaper piece, the group outlined its interest in acquiring the Asa Holt House to repurpose the building as a museum. The paper noted, "The main project of the Sidney Lanier Chapter of the United Daughters of the

Confederacy is raising funds to purchase a historic home of architectural significance for the establishment of a Confederate museum and to preserve one of Macon's fine old homes to be used as the group's chapter house."[249]

The article continued to remind readers that "Mrs. Frank F. Jones has been honorary president of the chapter since 1949 and is also registrar emeritus. She was recently named honorary president of the Georgia Division, UDC." The person who wrote the 1928 article commemorating the shell hitting was still involved in the preservation efforts of the Holt House. Interestingly, the article did include a picture of the front of the house. The text mentioned both the current owner, Mrs. Charles Canning, and Judge Asa Holt. However, there was not a single reference to the name "Cannonball House."[250]

Before the purchase, the Georgia Historical Commission placed a marker in front of the house in 1954; the organization used the name "Judge Asa Holt House." While the marker recounts the infamous cannonball narrative in appropriate but brief detail, it also notes the current resident at the time being a relative of the Holt family. However, nowhere does it say that the structure is the "Cannonball House" or was known as such.

As the purchase and museum project continued to gain steam, Blythe McKay provided an update in "One Will Be Preserved." Importantly, this

Historical marker of the Georgia Historical Commission at the Asa Holt House on Mulberry Street in Macon. *Author's collection.*

article recollected some of the key aspects of the house's story, including that the cannonball was in the possession of the Macon Volunteers, a gift to them from the Holt family. Supposedly, "Mrs. Holt kept the cannon ball on a parlor table until she gave it to the Macon Volunteers to put among their relics." Aware that the project to obtain ownership of the house was costly, the ladies used various means to raise money, including appeals to their brand of southern heritage. Apparently, in 1961, they had "sponsored a gala showing of 'Gone with the Wind' and attendant events raise funds for the project."[251]

At the same time, the article pointed to a potential confusion within the community. In a section titled "Canning-Cannon," McKay tried to shed some light on the issue by recounting a recent conversation. "Just last week a Maconite said, 'I always thought the house was the old Cannon house because a cannon ball hit it, I didn't realize it was the Canning house because the Cannings lived there.' But it was."[252] Could the name "Cannonball House" be a simple confusion with the name "Canning House"?

Once the Sidney Lanier Chapter took over the house, the name started to change. An article published on April 26, 1964, announced the opening of the house to visitors. For the first time, a new term appeared in the news coverage of the house: "[T]he 110-year-old Greek Revival Asa Holt house, known also as the Cannon Ball House because it was hit during the attack on Macon by Federal forces."[253] However, until only a few years earlier, the house had been the Asa Holt House, not the "Cannonball House"—this was an ingenious move by the new owners to alter the terminology.

In commemoration of the centennial of the first battle of Macon, the *Telegraph* ran an unsigned but clearly pro-Confederate story: "One hundred years ago today the War Between the States was in its fourth year and events were pointing toward an anguishing April day at Appomattox when Macon felt the excitement of its first raid by Federal forces." The article noted how General Stoneman's men had "hastily entrenched" near the Dunlap Farm and fired upon the city. The author then incorrectly claimed that Macon had earthworks that Confederate forces used to defend the city. As previous chapters indicate, those earthworks came into existence *after* the first battle of Macon.[254]

Downplaying the damages of the Rebel artillery to the Dunlap Farm, the author wrote, "Legend has it that a Confederate shot went through the house, but no sign remains to substantiate that." Ironically, the shot was mentioned in the Macon news coverage of the battle, which did not include the shot fired on the Holt House.[255] It seems odd that to make the Holt

House story look stronger, one has to dismiss the story of the other house getting hit—likely because a Rebel shell had hit the structure.

The article continued in its blend of fiction and reality by introducing then eight-year-old William Sims Payne, who supposedly "recalled vividly the events of the day" when he "heard the shot go over his head." The author claimed that "no one has put into print the account written many years later." The account, a treasured item held by the United Daughters of the Confederacy members, was supposedly written down in 1930, when Payne was seventy-four years old, nine years before he died. The author noted how closely the account aligns with the events; however, his recollection did occur after Mary Callaway Jones reminded the community about the cannonball.[256] We should naturally be cautious about the reliability of recollections sixty-six years later for an event witnessed by an eight-year-old.

Payne's recollection read:

> *As I was between eight and nine years of age when the fight took place, I remember many things connected with it quite well. My father, Dr. Geo. Payne, was a lieutenant in the Macon Volunteers Co. B., and was in the fight. When the report came that Gen'l Stoneman was going to try to take Macon, father took a squad of armed men and went around town pressing men into service to meet the enemy. He stopped at a certain corner and ordered all of the able bodied men to "fall in ranks." One very officious man stepped forward and said, "By what authority do you give these orders?" My father drew his sword, and said "By this authority, Fall in." He fell in. These were trying times, everything under military rule, and orders were strict. A short time after the above happened, I was sitting on some steps in front of our home on New St., listening to the cannon firing of Stoneman's men, when over my head I heard a curious noise as of something fluttering through the air. It was hard to locate, but I knew it was a shell. In a split second I heard it hit the ground and ricochet, crashing through a big column in the front of Mr. Asa Holt's house on Mulberry St. Passing through the house, it fell in one of the back rooms, unexploded. Several of the family were in the house at the time. The incident frightened me so that I ran in our home, which was a large brick house with a basement, being three stories on one side and two stories on the other, calling to my mother that one of the shells had just passed over me and as long as I could not dodge them, they seemed to be everywhere, tell me some place to go to get out of their way.*[257]

The rest of the article recounted his other experiences that day.

Based on the trajectory of the shot, the location of the building mentioned and Payne sitting in the front of his parents' house on New Street, thus facing east and likely close to Walnut Lane, he would not have been able to see the front of the Holt House where the shell hit the ground and rebounded toward the home. While Payne provides a second account, there is much in the account to be cautious about, and he is not an eyewitness of the hitting of the house.

After the centennial coverage, the new owners continued to struggle with raising sufficient funding to maintain the house. On April 12, 1965, Jane Brooks wrote a piece in the *Macon Telegraph* that indicated that the United Daughters of the Confederacy were about to host an antiques show to raise funds for its museum project. The article explained, "To establish the first museum of the early history of Macon through the time of the Civil Was [*sic*] is the dream of the Sidney Lanier chapter of the United Daughters of the Confederacy. Already the chapter has taken great strides in preserving the Old Cannon Ball House on Mulberry Street as one of Macon's beautiful and historic homes." The group had started to change the language in the city; instead of the Asa Holt House, people started to refer to the structure as the "Cannonball House." There was only one brief, passing reference to "Judge Holt (the builder of the house)."[258]

By the middle of the 1960s, the terminology transformation had seen success, and even the *Atlanta Journal* referred to the Asa Holt House as the "Cannonball House." Like previous stories, Frank Daniel recollected some of the odd and possibly apocryphal details of the story: "The cannonball tore through the front of the house, landed in the parlor, and rolled to the feet of the mistress of the mansion, Mrs. Asa Holt, who sat in the hospitably wide hallway, trying to compose herself by sewing to forget that the city was under siege. The shot was a dud." Besides mentioning Asa Holt's wife, all references to the house were now "Cannonball House"—not once referring to it as the Asa Holt House.[259]

Having established the term "Cannonball House" and successfully turned the property into a museum, the Sidney Lanier Chapter filed to add the house to the National Register of Historic Places. The application used the name "Cannonball House," not Asa Holt House. However, the name was not yet universally adopted. A survey of historic buildings in Macon, which likely came out after 1972, refers to the "Asa Holt–Canning House." However, all material provided by the UDC or showing the UDC as owners calls the house the "Cannonball House" and shows the UDC as owner and Asa Holt as only a previous owner.[260]

In more recent times, the terminology of "Cannonball House" has stuck, and some more additions got made to the property's history. In commemoration of a fifty-year-old article, Emily Cook reminded Maconites of the cannonball story and, intriguingly, indicated that the name "Cannonball House" was a modern invention. She wrote, "The Asa Holt home, now known as the Cannon Ball House, is operated by the Sidney Lanier, U.D.C., and displays the cannon ball in its Confederate museum."[261]

Even more, the United Daughters of the Confederacy continued to add to the mythology that surrounded the house. In a write-up for *U.D.C. Magazine*, Margaret Duncan allowed her imagination to add to the well-known but sparsely documented story. Like in other modern pieces, Duncan only briefly mentioned Judge Asa Holt as the person who owned the house, but she did refer to the structure as the "Cannonball House." However, she dramatically changed the story. Instead of the evidence presented earlier that the house remained known as the Holt House well into the 1960s, Duncan claimed that "the Holt home became known as the Old Cannon Ball House after it was hit by a cannon ball from Union forces under General George Stoneman during the battle of Dunlap Hill on July 30, 1864." Letting her imagination get the better of her, she added a new element to the well-worn story: "A small boy playing on the sand sidewalk

View of the Asa Holt House. *Author's collection.*

nearby saw it hit the sidewalk first." As clarified earlier, based on where Payne was at the time, he could not have seen the shell hit the road in front of the house—nor did he claim such.[262]

Another modern addition to the house was a cannon on a concrete base in the front of the house. The cannon was a Findlay Iron Works product from the U.S. Army's Rock Island Arsenal that the local Sons of Confederate Veterans obtained for the house on a "five-year renewable loan." The type of cannon displayed was not used by U.S. forces firing on Macon, but it is simply there because it was produced in Macon. After some controversy whether the barrel could remain in Macon, the SCV, with Congressional help, was able to retain the barrel in Macon.[263]

The Asa Holt House suffered damage during Stoneman's raid on Macon. However, there is much mythology today that surrounds the house. When the United Daughters of the Confederacy purchased the property, members altered its name and quickly erased Asa Holt House from the local language, turning the house simply into the "Cannonball House." As the story of the Asa Holt House became used by this Neo-Confederate organization, the Confederate shell hitting the Dunlap House disappeared from historic memory.

Chapter 8

Memorial Landscape

Over the years, since the creation of the first National Military Park at Chattanooga-Chickamauga in 1890, the country has added to the commemorative landscape of the rebellion with the addition of dozens of battlefield parks and hundreds of monuments. The battles in the Macon area are only partially preserved and monumented.

Throughout the region, there is a vast number of metal markers emblazed with Georgia's seal and placed by the Georgia Historical Commission (GHC). The commission came about in February 1951 under the direction of the state legislature. The commission erected some 1,800 markers and, in the course of the Civil War centennial, added more related to the rebellion. Governor James E. "Jimmy" Carter abolished the organization in 1973, folding some of its work into the Georgia State Parks.[264]

Unsurprisingly, the commission operated under the historic assumptions of the time, and many of its markers bear out that language. There are many criticisms leveled against the work of the commission, from a glorification of Sherman along the March to the Sea route to a saturation of certain Atlanta counties with markers at the expense of others. In addition, many markers include incorrect information. The latter should not surprise considering the use of Wilbur G. Kurtz Sr., who had consulted on *Gone with the Wind*, as historical adviser.[265] The commission added markers at the local battlefields, including Griswoldville.

One of the first indications that visitors are getting close to the Griswoldville Battlefield is a roadside marker placed by the GHC in 1957 about one mile from the battlefield and the U.S. line. The marker notes

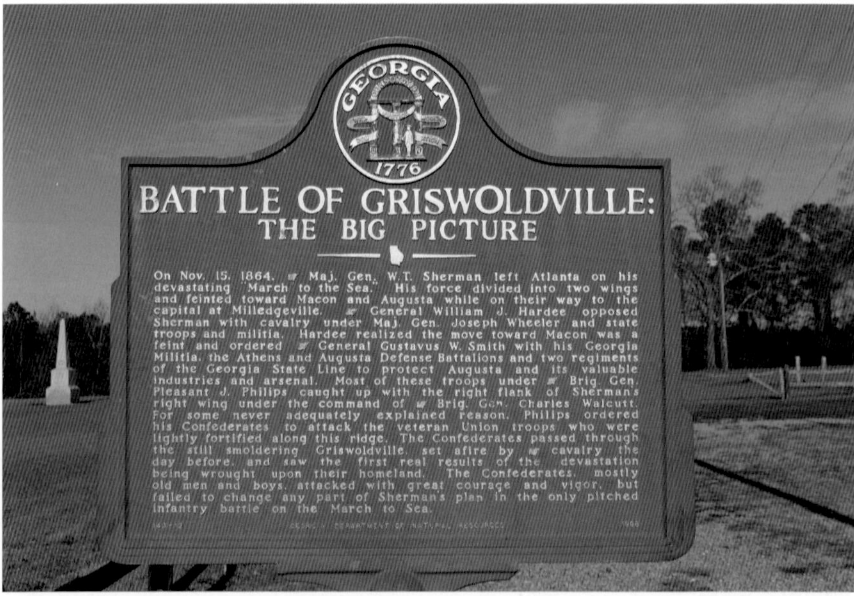

Marker placed by the Georgia DNR at the Griswoldville Battlefield. *Author's collection.*

the location where Rebel forces started their assault. Lacking entirely in context and solely focused on the Rebel side, the panel explains the very basics of the battlefield deployment of the Rebel forces. During a recent visit, the marker included a series of four faded Rebel battle flags and some newer work around the base.

The Griswoldville Battlefield Park is located 0.4 miles down Baker Road off Old Griswoldville Road. The park is situated where the cannons of the U.S. forces were in 1864. For the most part, visitors only find an empty grassy field with two monuments and a small gazebo. The location, bought in 1995 by the Association for the Preservation of Civil War Sites (a predecessor to the modern American Battlefield Trust), includes about twenty acres and cost $23,000 at the time.[266]

While the site is managed today by the Georgia State Parks, a division of the Department of Natural Resources (DNR), the property records indicate the owners as the Georgia Civil War Commission.[267] Georgia State Parks director Burt Weerts informed the Georgia Civil War Commission in April 1997 that he had received authorization to take title of the "Grizwoldville Civil War battlefield site."[268]

The small battlefield park includes two monuments. The most recent one was placed with DNR permission in 2012 by the Georgia Sons of

Left: Marker by the Georgia Historical Commission at the launch point of the Confederate assault at Griswoldville. *Author's collection.*

Right: Monument to the Confederate forces engaged at the Battle of Griswoldville. *Author's collection.*

Confederate Veterans' General Edward D. Tracy Jr. Camp. As per DNR policy, the SCV requested permission to erect the obelisk on the property. Based on the few documents available, it is not clear if the DNR was aware of who the sponsor of the monument was, but the reaction was notable. Director Becky Kelley felt that the "monument is impressive" and "would enhance the visitor experience."[269]

The monument is a remarkable modern celebration of the rebellion. Emblazed with a CSA on the front and back of the obelisk, the front of the middle base uses Georgia's seal and reads, "The Battle of Griswoldville November 22, 1864." On the reverse of this section of the monument is the seal of the Confederate States and the same text as on the front. Finally, the front base of the monument provides a list of the Confederate units involved in the battle. On the back of the base are special thanks to the Georgia Department of Natural Resources and the GA Division of the SCV, who helped in the erection of the monument in 2012.[270] The erection of such a monument only three years before the Emanuel African Methodist Episcopal Church massacre is illustrative.

Meanwhile, in Macon, the two overlapping battlefields are today largely part of the Ocmulgee National Historical Park (formerly Ocmulgee National Monument). However, with its focus on the Mississippian Mounds, the Civil War narrative of Ocmulgee largely disappears, and unless they are aware or looking for the evidence, few visitors realize that two battles took place on these grounds. The park places very little emphasis on the battles.

The "State of the Park" report acknowledged that the park included "Civil War earthworks" but suggested very little regarding their use, interpretation and integration into the park's narrative. Coinciding with the sesquicentennial events of the Civil War, the report included a few brief references about the park's participation in these commemorations. The park sponsored a reenactment in July 2014 and a lecture series in November. The park acknowledged the importance of the earthworks, which "represent the only skirmishes around Macon, GA." Besides the protection of the earthworks with the removal of trees, there is no indication of their future interpretive use or value.[271] Similarly, the park does not seem to have done a structural report on the Dunlap House to potentially confirm the cannonball hit.

Historical marker of the Georgia Historical Commission at Ocmulgee National Historical Park. *Author's collection.*

Historical marker of the Georgia Historical Commission at Ocmulgee National Historical Park. *Author's collection.*

The park also has two 1950s GHC markers on site, one devoted to the Dunlap House and the other to the July battle. The Dunlap House marker incorrectly notes, "Twice the Federals attacked Macon, emplanting their cannon on this farm." Kilpatrick's men never placed a cannon on Dunlap ridge since they only charged along the railroad trestle and against a redoubt at the nearby park entrance. The second panel, "Battles of Dunlap Farm," also misrepresents Kilpatrick's orders to demonstrate as intending to "capture" the city.

In addition, the park, relatively recently, in the course of the sesquicentennial commemorations, added a few text panels near the Dunlap Farm and the earthworks. Considering that the markers are less than a decade old, they show some serious wear from weathering. An image on "The Battle of Dunlap Hill–Stoneman's Raid" panel shows the Holt House, described as the "Cannonball House," with both the fence and the cannon emplacement. Using Robert Iobst's problematic study of Civil War Macon, the Ocmulgee NHS staff crafted and placed these markers in time for the sesquicentennial of the battle.[272]

While the panels do well in noting correctly that the shell fired from Dunlap hill struck "the home of Judge Asa Holt, now known as the Cannonball

House," the neighboring panel on Dunlap House illustrates how much the narrative in the Macon area is dominated by the Holt House myth. There is no mention that a Confederate cannonball hit the Dunlap House, forcing the mistress of the house to evacuate her residence.

The commemorative landscape in the Macon area is extremely limited. Besides the few makers placed by the GHC, both the Griswoldville and Ocmulgee parks protect the battlefields. However, these fields are inadequately documented for the uninitiated visitors, leaving much to be desired. Concerning is the lack of information at Griswoldville to contextualize the extremely new Rebel monument on site. The assault on Macon by General Wilson is entirely without signage along its final approach into Macon. While not every battlefield should or can be preserved, there is much need for adequate information about the battles at any of these sites.

Conclusion

Nobody in 1825, a few short years after Macon's creation, would have assumed that the town would eventually become a major transportation and industrial center thirty years down the road. Despite Macon's early transportation centering on waterborne vehicles, especially steamboats, to carry the region's cash crops down the Ocmulgee and Altamaha Rivers to the Atlantic Ocean, the arrival of the Central of Georgia Railroad and other railroad companies moved transportation from the muddy, clay roads of Georgia and the flood- and debris-prone rivers onto the reliable all-weather iron rails that stretched the country. Besides Atlanta, Macon was a central railroad hub.

Georgia's railroad network, as well the nation's, created new industries that supported the growing transportation network, especially iron factories. In Macon, a series of ironworks sprang into existence in the 1840s. These factories produced items for the immediate needs of the cash crops society around Macon, such as cotton gins. However, the ironworks also produced larger and heavier items like steam engines and replacement parts for the railroads. These industries allowed Macon to quickly transition from a peacetime to a wartime economy when some of the southern states rebelled against the national government in the aftermath of the constitutional election of Abraham Lincoln.

Macon's location in the heart of Georgia separated the city from enemy operations and allowed the city to be a safe environment for refugees from war-torn regions, elite girls sent to school and out of harm's way, wounded soldiers seeking recovery and, of course, industrial facilities. Until early 1864, Macon maintained its distance from the front lines and enemy armies. However, Sherman's advance on Atlanta in the summer changed everything.

In July, Macon's defenses and defenders faced their first test when U.S. cavalry under General Stoneman attempted to cut the connection between besieged Atlanta and points to the south. The city lacked fortifications at the time of Stoneman's raid; therefore, the various units defending the city faced the enemy on open ground. Thankfully for Macon, Stoneman and his officers had made some serious miscalculations. Nevertheless, the arrival of U.S. troops in East Macon meant that fear gripped the city. Repulsing Stoneman and, a few days later, seeing him as a captive created a high level of misplaced confidence. For the moment, Macon did not share Atlanta's fate.

Macon's sense of security was shattered once more when the city and Rebel authorities were left guessing about Sherman's intentions as he started to evacuate prisoners from Atlanta and accumulate a significant army around the city. The target of Sherman's famous March to the Sea, Savannah, remained unclear for the longest time; even when his forces were in the surroundings of Macon, city leaders assumed that he was headed to Augusta.

In contrast to July, Kilpatrick's cavalrymen only demonstrated against Macon, in this case shielding the movements of Sherman's infantry from Rebel attention. Kilpatrick encountered a fortified city with stubborn and ready defenders. A small number of his men engaged the enemy without pushing their advantage or seriously challenging the enemy position, while the rest of the troops brought destruction to the railroad infrastructure. For the second time in six months, Macon's defenders repulsed an enemy force and saved the city.

However, the elation of victory soon turned sour for Macon families when Rebel forces moved away from the city in pursuit of the enemy and encountered Kilpatrick's cavalry and a brigade of infantry in the vicinity of Griswoldville. The numerically superior Rebel forces were unable to gain an advantage against the veteran U.S. forces on the high ground. Many soldiers died in this utterly unnecessary engagement. Sherman bypassed Macon, allowing its military-industrial complex to continue unabated.

Sherman's departure granted Macon another five months of peace and tranquility as the war effort turned south for the rebellion in North Carolina, Virginia and Tennessee. Bringing destruction to the final untouched region, General Wilson's cavalry raid into Alabama once again took aim at the military-industrial heartland of the Confederacy. After the fall of Montgomery and Columbus, Macon's newspapers called for resilience among its defenders, but the authorities seemed reluctant to defend the city for a third time, especially with rumors that Robert E. Lee had surrendered in Virginia. When Wilson's cavalry approached, resistance quickly melted away, and Wilson's men occupied the city.

The end of the rebellion finally witnessed the fall of the city and its occupation by U.S. forces. Even more, the forces that captured Jefferson Davis were part of Wilson command and started their pursuit in Macon. There was never a battle at Macon on the scale of Gettysburg, Shiloh or Chickamauga, and most of the fighting involved only a few hundred men at best. However, in that regard, Macon's experience was representative of the rebellion. The vast majority of engagements were small skirmishes similar to those in Macon. Even more, Macon's emergence in the antebellum period as a transport hub and industrial city made the town a target for U.S. forces once they reached Georgia. The industrial capabilities of Macon and other cities allowed the rebellion to survive as long as it did, but the fighting certainly served as a reminder of the realities of war.

Notes

Chapter 1

1. Marsh, *Ocmulgee National Monument*, 4–5.
2. Bartram, *Travels through North and South Carolina*, 52–53.
3. Jenkins, "Ante Bellum Macon and Bibb County, Georgia," 15–17, 22–23.
4. *Acts of the General Assembly of the State of Georgia…November and December 1823*, 35, 162–63, 178, 222.
5. Jenkins, "Ante Bellum Macon and Bibb County," 3–4.
6. *Acts of the General Assembly of the State of Georgia…November and December 1823*, 35, 162–63, 178, 222.
7. Levasseur, *Lafayette in America in 1824 and 1825*, 70.
8. *Acts of the General Assembly of the State of Georgia…November and December 1826*, 78.
9. Ibid., 167–68.
10. *Acts of the General Assembly of the State of Georgia…November and December 1828*, 39.
11. Ibid., 39.
12. *Acts of the General Assembly of the State of Georgia…November and December 1829*, 181–82.
13. *Acts of the General Assembly of the State of Georgia…November and December 1834*, 240.
14. *Acts of the General Assembly of the State of Georgia…November and December 1833*, 129.

15. Ibid., 129.
16. *Acts of the General Assembly of the State of Georgia…November and December 1835*, 202, 211.
17. *Acts of the General Assembly of the State of Georgia…November and December 1836*, 43–44.
18. Ibid., 135–36.
19. *Acts of the General Assembly of the State of Georgia…November and December 1835*, 255.
20. *Acts of the General Assembly of the State of Georgia…November and December 1838*, 227.
21. Jenkins, "Ante Bellum Macon and Bibb County," 129–30, 132.
22. Reynolds, "First Annual Report of the President," 145.
23. Buckingham, *Slave States of America*, 1:190–91.
24. Ibid., 1:191, 193.
25. Ibid., 1:199–200.
26. Ibid., 1:194.
27. Ibid., 1:195.
28. Ibid., 1:209.
29. Ibid., 1:197.
30. Ibid., 1:207–8.
31. Jenkins, "Ante Bellum Macon and Bibb County," 46–48.
32. Ibid.
33. Phillips, *History of Transportation*, 252.
34. Ibid., 254, 258, 262.
35. Ibid., 263–64.
36. Ibid., 272.
37. Jenkins, "Ante Bellum Macon and Bibb County," 145–46.
38. Ibid., 161.

Chapter 2

39. Abrahamson, *Men of Secession and Civil War*, 94.
40. Jenkins, "Ante Bellum Macon and Bibb County," 56, 423. In the text, Jenkins claims a population of 16,291, but the appendix at the end disagrees with his number. Iobst states that the population of Bibb County was 8,838 white and 7,030 enslave people in Bibb County in 1860. Iobst, *Civil War Macon*, 1.
41. See Gagnon, *Transition to an Industrial South Athens*.

42. Richards, *Appletons' Illustrated Hand-Book*, 278.
43. Davis, *Cotton, Fire, and Dreams*, 13, 19, 24–25.
44. Ibid., 41–43.
45. Ibid., 47, 52, 67–68.
46. Robert Findlay, "Findlay's Iron Works Macon, GA," *Georgia Journal and Messenger*, November 2, 1853.
47. Davis, *Cotton, Fire, and Dreams*, 63.
48. Ibid., 86–87, 91, 94.
49. Ibid., 78–79.
50. Ibid., 119, 124.
51. *Weekly Georgia Telegraph*, "Findlay's Iron Works," February 25, 1860.
52. Davis, *Cotton, Fire, and Dreams*, 79.
53. T.C. Nisbet, "T.C. Nisbet, Founder and Machinist," *Georgia Telegraph*, April 10, 1855.
54. Davis, *Cotton, Fire, and Dreams*, 44.
55. *Weekly Georgia Telegraph*, "Schofield and Brothers Founders and Machinists," March 22, 1859; *Weekly Georgia Telegraph*, "Hardware, Iron and Steel at Carhart and Curd's," March 22, 1859.
56. Davis, *Cotton, Fire, and Dreams*, 46, 94.
57. See Schiller, *Sumter Is Avenged*.
58. Davis, *Cotton, Fire, and Dreams*, 128–29.
59. Ibid., 133, 140.
60. Ibid., 132, 139–40.
61. Iobst, *Civil War Macon*, 231, 235–36, 240, 242–43, 245, 250–51. Iobst ingeniously calls the slaves "laborers" to avoid a difficult subject.
62. Ibid., 179–80, 188.
63. Ibid., 194, 197, 204.
64. Ibid., 208.
65. Ibid., 104–5, 108–9.
66. Ibid., 107–8, 112–13.
67. S.H. Stout, "To the Good People of Macon and the Surrounding Country," *Macon Daily Telegraph*, July 22, 1864.
68. *Macon Daily Telegraph*, "Relieve the Wounded," July 22, 1864.
69. *Macon Daily Telegraph*, "Findlay's Battalion," July 14, 1864.
70. W.T. Morgan, "Attention! Militia Reserve of Bibb County," *Macon Daily Telegraph*, July 20, 1864.

Chapter 3

71. *Macon Daily Telegraph*, July 26, 1864.
72. Howell Cobb, "Headquarters Georgia Reserves," *Macon Daily Telegraph*, July 27, 1864.
73. Report of Major Haviland Tompkins, 14th Illinois Cavalry, Provost-Marshal of Operations, July 27–August 6, *OR*, series 1, vol. 38, 3:919–20; Sanford, *History of Fourteenth Illinois Cavalry*, 185.
74. Sanford, *History of Fourteenth Illinois Cavalry*, 186.
75. Ibid., 186.
76. Iobst, *Civil War Macon*, 302–3.
77. Report of Colonel Horace Capron, 14th Illinois Cavalry, commanding 3rd Brigade, July 27–August 6 (Stoneman's raid), *OR*, series 1, vol. 38, 3:926.
78. *Macon Daily Telegraph*, "The Raid on the Central Railroad," August 2, 1864.
79. Iobst, *Civil War Macon*, 305.
80. *Macon Daily Telegraph*, "The Raid on the Central Railroad," August 2, 1864.
81. Ibid.
82. Report of Major Haviland Tompkins, 14th Illinois Cavalry, Provost-Marshal of Operations, July 27–August 6, *OR*, series 1, vol. 38, 3:919–920; Sanford, *History of Fourteenth Illinois Cavalry*, 189.
83. Report of Colonel Horace Capron, 14th Illinois Cavalry, commanding 3rd Brigade, July 27–August 6 (Stoneman's raid), *OR*, series 1, vol. 38, 3:926.
84. *Macon Daily Telegraph*, "Raid on Macon," August 2, 1864.
85. Iobst, *Civil War Macon*, 307–8.
86. *Macon Daily Telegraph*, "Raid on Macon," July 30, 1864.
87. Iobst, *Civil War Macon*, 312.
88. Ibid., 311.
89. Ibid., 309.
90. Ibid., 310.
91. *Macon Daily Telegraph*, "Raid on Macon," August 2, 1864.
92. Report of Colonel Horace Capron, 14th Illinois Cavalry, commanding 3rd Brigade, July 27–August 6 (Stoneman's raid), *OR*, series 1, vol. 38, 3:926.
93. Report of Major Haviland Tompkins, 14th Illinois Cavalry, Provost-Marshal of Operations, July 27–August 6, *OR*, series 1, vol. 38, 3:920.

94. Sanford, *History of Fourteenth Illinois Cavalry*, 189–90.
95. Ibid., 190.
96. Ibid., 191.
97. *Macon Daily Telegraph*, "Raid on Macon," August 2, 1864.
98. Ibid.
99. J. William Blackshear to his wife, Macon, August 2, 1864, Blackshear Papers, quoted in Iobst, *Civil War Macon*, 313.
100. *Macon Daily Telegraph*, "The Raid on the Central Railroad," August 2, 1864.
101. Sanford, *History of Fourteenth Illinois Cavalry*, 190.
102. Report of Colonel Horace Capron, 14th Illinois Cavalry, commanding 3rd Brigade, July 27–August 6 (Stoneman's raid), *OR*, series 1, vol. 38, 3:926.
103. *Macon Daily Telegraph*, "The Latest from Stoneman," August 2, 1864.
104. *Macon Daily Telegraph*, "Arrival of Stoneman," August 2, 1864.
105. *Macon Daily Telegraph*, "Raiders in Eatonton," August 4, 1864.
106. Reports of Major General George Stoneman, U.S. Army, commanding cavalry, Army of the Ohio, May 7, July 13–15, July 27–August 6, August 6, 1864, *OR*, series 1, vol. 38, 3:914.
107. Ibid.
108. "Believer," "Prayer for the County," *Macon Daily Telegraph*, August 5, 1864.
109. *Macon Daily Telegraph*, "Christ Church—Thanksgiving Service," August 3, 1864.
110. *Historical Guide to Clinton, Georgia*, 10.
111. R.W. Bonner, "The Stoneman Raid, Clinton, August 2, 1864," *Macon Daily Telegraph*, August 4, 1864.
112. *Macon Daily Telegraph*, "Quantrell, The Guerilla Chief," August 4, 1864.
113. *Macon Daily Telegraph*, "Central Rail Road," August 8, 1864.

Chapter 4

114. William T. Sherman, Military Division of the Mississippi Special Field Order 120, November 9, 1864, *OR*, series 1, vol. 39, 3:713–14.
115. Ibid.
116. Ibid.
117. Ibid.

118. Ibid.
119. *Daily Chattanooga (TN) Rebel*, "The Defense of Macon," November 21, 1864.
120. Iobst, *Civil War Macon*, 328–31, 335.
121. *Macon Daily Telegraph and Confederate*, "From Up the Road," November 15, 1864.
122. *Macon Daily Telegraph and Confederate*, "The City" and "From Forsyth," November 18, 1864.
123. *Macon Daily Telegraph and Confederate*, "The Situation," November 19, 1864.
124. Iobst, *Civil War Macon*, 332.
125. *Carolina Spartan*, "From Georgia," November 24, 1864.
126. Judge Cole's son-in-law to Howell Cobb, November 22, telegram, Folder 12, Box 54, Howell Cobb, 1823–1969, Howell Cobb Family Papers, Hargrett Manuscripts, University of Georgia Libraries, Athens, Georgia.
127. *Carolina Spartan*, "From Georgia," November 24, 1864.
128. *Camden (SC) Daily Journal*, "From Macon," November 24, 1864.
129. *Macon Daily Telegraph and Confederate*, "The Emergency," November 19, 1864.
130. Iobst, *Civil War Macon*, 338, 341.
131. *Macon Daily Telegraph and Confederate*, "The Situation," November 21, 1864.
132. Judson Kilpatrick, December 27, 1864, *OR*, series 1, vol. 44, 362; Report of Major General William T. Sherman, January 1, 1864, *OR*, series 1, vol. 44, 8.
133. Judson Kilpatrick, December 27, 1864, *OR*, series 1, vol. 44, 362.
134. Itinerary of the Union Forces, November 1–December 31, 1864, Right Wing, 15th Army Corps, *OR*, series 1, vol. 44, 26–27.
135. Report of Major Asias Willison, 103rd Illinois Infantry, January 2, 1865, *OR*, series 1, vol. 44, 106.
136. Report of Brigadier General Charles R. Woods, U.S. Army, commanding 1st Division, November 23, 1864, *OR*, series 1, vol. 44, 97–98.
137. Howell Cobb to wife, November 19, 1864, Folder 12, Box 54, Howell Cobb, 1823–1969, Howell Cobb Family Papers, Hargrett Manuscripts, University of Georgia Libraries, Athens, Georgia.
138. Wheeler to Cobb, November 19, Folder 12, Box 54, Howell Cobb, 1823–1969, Howell Cobb Family Papers, Hargrett Manuscripts, University of Georgia Libraries, Athens, Georgia.

139. Report of Major General Joseph Wheeler, C.S. Army, commanding Cavalry Corps, December 24, 1864, *OR*, series 1, vol. 44, 406–7.
140. Judson Kilpatrick, December 27, 1864, *OR*, series 1, vol. 44, 363.
141. Report of Lieutenant Colonel Robert H. King, 3rd Kentucky Cavalry, *OR*, series 1, vol. 44, 379.
142. Report of Colonel Thomas J. Jordan, 9th Pennsylvania Cavalry, December 17, 1864, *OR*, series 1, vol. 44, 386.
143. Iobst, *Civil War Macon*, 349.
144. *Macon Daily Telegraph and Confederate*, "Attack on Macon, GA," November 30, 1864.
145. Ibid.
146. Report of Colonel Smith D. Atkins, 92nd Illinois Mounted Infantry, December 24, 1864, *OR*, series 1, vol. 44, 389–90.
147. *Ninety-Second Illinois Volunteers*, 176–77.
148. Report of Lieutenant Colonel Matthew Van Buskirk, 92nd Illinois Mounted Infantry, December 20, 1864, *OR*, series 1, vol. 44, 394.
149. *Ninety-Second Illinois Volunteers*, 176–77.
150. Report of Colonel Smith D. Atkins, 92nd Illinois Mounted Infantry, December 24, 1864, *OR*, series 1, vol. 44, 389–90.
151. Report of Lieutenant Colonel Matthew Van Buskirk, 92nd Illinois Mounted Infantry, December 20, 1864, *OR*, series 1, vol. 44, 394.
152. *Macon Daily Telegraph and Confederate*, "Attack on Macon, GA," November 30, 1864.
153. Report of Colonel Smith D. Atkins, 92nd Illinois Mounted Infantry, December 24, 1864, *OR*, series 1, vol. 44, 390.
154. Report of Lieutenant Colonel Thomas W. Sanderson, 10th Ohio Cavalry, December 22, 1864, *OR*, series 1, vol. 44, 403; *Ninety-Second Illinois Volunteers*, 176–77.
155. *Macon Daily Telegraph and Confederate*, "Attack on Macon, GA," November 30, 1864.
156. Report of Major General Joseph Wheeler, C.S. Army, commanding Cavalry Corps, December 24, 1864, *OR*, series 1, vol. 44, 407.
157. Report of Colonel Smith D. Atkins, 92nd Illinois Mounted Infantry, December 24, 1864, *OR*, series 1, vol. 44, 390.
158. Ibid.; Report of Lieutenant Colonel Matthew Van Buskirk, 92nd Illinois Mounted Infantry, December 20, 1864, *OR*, series 1, vol. 44, 394.
159. *Ninety-Second Illinois Volunteers*, 178.
160. Ibid., 177.

161. *Macon Daily Telegraph and Confederate*, "The Situation," November 23, 1864.
162. Ibid.
163. Iobst, *Civil War Macon*, 355.

Chapter 5

164. Report of Major General Joseph Wheeler, C.S. Army, commanding Cavalry Corps, December 24, 1864, *OR*, series 1, vol. 44, 407.
165. Report of Colonel Thomas J. Jordan, 9th Pennsylvania Cavalry, November 22, 1864, *OR*, series 1, vol. 44, 386.
166. Report of Colonel Robert F. Catterson, 97th Indiana Infantry, November 23, 1864, *OR*, series 1, vol. 44, 105.
167. Report of Major General Peter J. Osterhaus, U.S. Army, Commanding 15th Army Corps, December 26, 1864, *OR*, series 1, vol. 44, 82.
168. Report of Colonel Robert F. Catterson, 97th Indiana Infantry, November 23, 1864, *OR*, series 1, vol. 44, 105.
169. Report of Major General Peter J. Osterhaus, U.S. Army, Commanding 15th Army Corps, December 26, 1864, *OR*, series 1, vol. 44, 82–83.
170. Report of Major Asias Willison, 103rd Illinois Infantry, January 2, 1865, *OR*, series 1, vol. 44, 107.
171. Report of Colonel Robert F. Catterson, 97th Indiana Infantry, November 23, 1864, *OR*, series 1, vol. 44, 105.
172. Report of Major General Peter J. Osterhaus, U.S. Army, Commanding 15th Army Corps, December 26, 1864, *OR*, series 1, vol. 44, 83.
173. Report of Major Asias Willison, 103rd Illinois Infantry, January 2, 1865, *OR*, series 1, vol. 44, 107.
174. Report of Colonel Robert F. Catterson, 97th Indiana Infantry, November 23, 1864, *OR*, series 1, vol. 44, 105.
175. Ibid.
176. Ibid.
177. Report of Major Asias Willison, 103rd Illinois Infantry, January 2, 1865, *OR*, series 1, vol. 44, 107.
178. Reid, *Ohio in the War*, 851.
179. Report of Colonel Robert F. Catterson, 97th Indiana Infantry, November 23, 1864, *OR*, series 1, vol. 44, 105.
180. Report of Major Asias Willison, 103rd Illinois Infantry, January 2, 1865, *OR*, series 1, vol. 44, 107.

181. Ibid.
182. Reports of Brigadier General Charles R. Woods, U.S. Army, commanding 1st Division, November 23, 1864, *OR*, series 1, vol. 44, 98.
183. Report of Colonel Robert F. Catterson, 97th Indiana Infantry, November 23, 1864, *OR*, series 1, vol. 44, 105–6.
184. Report of Major Asias Willison, 103rd Illinois Infantry, January 2, 1865, *OR*, series 1, vol. 44, 107.
185. Report of Brigadier General Charles R. Woods, U.S. Army, commanding 1st Division, November 23, 1864, *OR*, series 1, vol. 44, 105–6.
186. Report of Major Asias Willison, 103rd Illinois Infantry, January 2, 1865, *OR*, series 1, vol. 44, 98.
187. Ibid., 107.
188. *Macon Daily Telegraph and Confederate*, "The Battle of Griswoldville," November 24, 1864.
189. *Macon Daily Telegraph and Confederate*, "From Gordon and Griswoldville," November 30, 1864.
190. Report of prisoners of war captured and property captured and destroyed by 3rd Cavalry Division during the campaign terminating with the occupation of Savannah, *OR*, series 1, vol. 44, 367.
191. Report of Major General Peter J. Osterhaus, U.S. Army, Commanding 15th Army Corps, December 26, 1864, *OR*, series 1, vol. 44, 83.
192. Reports of Brigadier General Charles R. Woods, U.S. Army, commanding 1st Division, November 23, 1864, *OR*, series 1, vol. 44, 98.
193. Oliver O. Howard to Peter J. Osterhaus, November 23, 1864, *OR*, series 1, vol. 44, 106.
194. *Columbus Times*, "A Proclamation. By Jos. E. Brown, Governor of Georgia," November 28, 1864.
195. *Macon Daily Telegraph and Confederate*, "Macon Is Safe," November 26, 1864.

Chapter 6

196. Reports of Brevet Major General James H. Wilson, U.S. Army, commanding Cavalry Corps, Military Division of the Mississippi, May 3, 1865, *OR*, series 1, vol. 49, 1:350.
197. Ibid.

198. *Macon Daily Telegraph and Confederate*, "From Alabama," April 13, 1865.
199. *Macon Daily Telegraph and Confederate*, "Is Columbus to Be Defended?" April 15, 1865.
200. Ibid.
201. Joseph E. Brown, "Attention, Militia!" *Macon Daily Telegraph and Confederate*, April 17, 1865.
202. Reports of Brevet Major General James H. Wilson, U.S. Army, commanding Cavalry Corps, Military Division of the Mississippi, May 3, 1865, June 29, 1865, *OR*, series 1, vol. 49, 1:350, 1:363–64.
203. Ibid.
204. *Macon Daily Telegraph and Confederate*, "The Battle of Columbus," April 18, 1865.
205. *Macon Daily Telegraph and Confederate*, "To the Rescue," April 18, 1865.
206. *Macon Daily Telegraph and Confederate*, "Fall In!" April 18, 1865.
207. *Macon Daily Telegraph and Confederate*, "Need Macon Fall!" April 19, 1865.
208. *Macon Daily Telegraph and Confederate*, "Send in Your Negroes," April 19, 1865.
209. *Macon Daily Telegraph and Confederate*, "Barricade the Streets," April 19, 1865.
210. Iobst, *Civil War Macon*, 385–86.
211. Davis, *Cotton, Fire, and Dreams*, 141.
212. *Macon Daily Telegraph and Confederate*, "The Virginia Situation," April 20, 1865.
213. *Macon Daily Telegraph and Confederate*, "From General Lee's Army," April 20, 1865.
214. Reports of Brevet Major General James H. Wilson, U.S. Army, commanding Cavalry Corps, Military Division of the Mississippi, June 29, 1865, *OR*, series 1, vol. 49, 1:350, 1:365; Reports of Colonel Robert H.G. Minty, 4th Michigan Cavalry, commanding 2nd Division, April 2–20, *OR*, series 1, vol. 49, 1:442.
215. Reports of Colonel Robert H.G. Minty, 4th Michigan Cavalry, commanding 2nd Division, April 2–20, *OR*, series 1, vol. 49, 1:442–43.
216. Reports of Brevet Major General James H. Wilson, U.S. Army, commanding Cavalry Corps, Military Division of the Mississippi, May 3, 1865, June 29, 1865, *OR*, series 1, vol. 49, 1:350, 1:365.
217. Ibid.

218. Reports of Brevet Major General James H. Wilson, U.S. Army, commanding Cavalry Corps, Military Division of the Mississippi, June 29, 1865, *OR*, series 1, vol. 49, 1:365.
219. Reports of Brevet Major General James H. Wilson, U.S. Army, commanding Cavalry Corps, Military Division of the Mississippi, May 3, 1865, June 29, 1865, *OR*, series 1, vol. 49, 1:350, 1:365–66.
220. Reports of Colonel Robert H.G. Minty, 4th Michigan Cavalry, commanding 2nd Division, April 2–20, *OR*, series 1, vol. 49, 1:443.
221. Iobst, *Civil War Macon*, 390.
222. Reports of Brevet Major General James H. Wilson, U.S. Army, commanding Cavalry Corps, Military Division of the Mississippi, June 29, 1865, *OR*, series 1, vol. 49, 1:366.
223. Cobb to Beauregard, April 20, 1865, Folder 7, Box 55, Howell Cobb, 1823–1969, Howell Cobb Family Papers, Hargrett Manuscripts, University of Georgia Libraries, Athens, Georgia.
224. Reports of Brevet Major General James H. Wilson, U.S. Army, commanding Cavalry Corps, Military Division of the Mississippi, May 3, 1865, June 29, 1865, *OR*, series 1, vol. 49, 1:350, 1:367.
225. Reports of Brevet Major General James H. Wilson, U.S. Army, commanding Cavalry Corps, Military Division of the Mississippi, January 17, 1867, *OR*, series 1, vol. 49, 1:371–72.
226. Ibid., 1:375–76.
227. Ibid., 1:376.
228. Ibid., 1:376–77.
229. Ibid., 1:377.
230. Ibid.
231. *Macon Daily Telegraph*, "Capture of Messrs. Davis and Reagan," May 13, 1865.
232. *Macon Daily Telegraph*, "Mr. Davis and Party," May 13, 1865.
233. *Macon Daily Telegraph*, "Capture of Mr. Davis," May 14, 1865.

Chapter 7

234. Mary Ann Lamar Cobb to mother, July 31, 1864, Box 57, Folder 18, Howell Cobb Family Papers, Hargrett Manuscripts, University of Georgia Libraries, Athens, Georgia.
235. *Daily Sun*, "The Raid on Macon," August 3, 1864.
236. Butler, *Historical Record of Macon and Central Georgia*, 264.

237. Reston, *Sherman's March and Vietnam*, 67. Reston did not provide documentation related to where this story came from.
238. Bozeman, *Macon*, 65.
239. Iobst, *Civil War Macon*, 311.
240. Cole, *Civil War Artillery at Gettysburg*, 81; Civil War Artillery Projectile and Cannon Home Page, "Basic Facts Concerning Artillery," http://www.civilwarartillery.com/basicfacts.htm.
241. *Official Automobile Blue Book*, 1922, 2:481.
242. Leckie, *Georgia*, 111–16.
243. Writers' Program of the Work Projects Administration, *Macon Guide*, 95–96.
244. Mary Callaway Jones, "Asa Holt Home Was Gun Target during Civil War," *Macon Telegraph*, May 20, 1928.
245. Lamar, *When All Is Said and Done*, 172.
246. See Cox, *Dixie's Daughters*.
247. Mary Callaway Jones, "Asa Holt Home Was Gun Target," *Macon Telegraph*, May 20, 1928.
248. Gus Bernd, "Ga. Cavalcade," *Houston Home Journal*, August 9, 1951.
249. *Macon Telegraph and News*, "UDC Hopes to Buy Historic Home Here," October 28, 1962.
250. Ibid.
251. Blythe McKay, "One Will Be Preserved," *Macon Telegraph and News*, January 13, 1963.
252. Ibid.
253. *Macon Telegraph and News*, April 26, 1964.
254. *Macon Telegraph and News*, "Federal Cannonball Fell on Macon Century Ago," July 30, 1964.
255. Ibid.
256. Ibid. An embellished version of Payne's story is included in Jacqueline Cook's novels.
257. Ibid.
258. Jane Brooks, "Antique Show to Add Funds for UDC Historical Museum," *Macon Telegraph and News*, April 12, 1965.
259. Frank Daniel, "The Cannon Ball House," *Atlanta Journal*, April 25, 1965.
260. *Historic Macon Building Survey*, vol. 14, 3,242–71.
261. Emily Cook, "Anniversary Noted for Cannon Ball," *Macon Telegraph*, July 25, 1989.
262. Duncan, "Old Cannon Ball House," 28.
263. *Blue and Grey Magazine*, "Cannon to Remain in Georgia."

Chapter 8

264. Jann Haynes Gilmore, "Georgia's Historic Preservation Beginning: The Georgia Historical Commission (1951–1973)," *Georgia Historical Quarterly* 63 (Spring 1979).
265. Ibid., 11, 13.
266. Battlefield Update, "APCWS Approves $3.5 Million Land Acquisition Package," American Battlefield Protection Program, NPS 56 (May 1995), 3.
267. QPublic, "Twiggs County, GA," Report T054004, https://qpublic.schneidercorp.com/Application.aspx?AppID=684&LayerID=11374&PageTypeID=4&PageID=4785&KeyValue=T054%20%20%20004.
268. Burt Weerts to Oliver Keller, April 15, 1997, provided courtesy of Judd Smith, Parks Historian, Parks, Recreation and Historic Sites Division.
269. Becky Kelley to L. Harris Churchwell, November 17, 2010, provided courtesy of Judd Smith.
270. The author reached out to the DNR for any documentation regarding the placement of the Confederate monument but has not heard back yet.
271. National Park Service, "State of the Park Report: Ocmulgee National Monument," 2014, http://www.npshistory.com/publications/state-of-the-park/ocmu-2014.pdf.
272. Angela Bates, e-mail correspondence, January 23, 2020. From the looks, the Ocmulgee Civil War markers were designed in house at the park using NPS templates and not with the support of Harpers Ferry.

Bibliography

Archive

Howell Cobb Family Papers. Hargrett Manuscripts. University of Georgia Libraries, Athens, Georgia.

Primary Sources

Acts of the General Assembly of the State of Georgia, Passed in Milledgeville at an Annual Session in November and December 1823. Milledgeville, GA: Camak and Ragland, 1824.

Acts of the General Assembly of the State of Georgia, Passed in Milledgeville at an Annual Session in November and December 1826. Milledgeville, GA: Camak and Ragland, 1826.

Acts of the General Assembly of the State of Georgia, Passed in Milledgeville at an Annual Session in November and December 1828. Milledgeville, GA: Camak and Ragland, 1829.

Acts of the General Assembly of the State of Georgia, Passed in Milledgeville at an Annual Session in November and December 1829. Milledgeville, GA: Camak and Ragland, 1830.

Acts of the General Assembly of the State of Georgia, Passed in Milledgeville at an Annual Session in November and December 1834. Milledgeville, GA: P.L. and B.H. Robinson, 1835.

Acts of the General Assembly of the State of Georgia, Passed in Milledgeville at an Annual Session in November and December 1833. Milledgeville, GA: Polhill and Fort, 1834.

Acts of the General Assembly of the State of Georgia, Passed in Milledgeville at an Annual Session in November and December 1835. Milledgeville, GA: John A. Cuthbert, 1836.

Acts of the General Assembly of the State of Georgia, Passed in Milledgeville at an Annual Session in November and December 1836. Milledgeville, GA: P.L: Robinson, 1837.

Acts of the General Assembly of the State of Georgia, Passed in Milledgeville at an Annual Session in November and December 1838. Milledgeville, GA: P.L: Robinson, 1839.

Automobile Blue Book Corporation. *Official Automobile Blue Book, 1922*. New York: Automobile Blue Book Corporation, 1921.

Bartram, William. *Travels through North and South Carolina, Georgia, East and West Florida, the Cherokee Country, the Extensive Territories of the Muscogulges, or Creek Confederacy, and the Country of the Chactaws*. Philadelphia, PA: James and Johnson, 1791.

Buckingham, James Silk. *The Slave States of America*. London: Fisher, Son and Company, 1842.

Levasseur, Auguste. *Lafayette in America in 1824 and 1825: Or, Journal of a Voyage to the United States*. Philadelphia, PA: Carey and Lea, 1829.

Ninety-Second Illinois Volunteers. Freeport, IL: Journal Steam Publishing, 1875.

Reid, Whitelaw. *Ohio in the War: Her Statesmen, Generals and Soldiers*. Cincinnati, OH: Robert Clarke Company, 1895.

Reynolds, L.O. "First Annual Report of the President and Engineer-in-Chief of the Central Railroad and Banking Company of Georgia." *American Railroad Journal and Mechanics' Magazine* 5 (September 1, 1838): 145.

Richards, T. Addison. *Appletons' Illustrated Hand-Book of American Travel*. New York: D. Appleton, 1860.

Sanford, W.L. *History of Fourteenth Illinois Cavalry and the Brigades to Which It Belonged*. Chicago: R.R. Donnelley and Sons, 1898.

United States War Department. *The War of the Rebellion: A Compilation of the Official Records of the Union and Confederate Armies*. 127 vols. Washington, D.C.: Government Printing Office, 1881–1901.

Writers' Program of the Work Projects Administration. *The Macon Guide and Ocmulgee National Monument*. Macon, GA: J.W. Burke, 1939.

Newspapers

Atlanta (GA) Journal.
Camden (SC) Daily Journal.
Carolina Spartan (Spartanburg, SC).
Columbus (GA) Times.
Daily Chattanooga (TN) Rebel.
Daily Sun (Columbus, GA).
Georgia Telegraph (Macon, GA).
Houston Home Journal (Perry, GA).
Macon (GA) Daily Telegraph and Confederate.
Macon (GA) Daily Telegraph.
Macon (GA) Telegraph and News.
Weekly Georgia Telegraph (Macon, GA).

Secondary Sources

Abrahamson, James L. *The Men of Secession and Civil War, 18591861.* Lanham, MD: Rowman and Littlefield, 2000.

Blue and Grey Magazine. "Cannon to Remain in Georgia" (June 2001).

Bozeman, Glenda Barnes. *Macon.* Charleston, SC: Arcadia Publishing, 2010.

Butler, John Campbell. *Historical Record of Macon and Central Georgia Containing Many Interesting and Valuable Reminiscences.* Macon, GA: J.W. Burke and Company, 1879.

Cole, Philip M. *Civil War Artillery at Gettysburg.* New York: Da Capo Press, 2002.

Cox, Karen L. *Dixie's Daughters: The United Daughters of the Confederacy and the Preservation of Confederate Culture.* Gainesville: University Press of Florida, 2003.

Davis, Robert S., Jr. *Cotton, Fire, and Dreams: The Robert Findlay Iron Works and Heavy Industry in Macon, Georgia, 1839–1912.* Macon, GA: Mercer University Press, 1998.

Duncan, Margaret H. "The Old Cannon Ball House and Macon Confederate Museum." *UDC Magazine* 49, no. 2 (February 1986): 28.

Gagnon, Michael J. *Transition to an Industrial South Athens, Georgia, 1830–1870.* Baton Rouge: Louisiana State University Press, 2012.

A Historical Guide to Clinton, Georgia: An Early Nineteenth Century County Seat. Marye Collection, Georgia Department of Archives and History, 1975.

Historic Macon Building Survey. Available at the Washington Memorial Library Archives, Macon, Georgia.

Iobst, Richard W. *Civil War Macon: The History of a Confederate City.* Macon, GA: Mercer University Press, 1999.

Jenkins, William T. "Ante Bellum Macon and Bibb County, Georgia." PhD dissertation, University of Georgia, 1966.

Lamar, Dolly Blount. *When All Is Said and Done.* Athens: University of Georgia Press, 1952.

Leckie, George G. *Georgia: A Guide to Its Towns and Countryside.* Atlanta, GA: Tupper and Love Book, 1954.

Marsh, Alan. *Ocmulgee National Monument: An Administrative History*. N.p.: National Park Service, 1986.

Phillips, Ulrich Bonnell. *A History of Transportation of the Eastern Cotton Belt to 1860.* New York: Columbia University Press, 1908.

Reston, James. *Sherman's March and Vietnam.* New York: Macmillan, 1984.

Schiller, Herbert M. *Sumter Is Avenged: The Siege and Reduction of Fort Pulaski.* Shippensburg, PA: White Mane Publishing Company, 1995.

About the Author

Niels Eichhorn is a historian and adjunct instructor in Macon, Georgia. He holds a PhD in history from the University of Arkansas. He is the author of two recent books, *Liberty and Slavery: European Separatists, Southern Secession, and the American Civil War* (LSU Press, 2019) and *Atlantic History in the Nineteenth Century: Migration, Trade, Conflict, and Ideas* (Palgrave, 2019). He has published a series of articles and blog posts on Civil War history and is now working on a diplomatic history of the Civil War era.

VANDERBILT BASKETBALL

TALES OF COMMODORE HARDWOOD HISTORY

BILL TRAUGHBER

THE History PRESS

Published by The History Press
Charleston, SC 29403
www.historypress.net

First published 2012

Manufactured in the United States

ISBN 978.1.60949.688.3

Library of Congress CIP data applied for.

Notice: The information in this book is true and complete to the best of our knowledge. It is offered without guarantee on the part of the author or The History Press. The author and The History Press disclaim all liability in connection with the use of this book.

To my beautiful daughter, Heather Jane,
and my grandson, Edward Ladd Jackson III, whom we call "Trip."
I am very proud of both.

Contents

Foreword

Vanderbilt basketball. That's a weighty topic. I think of Town and Country, Memorial Magic, the F-Troop, Clyde Lee and the balconies he built, Phil Cox, Shan Foster, Derrick Byars, Matt Freije, Coach Kevin Stallings, Coach Eddie Fogler, Coach Roy Skinner, Perry Wallace, Billy McCaffrey, John Jenkins, Kedren Johnson, Steve Grant's three to beat Georgia, Mario Moore's bomb to beat Oregon, Corey Smith's lay-up to beat Wichita State, "The Streak Continues…" so many images and feelings flash into my mind.

Of course, the most vivid and special of those memories come from the four years in the late 1980s when I was privileged to wear the black and gold. Coach C.M. Newton, Will Perdue and his Perdunks. Will's self-confidence and work ethic that made him a first-round draft pick, longtime NBA player and four-time NBA champion. My classmate, Barry Goheen, and all the shots that he made to pull us through.

The UT game in '86 when we were down eight points with forty-five seconds left and no 3-point line but managed to win in regulation. The tennis ball game that ultimately cost the '89 team and me our SEC championship rings. That one still hurts. Most importantly, I have great former teammates and friends in addition to those guys mentioned above—Frank Kornet, Charles Mayes, Eric Reid, Derrick Wilcox, Scott Draud, Steve Reece and so many others. Coach Ed Martin, Coach John Bostick, Glen Clem, Darrell Dulaney and Bobby Westbrooks…I could go on and on.

I have great memories of Vanderbilt fans packing the house virtually every night—15,626 (capacity) as the often-listed number for attendance.

Noise unlike anything I have ever heard before or since as we knocked off top-rated North Carolina, eventual national champion Indiana, some very good Kentucky teams and almost anyone who strayed into Memorial Gym. The NCAA Tourney win over Pitt that moved us into the Sweet Sixteen and the two threes by Goheen to force OT—unbelievable—and the reception that we received when we returned to Nashville that night. There was nothing like Vanderbilt basketball prior to the arrival of major professional sports teams in Nashville, and it was amazing to be a part of it.

Time marches on, the faces change, even Memorial Gym has changed, but Vanderbilt basketball remains unique, special, fun and an integral part of the life of the university, the Nashville community and the culture in the southeastern United States—just as it has been for so long. I am honored to have been part of this great story as a player and, even better, because my eligibility has lasted so much longer as a commentator.

Bill Traughber is thorough in his recording of this great story. He captures the history of Vanderbilt basketball from the perspective of someone who loves the subject—with passion and with the attendant curiosity to dig deeply. Like Vanderbilt basketball itself, Bill's book delivers great enjoyment and is instructive as to the value of hard work and perseverance. Importantly, Bill also delves into women's basketball and its great story.

Similar to my memories with men's and women's basketball, I think of Jackie Cowan, Carolyn Peck, Wendy Scholtens, Heidi Gillingham, Rhonda Blades, Sheri Sam, Ashley McElhiney, Chantelle Anderson, Carla Thomas, Christina Foggie, Coach Phil Lee, Coach Jim Foster, Coach Melanie Balcomb and the parade of great players that we've had. Above all, I think of my favorite Vanderbilt women's player, the great Karen Booker, who managed to lead the SEC in the unlikely statistical combination of steals and rebounding. She's a great sister too and part of why accepting the offer to attend Vanderbilt was one of the easiest big decisions of my life.

I think of how Karen and I grew up as the youngest of twelve children from Franklin, Tennessee. I think of how our experience at Vanderbilt University and particularly with Vanderbilt basketball has changed our lives so dramatically. For me, those four years were so wonderful, and it's impossible to imagine how my life would have developed without Vanderbilt basketball. I think that is the best part of the story—how much Vanderbilt basketball has impacted the lives of so many people in a positive way.

Enjoy the remarkable and rich history of Vanderbilt basketball. No doubt, there are stories here that you have only heard about and maybe some of which you are completely unaware. Bill's gift for capturing that history and describing it so well will help you to appreciate what Vanderbilt basketball has become that much more. Enjoy it. Go 'Dores!

Barry Booker
Vanderbilt Guard (1986–89)
Jefferson Pilot TV Basketball Commentator

Preface

My earliest recollections of Vanderbilt basketball came when I was about eleven years old. I was walking into a 7-11-type market in Green Hills with my older sister and twin brother. This must have been about 1965. Inside the market, we came across Clyde Lee and another Vanderbilt basketball player. Lee was well known and very popular in Nashville. I recall we were talking about how they towered over us. Vanderbilt basketball was huge in those days.

I do remember looking in a telephone book for Lee's address to send a letter asking for an autograph. There were a few "C. Lee"s listed, and I never received a response. I realized later that he lived in a dorm on campus. I probably sent the letter to the wrong Lee. But I knew who Clyde Lee was.

In that time, Nashville sports were lacking. There was no professional minor-league baseball team, NFL team nor NHL team. The old Nashville Dixie Flyers hockey club was in existence and successful on the ice but not in attendance. Memorial Gym was a much more pleasant sports venue than the Municipal Auditorium. Vanderbilt football was not finding success on the gridiron, but the basketball 'Dores were displaying their best records in school history.

I have an old, torn game program from the 1965–66 season, but I don't remember going to games at that time. I would attend games once in a while and always listened on the radio. I purchased season tickets during the C.M. Newton and Eddie Fogler eras, which were exciting times in Memorial Gymnasium.

I had a big sports day on December 5, 1987, when I watched my high school football team, Brentwood Academy, win a state championship on Dudley Field. After, I walked over to Memorial Gym and witnessed the Commodores upset Dean Smith and his No. 1–ranked North Carolina Tar Heels.

Later that basketball season, Vanderbilt went through a stretch of games when it was just dominating the competition at home. I was so excited just walking toward Memorial Gym from the parking lot in anticipation of some great college basketball. Will Perdue, Barry Booker, Frank Kornet and Barry Goheen were part of those exciting times.

Speaking of Goheen, what a clutch player. In January 1989 against Georgia, Goheen banked a mid-court shot at the buzzer just before halftime. I am sad to say I missed that. I had left my seat early to beat the crowd to the concession stand. As I was walking down the stairs (my season ticket seats were in 3L), I heard the gymnasium explode with cheers. A man exiting his sitting level below mine grabbed me and was shouting about that miracle shot by Goheen. He couldn't believe it.

But later in that same game, with Vandy down by two points in the final seconds, Booker brought the ball down and passed to Goheen. Goheen dribbled, looked up at the clock and stepped back behind the 3-point line. I was screaming, "Shoot, shoot!" I wanted overtime. But Goheen made the 3-pointer to win the game.

It was at this time that Vanderbilt was offering a contest for Vanderbilt fans. At home games, fans could fill out a slip of paper with their name and seat location. Three people were chosen to a shooting contest at halftime. I will admit I stuffed the entry box with several entry slips. American Airlines sponsored the contest, with a prize of free airfare for two. Each contestant had a shot from mid-court for a trip to Australia, one from the 3-point line for a trip to San Juan, Puerto Rico, and one from the foul line for airline tickets to choose from Los Angeles, San Francisco or San Diego. Only one contestant could win. I had California on my mind. After the game started, a couple of guys wearing American Airlines shirts arrived at my section. I just knew they were looking for me. They told me to be at the floor level near the visitors' bench a few minutes before halftime.

So there were two other guys and I at halftime on the floor of Memorial Gymnasium, which was packed. Vandy was playing Mississippi State. Nobody came close to making the mid-court shot. I made a try at the top of the 3-point line—straight up. I swished it through the goal—nothing but nylon. The fans cheered. I kept saying to myself, *I won, I won*. And I did! The last two guys missed their shots. The representatives gave me an envelope with airline ticket information. That summer, I received the free airline tickets and stayed in San Juan for a week. I can say my career shooting average in Memorial Gymnasium is 50 percent. That was my Memorial Magic moment.

When Eddie Fogler arrived on campus, he took the Commodores up another level. That 1992–93 SEC championship was great. Billy McCaffrey was special teaming with another transfer, Chris Lawson. I was very disappointed when Fogler left Vanderbilt for South Carolina. I did send Fogler a wooden plaque with the Commodores' home court markings to be signed. SEC championships are nearly impossible to win.

I gave up my season tickets but still followed the team closely. Then I became a contributing writer for vucommodores.com, writing Vanderbilt sports history stories (Commodore History Corner). With a media pass, I am able to watch Vanderbilt basketball up close. My fondest memories in recent years are upsets over No. 1 Florida and No. 1 Tennessee. And when Coach Kevin Stallings would not give Florida's Joakim Noah the basketball after a turnover near the Vanderbilt bench was entertaining.

Though it is always a great moment to beat Tennessee and Kentucky, Shan Foster's amazing shooting performance (forty-two points) on Senior Night 2008 was unbelievable. Going into the media room after games is special (and a good place to kill time as outside traffic clears). You can see these athletes as college men instead of performers on the court. I will say that Shan Foster was the flashiest dresser and caught the attention from the media.

I'd like to thank the following people in the Vanderbilt Athletic Communications office for assisting me with this book and in the past on my stories: Rod Williamson (director), Andy Boggs (men's basketball contact), Michael Scholl (women's basketball contact), Ryan Schulz, Chris Weinman, Kyle Parkinson, Brandon Barca, Larry Leathers, Brock Williams (director of sports operation) and Eric Jones (Vanderbilt ticket manager). I'd like to give special thanks to Barry Booker for writing such a complimentary foreword to this project and Molly Blatt, Coach Stallings's administrative assistant.

The Vanderbilt University Special Collections and Archives helped me with photographs for this project and other previous stories for vucommodores.com. I want to thank Henry Shipman and Philip Nagy (digital imaging specialists) and Juanita Murray (director).

These would be the members of my all-time Vanderbilt basketball team, judged from the times I've followed closely: Will Perdue, Billy McCaffrey, John Jenkins, Shan Foster and Dan Langhi. The bench would be phenomenal.

The 2012–13 season can prove to be historic for both Kevin Stallings and Melanie Balcomb. Stallings is eighteen wins away from passing Roy Skinner as the men's all-time winningest coach, while Balcomb is nineteen victories away from passing Jim Foster to become the women's all-time winningest coach.

There is something very special about Vanderbilt basketball and Memorial Gymnasium. It cannot be challenged that Vanderbilt basketball has a tradition and a history. It is sacred.

CHAPTER 1

Vanderbilt Was First College Team in 1893

In the fall of 1891, Dr. James Naismith needed an indoor sport to avoid the bitter winter weather in Springfield, Massachusetts. He was asked to instruct the physical activities for the participants of the Young Men's Christian Association Training School (later Springfield College). At that time, the YMCA was a base for training physical instructors and general secretaries for the YMCAs within the United States. Outdoor sports, such as football and rugby, failed to be converted to indoor sports. A small gymnasium was not equipped for a game requiring an enormous playing area.

Naismith's solution was to invent the game of "basket ball." Peach baskets were secured from the custodian and hung from the gym's balcony, which just happened to be ten feet from the floor. Naismith devised a set of rules that required nine players on a team and a soccer ball. The number of players on a team was derived to accommodate the eighteen students in Naismith's original class.

The new game began to spread within the United States and was the winter sport for the YMCAs in the country. Eventually, colleges and athletic clubs acquired the game for their activity. Nashville, with its YMCA and athletic clubs, was quick to learn the game. Vanderbilt's interest in the game was evident when the university's newspaper, *Hustler*, printed the rules in its December 21, 1893 edition. At the time, football, baseball and track were the featured sports on the Commodore campus.

The Old Gym built in 1880 still exists today and housed Vanderbilt student basketball games. The first recorded basketball game played by

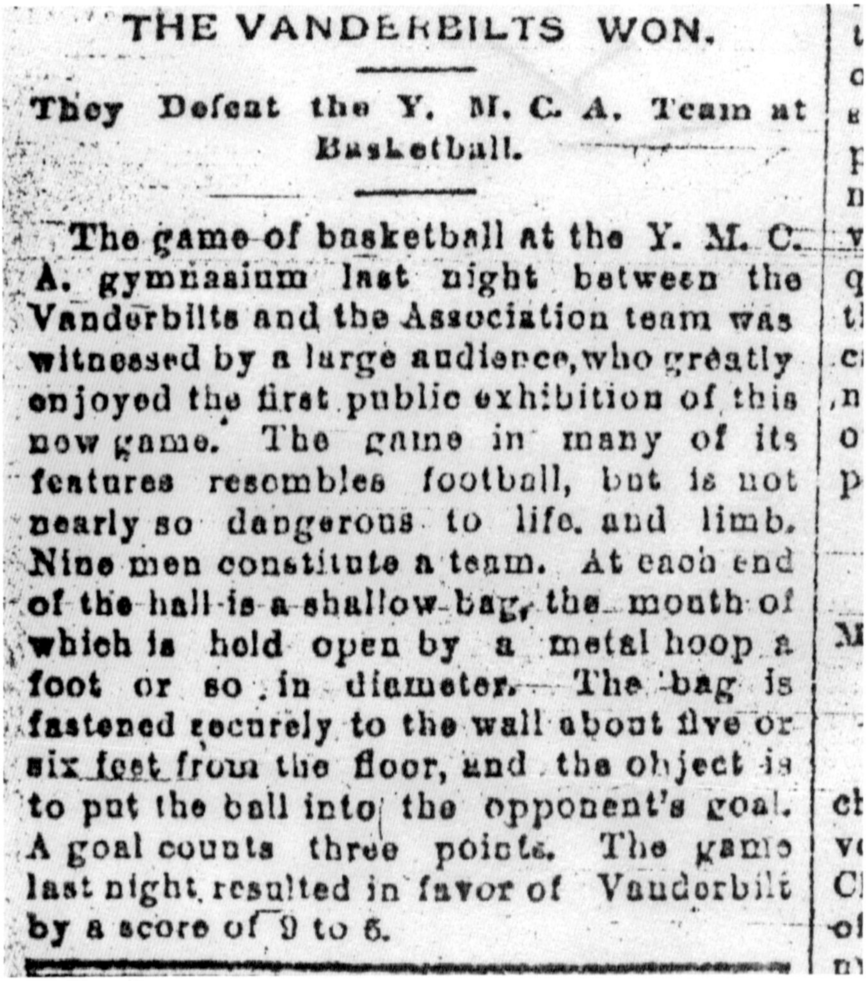

THE VANDERBILTS WON.

They Defeat the Y. M. C. A. Team at Basketball.

The game of basketball at the Y. M. C. A. gymnasium last night between the Vanderbilts and the Association team was witnessed by a large audience, who greatly enjoyed the first public exhibition of this new game. The game in many of its features resembles football, but is not nearly so dangerous to life and limb. Nine men constitute a team. At each end of the hall is a shallow bag, the mouth of which is held open by a metal hoop a foot or so in diameter. The bag is fastened securely to the wall about five or six feet from the floor, and the object is to put the ball into the opponent's goal. A goal counts three points. The game last night resulted in favor of Vanderbilt by a score of 9 to 6.

This article is from the February 8, 1893 issue of the *Republican Banner* and reveals Vanderbilt's first organized basketball game, defeating the YMCA 9–6. *Courtesy of the author.*

Vanderbilt as a team is mentioned in the *Comet*, the university's yearbook. The *Comet* reviews the 1893 "season," which consisted solely of a 9–6 victory over the Nashville YMCA. Also included in this yearbook are the names and positions of the nine Vanderbilt players. That Vanderbilt game was played on February 7, 1893, which credits the Commodores with being the first college to field a basketball team and play an organized game. With the caption "The Vanderbilts Won," the *Republican Banner* reported on the historic game:

> *The game of basket ball at the Y.M.C.A. gymnasium last night between the Vanderbilts and the Association team was witnessed by a large audience, who greatly enjoyed the first public exhibition of this new game. The game in many of its features resembles football, but not nearly so dangerous to life and limb. Nine men constitute a team. At each end of the hall is a shallow bag, the mouth of which is held open by a metal hoop a foot or so in diameter. The bag is fastened securely to the wall about five or six feet from the floor, and the object is to put the ball into the opponent's goal. A goal counts three points. The game last night resulted in favor of Vanderbilt by a score of 9 to 6.*

Basketball became popular for several years as an intramural winter game on the Vanderbilt campus. The University League was formed, containing teams from the dental school and undergraduate students. Then, in February 1899, Dr. William L. Dudley, the Athletic Association's president, sent a letter to *Hustler* expressing his concerns. Dudley's letter was printed as follows:

> *The Executive Committee of the Athletic Association desires to express the hope that all students who expect to be candidates for the track, baseball and football teams of the university, in fact, all who have athletic ability, will avoid the game of basketball as played in our gymnasium.*
>
> *Our athletics have had bitter experiences with this game in the past, and therefore the committee desires to give warning in due time.*
>
> *The gymnasium is not adapted to the game, and the practice of playing it in their gymnasium suits is considered unsafe by all experts.*
>
> *This game cost us the track championship of the Southern tournament last year and it is hoped that this year we may have winning teams in the field. To bring this result about we must have hearty cooperation of every*

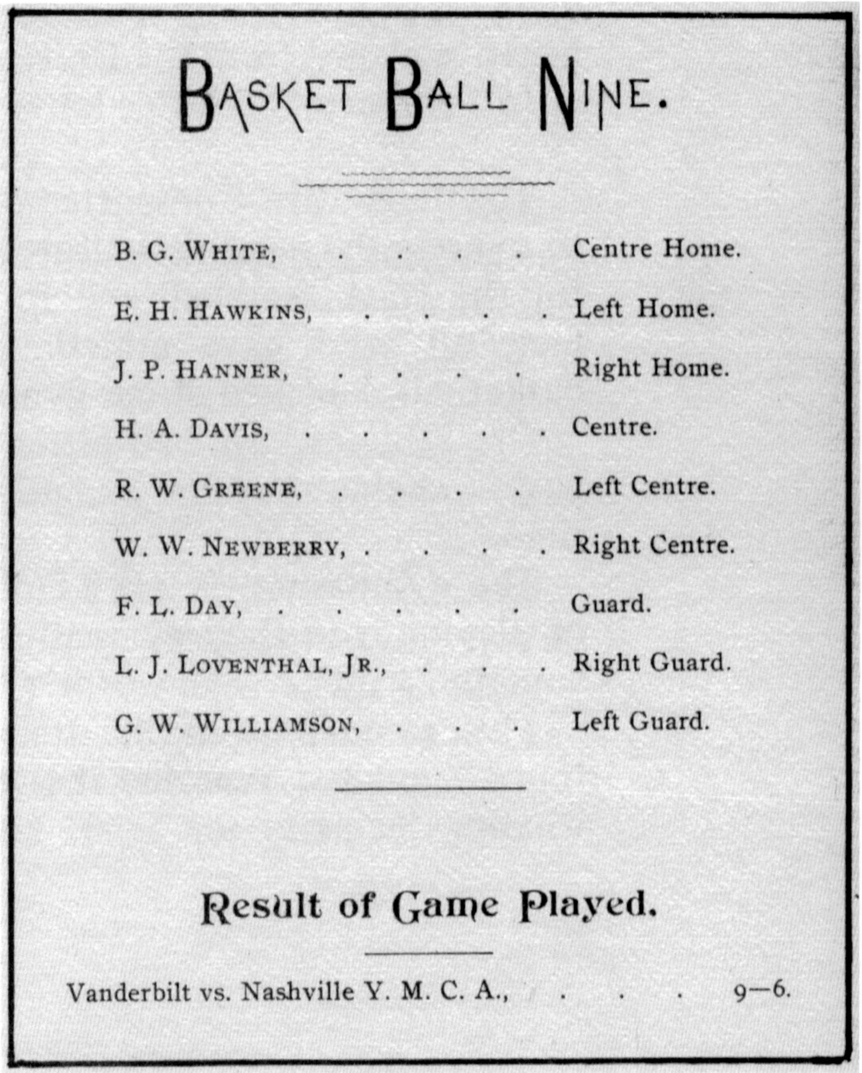

Basket Ball Nine.

B. G. White,	Centre Home.
E. H. Hawkins,	Left Home.
J. P. Hanner,	Right Home.
H. A. Davis,	Centre.
R. W. Greene,	Left Centre.
W. W. Newberry,	Right Centre.
F. L. Day,	Guard.
L. J. Loventhal, Jr.,	Right Guard.
G. W. Williamson,	Left Guard.

Result of Game Played.

Vanderbilt vs. Nashville Y. M. C. A., ... 9—6.

The *Comet* reviews the 1893 season. *Courtesy of Vanderbilt Athletic Communications.*

> *student, and no chances should be taken in a game like basketball in which there is nothing at stake.*

Dudley's advice to the students went unheeded, as a team was formed to accept a challenge from the YMCA in what would be Vanderbilt's first official games. A three-game series was scheduled with the YMCA, with the first contest played on December 15, 1900.

W.D. Weatherford became the first Commodores' coach and only had one week of practice to prepare Vandy for the more experienced men at the YMCA. By this time, the number of players in the game had been carved down to five. Weatherford's starters were Walter Simmons, Ernest Reese, Tom Motlow, Herbert Gannaway and E.L. Woolf.

The first game was played at the Y's gymnasium, and the host won, 22–19. The Commodores faced a problem as a visiting team. They were not accustomed to the goals, as a writer for *Hustler* reported:

> *The game was handicapped by lack of team work, having had only one week's practice, while Nashville's team work was excellent, her team being for the most part composed of men who have played together for several years.*
>
> *Another handicap to the Varsity was the fact that the baskets, instead of having solid wood backing from which the ball would rebound, as the rules require, had wire netting behind them and a ball pitched just above the basket would almost invariably drop in it. The Y.M.C.A. team was accustomed to the gymnasium and made use of this fact, in pitching goals.*

Vanderbilt trailed the game at halftime, 16–4, when Simmons, "who was all over the floor and who pitched nearly all of the goals," led a Commodore comeback with two minutes left in the game. Vandy cut the lead to 20–19, but the final basket by the Y-men ended the game at 22–19.

The second game of the series was played the following February with a surprising 24–9 Vanderbilt victory. Preceding the game in the Y's gym was a gymnastic exhibition provided by members of the Vanderbilt gymnastic team.

The final game of the series was played in March, as *Hustler* reported:

> *In the Y.M.C.A. gymnasium on Tuesday evening the basket ball team won the third and deciding game of the series with the Y.M.C.A. team by the very close score of 14 to 12. The Y.M.C.A. team's play was surprisingly strong and the game was very exciting.*

This 1900–1 Vanderbilt basketball team played its first schedule with four games. *Courtesy of Vanderbilt Athletic Communications.*

> *At the end of the last half the score stood 8–6 in favor of Vanderbilt. In the last four minutes of play Y.M.C.A. secured a lead of 2 points, but the Varsity immediately pitched another goal, making the score a tie, 12 to 12 at the end of the second half. In deciding the tie the play was fast and furious, but Perry finally landed the ball in the basket, winning the game for the Varsity.*

The final game of Vanderbilt's inaugural basketball season was played a week later at the Nashville Athletic Club (NAC). The gymnasium was packed, "and the crowd was about evenly divided in its sympathies." *Hustler* reported on the NAC's 13–11 victory over Vanderbilt:

> *The basket ball game was one of the finest seen in Nashville this season. The N.A.C. team was composed of men who have played together for several years. They were all, with one exception, six footers and outweighed*

> *the Varsity at least twenty-pounds to the man. They expected to win an easy victory.*
>
> *In the latter part of the first half the N.A.C. team seemed to play all around the Varsity, and when the whistle blew the score stood N.A.C. 10, Vanderbilt 5. The different arrangement of the goals in N.A.C. gymnasium seemed to greatly handicap the Varsity, for most of the pitches went wild and there was none of the team's usual accuracy in pitching goals.*

Simmons led a desperate Commodore comeback in the second half, as *Hustler* continued:

> *Trusting to their superior weight, the N.A.C.'s began to play a rough game in the second half, and fared ill at it. Simmons brought down the house, figuratively, and almost literally, by throwing over his shoulder two of the N.A.C. men at once, each of whom were larger than he, in a way that was rather humiliating to the N.A.C. rooters. Simmons' play throughout the game was remarkable.*

Simmons was also a four-year starter for the Commodores' football team. Vanderbilt's inaugural season concluded with a 2-2 record.

The Vanderbilt basketball tradition began in the Old Gym. With the growth of basketball, leagues were formed, with Vanderbilt joining the Southern Intercollegiate Athletic Association, Southern Conference and Southeastern Conference (SEC).

As the sport gained popularity in the South, Vanderbilt struggled to find an appropriate home. The Old Gym was used as a practice site, but it was too small to accommodate a meaningful crowd. The Commodores would schedule future games at the old Hippodrome, YMCA, area high schools, the Navy Classification Center and David Lipscomb College's McQuiddy Gym. Then, on December 6, 1952, the dedication game of the university's long-awaited campus gym was played against Virginia. Memorial Gymnasium was named for the Vanderbilt alumni who died in World War II.

Since joining the SEC in 1932, the Commodores have made it to the NCAA Tournament thirteen times with a 10-13 all-time record. The 1964–65 squad made it to the Elite Eight. The Commodores have been invited to the NIT eleven times with an 18-10 record. They were NIT champions in 1990 and runners-up in 1994.

The following Commodores have been honored as all-Americans: Bill Joe Adcock (1950), Clyde Lee (1965, 1966), Tom Hagan (1969), Jan van

Breda Kolff (1974), Will Perdue (1988), Billy McCaffrey (1993), Dan Langhi (2000), Matt Freije (2004), Derrick Byars (2007), Shan Foster (2008) and John Jenkins (2011, 2012).

Vanderbilt has been successful in recruiting outstanding players who have been honored as first-team all-SEC: Bill Joe Adcock (1948, 1950), Dave Kardokus (1951), Dan Finch (1954), Al Rochelle (1956, 1957), Jim Henry (1958, 1959), Bill Depp (1960, 1961), John Russell (1962, 1963), Clyde Lee (1964, 1965, 1966), John Ed Miller (1964, 1965), Bob Grace (1965), Keith Thomas (1966), Tom Hagan (1967, 1968, 1969), Bo Wyenandt (1967), Bob Warren (1968), Perry Wallace (1970), Thorpe Weber (1971), Terry Compton (1973, 1974), Jeff Fosnes (1975, 1976), Charles Davis (1979), Mike Rhodes (1980), Willie Jones (1982), Phil Cox (1983, 1985), Will Perdue (1987, 1988), Frank Kornet (1989), Barry Goheen (1989), Scott Draud (1991), Billy McCaffrey (1993, 1994), Drew Maddux (1998), Dan Langhi (2000), Matt Freije (2004), Shan Foster (2006, 2008), Derrick Byars (2007), Jermaine Beal (2010), John Jenkins (2011, 2012) and Jeffery Taylor (2012).

SEC Players of the Year include Clyde Lee (1965, 1966), Jan van Breda Kolff (1974), Will Perdue (1988), Billy McCaffrey (1993), Dan Langhi (2000), Derrick Byars (2007) and Shan Foster (2008). Vanderbilt has retired two jerseys in its long, proud history—those of Clyde Lee and Perry Wallace.

CHAPTER 2

Commodore Women Played in the Nineteenth Century

Toward the end of the nineteenth century, Stella Vaughn (a student-player coach and one of the first women to graduate from Vanderbilt) became a pioneer in developing basketball as a sport not only at Vanderbilt but also in Nashville. Miss Vaughn's "coed" teams, as they were known, had such a modest beginning that men were not allowed to watch their games or practices. The doors and windows of the gym were blocked and guarded by female teachers to screen all interested in viewing the inaugural game.

Wearing bloomers, tie-down shoes and voluminous blouses, these women played their first recorded game in March 1897. This basketball game was played against Ward Seminary at the Old Gym, which was built in 1880 and remains on campus today. Ward Seminary was the first women's team in Nashville and the South. Later, the school became Ward-Belmont, and it is known today as Belmont University.

The following newspaper article from the March 14, 1897 edition of the *Nashville American* describes that first recorded women's basketball game for Vanderbilt:

> *The "co-eds" of Vanderbilt and the Ward Seminary team played a game of basket ball in the University gymnasium yesterday morning which the former won by a score of 5 to 0.*
>
> *Reporters were debarred, but the contest is said to have been one of spirit, evidenced by the sunny locks found on the floor later by the janitor. There were no broken bones, black eyes or scratched faces reported, however, and*

This 1897 Vanderbilt women's basketball team played its first game against Ward Seminary (Belmont) for a 5–0 victory. *Courtesy of Vanderbilt University Special Collections and Archives.*

> *the members of either team were willing to sacrifice a few strands of hair to the good cause.*
>
> *The throwing was pronounced somewhat erratic at intervals, but at least one time proved the very thing. The lucky cast was made by Miss (Elizabeth) Buttorff of the co-educational contingent. The players on the other side aver that she had no idea it would be successful, and that it was all luck.*
>
> *Be that as it may, it won the game, though bouncing from the wall at the time it landed in the basket. Much interest was manifested in the game both by the participants and the attendance, which was very large.*

A male reporter of the *Hustler* provided a detailed account of this game. The reporter admitted he sneaked into the gym and hid in a dark corner to witness the game. This clandestine reporter, who was nameless, gave this personal account:

> *In spite of the precautions and vigilance of don't-let-a-man-come in girls, teachers and instructors, I gained admission to the gymnasium and hid myself in a corner and awaited developments.*

> *Soon the crowd began to gather, consisting of the girls' schools, old and young ladies. On the faces of the sweet schoolgirls were not seen the usual bewitching smiles. Something was lacking. What was it? It could not have been a girl friend, for all kinds of femininity was there.*
>
> *It must have been the absence of the college boys, whom, alas, the teachers had excluded from the rare sight of seeing girls play basket ball. There was a look of expectancy on many faces, as if they expected that some "man" would run the gauntlet and make his way in. But they were doomed to disappointment. Only "Little Gardiner" and the other girls were to be seen.*

The rules were different for the women, as a field goal was awarded five points. The game was 0–0 until the very end, when Vaughn passed the ball to Buttorff, who threw up a desperation shot at the goal. It was reported that the referee's whistle sounded just as the ball left her hand. The ball went in for a goal.

There was a "lively discussion" at the conclusion of the game as to the validity of the goal. The referee declared that the ball was in the air when the whistle blew and the goal counted. Vaughn would have been credited with the first assist as a female Vanderbilt player if assists existed.

This shy reporter from the *Hustler* also gave his thoughts and observations:

> *After the doors and windows had been barred and locked and a guard (female teachers) placed at each, time was called for the game to begin. "Now," thought I, "we will see some scratching and hair-pulling and hear a half dozen screams." I was not deceived; they showed that they were still girls.*
>
> *The agility of some of them was really surprising, as they got around after the ball in a manner that would put some of our gym graduates to shame. The teams seemed pretty evenly matched, the co-eds having a little advantage in the matter of weight. The Ward girls made several pretty throws at the basket, but failed to score.*

Only traces of information are available for these early years. Some publications indicate that the girls began playing a regular schedule in 1902, and some report 1905. By this time, crowds, including men, attended games. Vaughn remained a coach for twenty years and director of the coed gymnasium activities.

The women generally played a five-game schedule, which was expanded as more area schools supported and produced women's teams. Later, as

The 1914 Vanderbilt women's basketball team. *Courtesy of Vanderbilt University Special Collections and Archives.*

the game became a national sport, the Commodore women played other colleges. They would travel to Kentucky, Cincinnati and other cities in the years after 1910.

By this time, rosters and statistics would be recorded for publication in the school's newspapers and nearly received as much press as the men. Coach Vaughn's lineups would be listed as "Miss Johnson," "Miss Miller" and so forth. Team members are listed through 1919, but information on the women began to fade in the late 1920s.

The Girl's Athletic Association, an intramural league, was formed in 1928. Later, this became the Women's Athletics Board, which organized Vanderbilt's women's sports.

When the federal government implemented Title IX, the administration turned to basketball. In 1977, Joe Pepper was named the first Vandy women's coach, which was a part-time position. During that revised season in 1977–78, the women posted a 15-9 record. As the competition became fiercer, scholarships were added throughout the next several years.

Stella Vaughn would be fascinated with the progression of the women's game and the gymnasiums packed with fifteen thousand fans. She would be more fascinated if she had a Heidi Gillingham (six feet, ten inches) at her post.

Also, who was "Little Gardiner"?

CHAPTER 3

THE 1909–10 MEN'S AND WOMEN'S TEAMS

The following is a testimony from former Vanderbilt basketball player Samuel A. Weakley (1908–10) about the Commodores' 1909–10 basketball season. In letter form, the undated testimony was sent to Vanderbilt head basketball coach Bob Polk (1948–58, 1960–61) sometime in the 1950s. These are Weakley's reminiscences of that season:

> *When practice began for the season, it was clearly evident that Vanderbilt was to have another fine basketball team for McGehee, Neely, Martin, Sorrells, and Brown, the first line men of the team of the previous year, were on the floor in uniform. Weakley was the only sub left from the previous year, but with Pentecost, Freeland, and Nelson (one of Vanderbilt's great "little men," a Slator Martin of his day) on hand they constituted a formidable second line.*
>
> *The first road trip demonstrated the caliber of the team. Playing five games on five consecutive nights in five altogether different size gymnasiums, the team won four games. The game that was lost was in the miniature gym at Columbus, Georgia where the crowd was four deep between the playing floor and the wall; no out of bounds as such. One account of the game stated that "At one point in the game one of the spectators reached out and grasped Neely by the throat while he was struggling for the ball with one of the Columbus players." Another "assist" from the spectators was to extend their legs out on the floor as Vanderbilt would pass. So you see, a player never knew how many would be in the act when the play was near the side line.*

The 1909–10 Vanderbilt men's basketball team. *Courtesy of Vanderbilt University Special Collections and Archives.*

The gym in Mobile was lined along the foul line with chicken wire so that there was an out-of-bounds. On the trip between Columbus and Montgomery the train was delayed several hours behind a wreck at Union Springs, Alabama and the team did not arrive until shortly before game time. Likewise on the next day the team did not arrive in Mobile until late in the afternoon and had very little rest before game time. It speaks well for the fine physical condition and stamina and mental attitude of the players that they could play such basketball under such conditions.

In the Mobile game, Vanderbilt was one point behind when Neely passed the ball down the floor to Brown, who was in no position for a sure shot; but Neely realizing that time was about up, yelled to Brown to take a shot, which he did. The ball went through the hoop, putting Vanderbilt ahead by one point. Just then the final whistle blew, ending the game. (Brown to this day does not know how he was that good at goal shooting.) This game was plenty rough, 49 fouls being called. A banquet was held after the game when the delicacies of the Holiday season were served.

On the way home Vanderbilt defeated the Birmingham Athletic Club by a score of 50 to 30. It should not be overlooked that the YMCA and Athletic Clubs of those days had fine teams made up of men who had played together for years and in some cases with men who had previously played on Northern and Eastern University teams.

The next game was against an Alumni team, on Feb. 7th, on which were such great players as Stein Stone, Gene Lockhard, Dan Blake and Willard Throop. Only four alumni showed up for the game so Weakley was loaned to them as a fifth player. The Varsity won 41–21 and it was stated in one account that "Youth must be served for the come-back road is a hard one." This proved true, for Weakley a "youth" on the alumni team scored half of their points. One of the largest crowds ever to assemble in the V.U. gym was there, and the student band, 18 strong, made their first appearance in their new uniforms. "When playing at their best they ripped off such seductive strains as, tease, squeeze, lovin and wooing; Oh babe what are you doin." Or at least that was the way it sounded to the news reporter.

Cumberland University and Sewanee were defeated in turn, in a decisive manner. The Sewanee game was referred to in the news accounts as "rough but not barbaric." In the Sewanee game Nelson put on a fine exhibition and made six field goals. During the halves of these two games the Gym team of Heriges, Howe, Morrison, Raff and McClure put on a fine exhibition of acrobatics.

During the latter part of February, during severe cold weather and blizzards, the team made what proved to be a very disastrous four-day trip into Central Kentucky. Neely and Brown were unable to make the trip and Sorrells had a carbuncle on his neck as big as a walnut and could play only a part of the games and Weakley had a boil on the end of his nose which had that olfactory organ swelled to twice its normal size and Nelson had tonsillitis. Even at that, two of the games were in the win-column. In the Louisville game a new Vanderbilt record was set, fourteen field goals by Weakley. The largest number of field goals scored in a game by a Vanderbilt player previously, was eleven by Bob Blake on February 5, 1904 against the Nashville YMCA team and eleven by Bill Neely on February 9, 1910 against Cumberland University (February seemed to be a good month in which to make records).

The team and players were referred to in local and out of town news accounts in many instances, such as; "Commodores are a great all round team; when at strength, probably the greatest in the South." "Played suburb basketball." "Greatest all-round exhibition ever seen." "One of the best

> *squads ever to represent Vanderbilt." There was hardly a game in which Neely, McGehee, and/or Martin were not cited for their brilliant work. (Another great team of the early days of basketball of Vanderbilt was the team of 1906–07).*

Also included in the Weakley letter is a testimony from Ada Raines, the captain of the 1909–10 Vanderbilt women's basketball team. Stella Scott Vaughn was the women's coach, and Weakley is credited as a co-writer of this summary of the ladies' 1909–10 season:

> *The co-ed teams always had a way of winning their games under the excellent coaching of Miss Stella Vaughn. The season of 1909–10 was no exception. The season opened on Saturday, November 20, 1909 in the Vanderbilt Gym when the Vanderbilt co-eds crumpled the hair of the Cumberland University lasses to the tune of 24 to 8.*
>
> *The Cumberland team acted the part of the dark cloud which bade fair to make sailing rough and if possible to upset the equilibrium of a Vanderbilt victory; but Capt. Raines steered her cargo of precious freight through the tempest with only the loss of a few hair pins. Thus it looked through the eyes of the reporter.*
>
> *Lamar Ryals well remembers to this day how the butterflies flitted in her stomach the night before the game and she was unable to sleep, obsessed with the feeling that she would be unable to make a credible showing in throwing goals. But when the pre-game practice was underway the butterflies left and returned no more, for, the frame as one reporter stated "Miss Ryals, the goal throwing terror, was upon the verge of being the whole thing; she ringing up 10 of the 24 points; all this in addition to the plucky way in which she played after being wafted into dreamland by a sleep-producing jolt upon her auburn curles. Capt. Raines and Miss Young allowed only two field goals to be scored against them during the game. Scores were made by Ryals, 5 field; Stocks, 2 field and 4 foul.*
>
> *After this successful beginning of the girls, on Saturday, December 11th, 1909, played a team of former Vanderbilt co-eds players. It was stated that the Commodoresses spoiled the curls of the Alumni girls 26–19. Quoting further: the game was snappy and fast except the times taken out by the alumni on account of lack of breath and one knockout administered by the younger aggregation. Miss Stella Vaughn did the best playing for the alumni. Capt. Raines when interviewed expressed the opinion that the team would continue to play winning ball. The alumni team was composed of*

The 1909–10 Vanderbilt women's basketball team with child mascot. *Courtesy of Vanderbilt University Special Collections and Archives.*

> *Florence Gates, Lois Amanda Godbey, Mary Lipe, Rose Nelson, and Stella Vaughn (Capt.). These games were played before a feminine audience only and behind guarded doors as had always been the case with Vanderbilt co-ed games. No other outside games were played by the team.*
>
> *'You varsity players look back and think your games were rough; what do you think of our games;' says Ada Raines."*

The 1909–10 men's basketball team recorded a 10-3 mark, while the ladies' games were not officially recorded.

CHAPTER 4

VANDERBILT IS 1920 SIAA CHAMP

Vanderbilt had been a member of the Southern Intercollegiate Athletic Conference (SIAA) from 1895 to 1924. The Commodores then became members of the Southern Conference (1924–32) and finally the Southeastern Conference (1932–present). During the 1919–20 basketball season, there were about twenty-four teams included in the SIAA. Teams ranged from Texas to Florida to Kentucky, including such small colleges as Centre (Kentucky), Mercer and Howard (Samford).

With such a large membership, the best record determined the championship, and obviously with so many teams, a true champion could not be determined. A few colleges were allowed to compete for the championship though they were not official members. Some members of the league played more conference games due to a larger number of teams in their region.

Ray Morrison, a former Commodore all-American football player and assistant football coach under Dan McGugin, coached Vanderbilt. The Commodore players were Dick Gleves, Alf Adams, Tommie Zerfoss, Josh Cody (Vandy football all-American), Rolly Norton, L.M. Graves, Johnny Floyd and Gus Morrow. During the season, Zerfoss was declared ineligible when it was discovered that he had played one year of basketball at Kentucky before transferring to Vanderbilt.

The *Tennessean* reported on the final conference game played at the Nashville YMCA (Vandy home court) against Georgia Tech:

Much of the sting of old gridiron defeats at the hands of the Tech congregation was completely wiped out by the Commodores last night when they annihilated the Yellow Jackets by the score of 32–3. Only twice during the whole game did the Techites break into the scoring column, once by a weird shot by Jenks from somewhere near the center of the floor and once when Martin sent one through the hoop on a foul shot.

The game was a riot from the start. For a long time it looked as if the big zero was a permanent fixture on Tech's side of the scoreboard. Vandy had run up a total of 21 points before Tech came through with a single tally. At the end of the first half the score was 9–0. At the end of the game it was even worse. It was 32 to 3.

For the Commodores, Norton was the highest individual scorer, making six field goals and two fouls. He was like an eel, darting about over the floor and shooting from every place except out of bounds. Staton and Mayer gave up trying to head him off. It was too late.

The YMCA teams within the Commodores' region dominated Vanderbilt's schedule. These Y teams were in Nashville, Mobile, Montgomery, Chicago, Memphis, Macon and Chattanooga. The university's 1920 yearbook, *Commodore*, gave this summary of the Vanderbilt basketball players of 1919–20:

Gaze, O Gentle Reader, upon this greatest of great forwards for the last time in garb of the Gold and Black, for Tommie Zerfoss has caged his last basket for his Alma Mater. For four long years he has held this berth, and for the last two of them, at least, he has been All-Southern Collegiate forward. The S.I.A.A. powers-that-be ruled him ineligible on the four-year rule in the middle of the past season, but not before the gallant Commodore captain had won several contests by his expert dribbling, accurate passing, and deadly, sure-shot shooting from all angles.

And now, we introduce you to another brilliant light in Southern basketball circles, Dr. Graves, the high-jumping medico. This young Apollo has held down the center job for three years, during which period he has played a good game consistently. This South-side star was ever in the thick of the fray, eternally scrapping and passing from whistle to whistle, and, at any moment, unexpectedly leaping out of a scramble and batting the globule into the netting. His work was as polished as that of any man on the team.

The militant and pugilistic physiognomy to your left is the personal property of none other than Alf Adams. For four seasons, off and on, Alf

Members of the 1920 Southern Intercollegiate Athletic Association Championship team. *Courtesy of Vanderbilt Athletic Communications.*

has planted himself firmly in the hole under the enemy's goal, and has hurled back the hostile onslaughts of all comers, big and little. Very few goals have gone over this rugged Commodore without a desperate struggle, for Shug is a power of strength. Alf always plays an aggressive game—the opponent who hesitates in shooting surely is lost. He is another mighty cog that will be missed in the 1921 basketball machine.

Whe—ee-e Gleaves! Yes, that is the Arch-Chance posing there. He stepped up with the intention, no doubt, of making a speech, but if we can keep him still for about two minutes we will tell you something of his basketball ability. It was he who kept Georgia Tech from shooting more than one goal, and how that happened Dick does not know. He showed real ability in that game, and since Dick has been in school but twelve years, we may expect to hear more of him.

Here we have with us "Chicken-foot" Morrow, the sturdy youth who rambled about at top speed as running guard of the Commodore quintet. All forwards look alike to young Morrow, and he bustled up shot after shot in both of the Rambler games. On the offensive, Morrow shifts quickly,

> *pivoting, dodging, dribbling, or passing to the constant discomfort of the enemy, and many the time has he caged goals on one of his springing jumps, the like of which has been rarely seen on the local "Y" floor. His style of playing is ideal for a running guard, and the Commodores are lucky to have such a man back to lead the '20–'21 squad as captain.*
>
> *This isn't Hercules, nor his side-kick, Atlas, nor old man Samson. Just to relieve the suspense, we'll announce that this is Joshuway Cody, the interference-smashingest, goal-cageingest, home-run knockingest, super-athlete in all Dixie. With old Josh and Tommie, the Commodore quintet had a pair of forwards that broke through the best defense in this part of the land. Josh, in spite of his massiveness, handles himself wonderfully well, and his absence next year will leave quite a gap in the Gold and Black five, as well as a yawning chasm on the gridiron and on the diamond.*
>
> *This is Rolly, the rosy-lipped, curly-headed lad from the Windy City, where he learned many of the fine points of the old goal-caging game. "Diminutive, but deafening," or in common parlance, "Little, but loud"; that's Rolly all over. Fast as a streak, and possessing an unerring eye for the old basket, Norton stepped right into Captain Zerfoss' shoes when the latter was ruled ineligible, and darned near filled them too. This is his second year on the team, and we all expect loads from Rolly Norton in 1921.*
>
> *This young gentleman is Mr. Johnny Floyd, he of the sorrel top. Everyone knows his football, but there are some who do not know that this halfback is far from being a back in the fine art of basketball guarding. In the Georgia Tech game, he and V-chance made the Tornado look like the doldrums. His guarding was first class, and he shot a few goals just to show us that he could do it.*

Vanderbilt finished the season 14-4 with conference wins over Georgia (40–18), Georgia Tech (29–21), Centre (29–18) and Georgia Tech (32–3) in Nashville. The team also defeated Maryville College (22–10), which attempted to claim the title as a non-league member. The Commodores lost their final game of the season to the Nashville Ramblers, their second in as many games. The Ramblers were proclaimed Nashville City champs; for years, they had been a city power in amateur basketball. The Commodores played their home games in the Hippodrome.

The Commodores were awarded the SIAA championship by going undefeated (6-0) against the college teams. The championship trophy was mailed to the Vanderbilt Athletic Association. Morrow is quoted in Roy M. Neel's book *Dynamite! 75 Years of Vanderbilt Basketball*: "You've got to

More members of the 1920 championship team. *Courtesy of Vanderbilt Athletic Communications.*

understand that since there was no real seating for students or fans, we really didn't have much interest. It was fun to win, of course, and the conference championship was a real thrill for the players, but it was no big deal for anyone else."

CHAPTER 5

The 1927 Southern Conference Champions

Before the 1926–27 Vanderbilt basketball season, Head Coach Josh Cody announced he was leaving Vanderbilt at the end of the season. Cody was a Vanderbilt football (1914–16, 1919) all-American tackle in 1919. He was also in a dual role of head basketball and assistant football coach. Cody accepted a job as Clemson's head football coach.

Vanderbilt was a member of the Southern Conference in this era. The Commodores went into the 1926–27 season with a determination. They were led by center Jim Stuart (six feet, four inches), guard John McCall (six feet, three inches) and guard Malcomb Moss (six feet), with forwards Frank Bridges (five feet, ten inches) and Dave Baker (six feet, one inch).

The previous year, Vanderbilt had been 8-18. The team opened this historic year with a loss to Evansville, a victory over Marquette and a humiliating loss to Loyola (31–7). Roy Neel quotes Moss in his book *Dynamite! 75 Years of Vanderbilt Basketball*:

> *We were panicked and demoralized after the whipping Loyola had given us. Loyola had stalled the ball in the backcourt (there was no 10-second rule then) until we had grown so frustrated we committed mistakes, and they scored easily. We sat in the locker room for nearly an hour without talking. Cody said nothing. We simply had not been able to adjust. But we learned a lot that night.*

Vanderbilt went to the conference postseason tournament in Atlanta with a 16-4 record and a No. 4 seed. Raymond Johnson of the *Tennessean* gave this report:

> *Cody has turned out a basketball team this season that ranks with the best in Dixie. It has been a fighting team, one that did not know when it was beaten and on numerous occasions has come from behind in the last half to eke out a victory. Great things are expected of the Commodores in the Atlanta meet. Even down in the Cracker town, they are conceding Vandy more than an outside chance.*
>
> *The Commodores have played a fine brand of basketball this season. Auburn, Tennessee, Mississippi, Mississippi Aggies, Sewanee and Kentucky victims. On the other hand, the Gold and Black tossers have met only one defeat in the Conference. That was to Georgia Tech on the latter's floor.*

North Carolina was the conference leader, but the winner of the postseason tournament was recognized as the Southern Conference champions. The conference contained a remarkable twenty-three members. Vanderbilt won its first two games over Washington and Lee (44–32) and Mississippi (32–20). The Commodores were set to play South Carolina in the semifinals. The *Nashville Banner* reported on the events following the game with the Gamecocks:

> *Just one more hurdle to leap and the basketball championship of the Southern conference will be on the way back to Nashville. That hurdle, strange as it may seem, is none other the University of Georgia, which last night sponged out the Tar Heels, champions for the past three years.*
>
> *Tonight at 8 o'clock the Commodores will start in quest of bacon. They beat South Carolina 31 to 25, to get there. That they should have to meet Georgia to get this bacon is one of those things that happen with no explanation available. Georgia has been whipped three times this season by Tech, once by North Carolina, once by Maryland, and once by about everyone else they have met. They were placed in the bracket so that they could win one game. After that they were not figured as a possibility. They are one of the poorest teams in the tournament suddenly gone wild.*

It was reported that the Vanderbilt/Georgia finals attracted the largest crowd ever to see a basketball game in the South at that time. Of course, the partisan Bulldog fans dominated the crowd. Their "hostile" fans, with a deafening band, motivated Georgia as they held a 26–18 halftime lead. With two minutes remaining in the game, Vanderbilt fought back and led 43–42. After Moss made a field goal, Georgia called a timeout. Since

This 1927 Vanderbilt men's basketball team won the Southern Conference title. *Courtesy of Vanderbilt Athletic Communications.*

the Bulldogs were out of timeouts, they were given a technical foul. Moss converted the technical, the Commodores added a basket and Vanderbilt led 46–42. Georgia managed one final basket as Vanderbilt ran out the clock for a 46–44 victory.

The *Banner* gave this report:

> *The ability to take it to the jaw and keep boring in has decided many a fight. It decided one here in the City auditorium last night. It meant more than that. The championship of the Southern conference basketball world came to Vanderbilt when the Commodores took all the Georgia Bulldogs had to offer, shook it off and plunged from the blackness of impending defeat to the championship. The score was 46–44.*
>
> *There was a stinging about the eyes for the Vanderbilt men here last night when the crack of the timer's pistol ended that titanic struggle and Josh Cody rushed out to his players. It was Josh Cody's last appearance as a Commodore coach and his boys had brought him a Southern championship.*

This drawing from the 1927 *Commodore* boasts of Vanderbilt's Southern Conference championship. *Courtesy of Vanderbilt Athletic Communications.*

> *He rushed out and caught the tall form of sweaty Jim Stuart in his arms. He grabbed the others as they came off, their faces strained, their eyes deep-set.*
>
> *The strain of tournament play all the way to the finals is no small thing. These boys had been through a week of terrific effort that reached its climax in the nerve-wrecking, pulse-shattering thing of last night when the Georgia Bulldogs were battered down in that test to determine who could take it the longest and still not break.*

Stuart led all scorers with an impressive nineteen points to cap a 20-4 record. McCall joined Stuart on the all-Southern team. Cody returned to Vanderbilt as the top football assistant in 1932. He was also given the basketball head coaching position, though he never again achieved the success of his 1927 squad. Cody's all-time basketball coaching record (1924–27, 1932–36) at Vanderbilt was 98-100. Moss also said about Cody in *Dynamite*, "He was an excellent coach. No razzle-dazzle, but great fundamentals and strong on conditioning. He was truly a great motivator out there."

This would be Vanderbilt's second championship. It won the Southern Intercollegiate Athletic Association championship during the 1919–20 season with a 14-4 record. After 1927, Vanderbilt would not win another championship until the 1964–65 season.

CHAPTER 6

TOM HENDERSON PLAYED BEFORE THE SEC

This interview between Tom Henderson and Bill Traughber is from January 1999. Mr. Henderson passed away on December 19, 2002, at age ninety.

During the early part of the century, college basketball struggled to be recognized as a national sport. In Nashville, Vanderbilt was prominent in developing basketball in the city with competition against local athletic clubs, including the YMCA. Vanderbilt expanded its schedule each decade with tougher teams as James Naismith's invention began to catch on.

At least one of Vanderbilt's players from that era is still around to talk about it. "Yep! I'm still alive," responded Tom Henderson when told that he is the oldest living former Vandy basketball player.

Henderson, who is eighty-six years old, is from the Vanderbilt class of 1933. He was on the court in 1931, playing against Kentucky's Adolph Rupp, who was in his first season as a twenty-eight-year-old head coach.

"We were the first Vanderbilt team to beat Kentucky in their old gymnasium in Lexington," Henderson said. "We beat them by one point up there [in 1932]. A young man from Nashville by the name of Harold Huggins, who worked for the paper, was one year behind me in basketball. He was the one that played the best game and was instrumental in us beating Kentucky."

Originally from Franklin, Tennessee, Henderson graduated from Battle Ground Academy and then spent one year at Riverdale Military Academy

The starting five for the 1931 Commodores, *standing, left to right*: Bill Schwartz, Shelby Coffee, Bertram Chalfant; *kneeling, left to right*: Tom Henderson and Bill Young. *Courtesy of Vanderbilt Athletic Communications.*

in Georgia. After this one year of prep school, he began his college career at Vanderbilt. Henderson was also a member of the Commodores' football and baseball teams.

The 1932–33 season was the first for the newly organized Southeastern Conference, where Kentucky was the first champion under Rupp. During Henderson's first two seasons, Vanderbilt was a member of the Southern Conference, which consisted of twenty-three teams. Even in those early days, Henderson knew Rupp and Kentucky were on the verge of becoming a force on the national level.

"Beating Kentucky in those days was a big event," said Henderson. "Adolph Rupp came by the hotel room that night to see us after we beat them. We were quite small, and Huggins weighed only 135 pounds but played a great night. He wanted to see Huggins, who had beaten him that night. It was an interesting interview that night as he came up on his own volition."

Today's players have the luxury of traveling in commercial and charter air flights. The teams back then had to travel throughout the country by train. "The schedule called for Vanderbilt to leave Nashville by train," Henderson recalled. "We'd go to Lexington by train, then across to Knoxville and back into Nashville. We had the best quarters; we had the Pullman and conductors. Everyone knew who we were. The porters would put the beds up for us, and it was really something. When we played football, we traveled on the train to Minnesota and Ohio State."

In those days, there was no Memorial Gymnasium. The Commodores played in what is now the Fine Arts Building (the Old Gym) on the Vanderbilt campus. A visit to the old place today reminds one of an old English cathedral built by stone. Henderson, who was team captain his senior year, said:

> *The original gym wasn't much bigger than a handball court. There was no air conditioning, just opened windows. We practiced at the gym and played some of the games in the back part. They built a rectangular building about the size of a basketball court onto the old gym.*
>
> *Spectators sat upstairs where they had a gallery around it. We played some of our games at East High. They had a new gym with adequate seating. We practically played on the stage over there; it was an unusual situation. We played teams like Kentucky and LSU in the new East gym.*

Henderson worked for the National Life and Accident Insurance Company, where he became a vice-president. He was a member of the Battle Ground Academy Board of Trust.

Since his playing days, Henderson has remained loyal to the Vanderbilt basketball team by being its biggest fan. "My wife and I gave up our tickets two years ago," Henderson said, "when it became more difficult to get around."

CHAPTER 7

BILLY JOE ADCOCK EARNS FIRST SCHOLARSHIP

The modern era of Vanderbilt basketball had to begin somewhere. Billy Joe Adcock (1947–50) can be given that distinction for his achievements over sixty years ago. Adcock accumulated several firsts as a Commodore basketball player, including being awarded Vanderbilt's first basketball scholarship. He was born in Evansville, Indiana, but the family moved to Jackson, Tennessee, and later to Nashville for economic reasons when Adcock was six years old.

"I was about twelve years old when I learned to love the game of basketball," Adcock said. "I was influenced by several players when I used to slip on the court up at Peabody and watched a lot of basketball players in the summertime. The neighborhood that I lived in had outdoor basketball courts, but my father put in a court with lights in our backyard. Though I liked baseball and football, I played basketball all the time."

Adcock was playing his high school sports at West End High School. He played in a high school football all-star game on Dudley Field in 1945. Adcock would provide an upgrade to the basketball team's quest for championships. He said:

> *When I was at West End High School, my father was watching me practice one day. My dad had never met my basketball coach,* [Emmett] *Strickland. During this practice, Coach Strickland was all over my butt all day. He'd stop the practice to show me something. After practice, Coach looked up and saw this man in the stands he did not recognize.*

He went over and met my father. My dad said to Coach Strickland, "You were awfully tough on my son. Why are you doing all that?" Coach said, "I see something in him where he could be a great player. And I am going to work on him during his time at West End High School." I thought that was great.

We played in the state championship two years in a row. In my sophomore year, I was on the second team, and there were some great players there, including George Kelley [future Vanderbilt player]. *He was on the starting five. We won the state title that year. Then in my junior year, we were playing in the state tournament and got beat by Chattanooga Central in the semifinals.*

The thing that I regret, we were down by one point with a few seconds to play and Coach Strickland drew up a play where I'd get the ball and try to get the winning basket. I got the ball and missed the shot, and we didn't make it to the finals that year. Then my senior year, we went through every tournament we played and won them all. We won the state championship.

Vanderbilt basketball was not that serious of a sport to the university or fans. Norm Cooper was the Commodores' coach in a part-time role. Vanderbilt didn't have a full-time basketball coach until Adcock's sophomore season. Before Adcock's arrival on the Vanderbilt campus, the Commodores were 7-8 (SEC, 4-7) and not respected. With several teams interested in signing Adcock to a scholarship, he chose Vanderbilt. Adcock said:

Nashville is my home, and that is where I grew up. We didn't live far from Vanderbilt, and I'd go to Vanderbilt football games while keeping up with their sports through the newspapers. I just got enthused about Vanderbilt and always followed them, especially in football. In basketball they were not very good, but they had some good football teams in those days. Baseball was not really an entity in those days, especially in the SEC. I always wanted to go to Vanderbilt and take engineering. I developed an interest in engineering.

Adcock said that Tennessee, Alabama and Kentucky were recruiting him. Kentucky's Adolph Rupp wanted Adcock for his championship-caliber teams. A local basketball official, Fred "Cab" Curtis, had played basketball for Rupp and tried to influence Adcock to play in Lexington. Though Kentucky was a power in basketball, Adcock wanted to be part of a building program. He said:

Billy Joe Adcock (right) with teammate George Kelley. *Courtesy of Vanderbilt Athletic Communications.*

Vanderbilt didn't have basketball scholarships back in those days. The scholarship I was offered was really a football scholarship. If you got an athletic scholarship at Vanderbilt, you were expected to play football. There was a guy named Willie Geny [former Vanderbilt athlete] *who was very active with the Vanderbilt alumni. He pushed me to go to Vanderbilt. Through him, I got an offer to go there. When I went over to meet Coach* [Red] *Sanders* [head football coach and athletic director] *to sign up, he told me it was not a basketball scholarship.*

He said they didn't have them and I had to play football as well as basketball. I said, "Coach, I really want to concentrate on basketball because that is my best sport, and I want to concentrate on my studies in engineering." He said, "I'm sorry, son, we just don't give basketball scholarships." That was the end of the conversation, and I called Mr. Geny to tell him it looked like I was going to contact Cab Curtis and go to Kentucky. He told me not to make any decisions for about an hour and he'd get back to me.

I got a telephone call within an hour, and Mr. Geny said, "Son, we are going to give you the first basketball scholarship Vanderbilt has ever given." I was very fortunate as a young man. I had a lot of chances and lot of honors given to me. You get those honors because of the people you are playing with, teammates, etc. Getting the first basketball scholarship at Vanderbilt was a great honor.

As a freshman in 1946, Adcock was eligible for varsity play since there was a shortage of players with World War II's recent ending. As head basketball coach, Cooper was also the defensive line coach for Sanders in football. Adcock said that Cooper was a great football coach but was lacking in coaching skills for basketball.

Another problem with Vanderbilt basketball in this era was the lack of a home court and decent practice facilities. For a number of years, Vanderbilt had been playing its home games at the Hippodrome, a skating rink near the campus. During Adcock's tenure, home games were played in a gymnasium in the Navy Classification Center on Thompson Lane, Father Ryan High School, East High School and David Lipscomb's McQuiddy Gym. As a freshman, Adcock played in the game that was considered a wake-up call for Vanderbilt basketball. In the 1947 SEC Tournament, the Commodores were humiliated by Kentucky, 98–29. He recalled:

During my freshman season, there were a lot of returning veterans, and I was fortunate to play with them. Most of them were football players. There were people like Tommy Owen, Joe Kraft, Felix Ray, Mike Craig and Bobby Lawrence. They came back from World War II and played on the team with me. I was the only basketball scholarship player, as the rest were on football scholarships.

When we got into the SEC Tournament that year, Kentucky beat us bad in both games during the regular season in Lexington and Nashville. We had the worst SEC record, so we played Kentucky in the first game. They were one of the best teams in the country during my freshman year. They had two all-Americans from the previous year that could not make the starting five. They were that deep.

Rupp made an example of us, beating us 98–29. He did that on purpose. He was telling Vanderbilt either put up or shut up. Have more respect for basketball or we are going to continue to run you down. Coach Cooper at halftime said something like, "Okay, guys, we are going to go out there and run with them in the second half." We froze the ball the last minute and a half to keep them from scoring 100 points. We got booed off the floor.

Adcock scored a team-high seven points in that infamous game. Sanders decided it was time to get serious about basketball on the Vanderbilt campus. In the spring, he searched for a full-time coach. Ted Hornback was hired from the staff of Western Kentucky. After a few weeks of drills, Hornback resigned and went back to Bowling Green. Sanders found the right man with the hiring of Bob Polk, a Georgia Tech assistant. Polk (1948–58, 1960–61) is Vanderbilt's third-winningest coach (197-106) behind Roy Skinner and Kevin Stallings. Adcock said:

As far as I am concerned, Polk is the instrument in getting Vanderbilt basketball turned around. Polk built the team around me, and then he started getting recruits from Indiana, Ohio and other places. Polk was tough on you. He was a great disciplinarian, and he always challenged you as a player. He suggested that we learn to shoot more jump shots.

While we were traveling around the country, we were shooting jump shots while most players were shooting two-handed set shots. There was an all-American at Stanford who was the first one to shoot one-handed jump shots from the outside. It fascinated the New York area so much that when he went to the East Coast, players started shooting jump shots. That is how they developed into the great players of the day.

With the inadequate playing facilities for college basketball, the Commodores were forced to practice in the historic Old Gym, which was built in the 1880s. Adcock said:

> *The Old Gym was a tiny place that had the track around the top. There was probably three feet distance from where the basketball court ended and the gym wall. It was a tiny place, just big enough to practice but not large enough to play a basketball game. We had a locker room in the basement that we shared with wrestlers and other Vanderbilt athletes. We would dress at the Old Gym and bus over to our home games. It was not a first-rate operation.*

Adcock was told as a sophomore that a new gymnasium was going to be built in the coming years. Memorial Gymnasium did not open until 1952. In Polk's first season (1947–48), the Commodores were 8-14 (SEC, 4-11). Adcock would lead the SEC in scoring (17.1 ppg) and was ranked thirteenth in the nation in scoring. He said:

> *It couldn't have been any worse than my freshman year. That was a year you really didn't want to go through as a player. We still had to practice in the Old Gym and go over to Father Ryan and play. My sophomore year was my best in college. I had some great players that came along, like Haworth Parks.*
>
> *We had some players that developed. We didn't really have any great players. I was fortunate enough to be the focus of the offense; therefore, I had a very good scoring average. I made all-SEC that year, and I was all-SEC with four Kentucky players. It was* [Wallace] *Jones,* [Alex] *Groza,* [Ralph] *Beard and* [Dale] *Barnstable with me on the first five.*
>
> *Coach Polk and I were encouraged by what we could see happening at Vanderbilt. I always was a good shooter—fast and quick. I was able to maneuver around people well. What made it special was the improvement in the team itself. Polk was out trying to get good young players to compete with Kentucky. I always wanted to beat Kentucky but never did. UK was the biggest game and the one we wanted to win the most. I always wanted to beat Adolph Rupp.*

During Adcock's junior season, the Commodores were a much-improved 14-8 (SEC, 9-5). Polk expanded the schedule, and the distances the team would travel for quality games placed Vanderbilt basketball in the national sporting news. Adcock recalled:

Billy Joe Adcock was Vanderbilt's first basketball scholarship player, first all-American and first player to record 1,000 points. *Courtesy of Vanderbilt Athletic Communications.*

> *We had a very good year in my junior season, and we did it without many new players. We did have Dave Kardokus, Bob Dudley* [Smith] *and* [Gene] *Southwood, who were able to play my senior year. I had an entire new group of players in my senior year. George Kelley* [transferred from Tennessee] *joined us for my junior and senior years. Kelley was a helluva forward for us. We had a gutsy center named Pete Robinson who was six foot five, the tallest man we had. I played forward until my senior year when they moved me to guard, not a point guard. We didn't have point guards in those days. I was six foot three.*
>
> *We played in Vanderbilt's first Christmas tournament in Des Moines* [Corn Bowl Tournament] *but lost to Drake and Dartmouth. That was the first time I'd seen a seven-foot center. He was a guy named Jim McIntyre who played for the University of Minnesota. There was a great guard named* [Whitey] *Skoog that played at Minnesota, and both went into the NBA.*
>
> *We traveled any way we could get to a game. When I was a freshman, we drove everywhere. We'd drive to Birmingham, Lexington, Auburn and Knoxville. We drove automobiles.* [Coach] *Cooper, the trainer and one of the older players would drive in three or four cars. Then my sophomore year we began traveling by train throughout that year and most of my junior year. When we went to Oklahoma or in the East my senior year, we'd go by airplane. But we'd take the bus to Knoxville and Lexington.*

There were a couple of memorable games for Adcock and his teammates during that junior season. One was an upset in Nashville against No. 6 nationally ranked Tulane and a scoring-record game for Adcock. He said:

> *We played Tulane right to the wire. They had a lot of gunners, and all of them were from Indiana. Their coach was from Indiana. We won in the last minute 56–54 in Nashville. A few games earlier, I set the SEC single-game scoring record with 36 points against Mississippi State, and that was done at East High. I broke Alex Groza's record, which was 34 points.*
>
> *Coach Rupp set up Groza to regain the record within a week. Rupp kept him in the game against some team and scored 38 points. Rupp didn't want me or anybody from Vanderbilt to have that record. We were improved that year due to Coach Polk's coaching and more talent with basketball scholarship players.*

The confident Commodores were 17-8 (SEC, 11-3) in 1949–50, good enough for second place in the conference. This was Adcock's final season as a Vanderbilt basketball player. The additional scholarship players led to more success. He said:

> *Coach Polk got three from Indiana in Jack Heldman, Kardokus and Southwood. He also got* [George] *McChesney from Ohio. My senior year was the best team we ever had. We made a great deal of progress when Polk came there. Going from where we did and traveling all over the country like New York and Philadelphia made us improve.*

In New York, Vanderbilt surprised heavily favored New York University in overtime, 65–59, in Madison Square Garden. The Commodores then lost to Temple in Philadelphia for their next game, 55–35. Adcock recalled playing in the multipurpose Garden:

> *The only problem I had was with the floor. They put the floor over ice, which caused slick spots. You'd be dribbling on the court and the ball wouldn't come back up. A big country boy from Tennessee going to the Big Apple was something else with all those tall buildings. I'd just walk down the street and look up at those high buildings and all the people. That was one of the most exciting experiences for me, going to New York City.*

In his four years at Vanderbilt, Adcock wore three jersey numbers—No. 27 (freshman), No. 33 (sophomore and junior) and No. 9 (senior). He graduated from Vanderbilt in 1950 with a degree in engineering.

Not only was Adcock Vanderbilt's first basketball scholarship recipient, but he was also named all-SEC for three seasons (first team—1948 and 1950, second team—1949). Adcock was Vanderbilt's first all-American (1950), SEC all-tournament second team (1948-50), became Vanderbilt's all-time leading scorer and first member of the 1,000-point club with 1,190 points. He ranks thirty-second in all-time scoring. Adcock gives credit for his success on the hardwood:

> *I had a desire to win with hard work, practicing a lot and was dedicated. There were two people that inspired me in my basketball career. There was Emmett Strickland at West End High School. He was my first great coach that taught me about being a good person. Then Bob Polk came along and taught me more basketball skills and to be a man. They both taught me how*

to be a teammate. My father was a great man and taught me to persevere and be the best I can with TLC.

In the summer after graduation, Adcock played in a college East-West all-star game in Madison Square Garden. He was one of ten players on the East squad with future NBA Hall of Famer Bob Cousy as a teammate. Adcock also had a chance to play in the NBA for the Minneapolis Lakers (now the Los Angeles Lakers). He said:

> *I never seriously considered playing professional basketball. I was married at the time. My wife and her father really wanted me to work. Her father went to Vanderbilt and was an engineer, which influenced me to begin a career. They* [the NBA] *weren't paying very much.*
>
> *They told me if I made the squad I was going to make $7,500 a year. Minneapolis had five great players, and they won the NBA title that year with George Mikan and others. I probably would not have made the first five and probably not even the second five. I just don't know.*

Other recognitions that Adcock has achieved are memberships in the Tennessee Sports Hall of Fame and Tennessee High School Sports Hall of Fame, and he was the second Vanderbilt basketball player named as its Legend of the SEC.

Adcock lives in St. Louis and is retired from Monsanto Chemical Company, where he was the national account manager. Previously, he lived and worked in Cleveland and Chicago.

Adcock has fond memories from his playing days in a Commodores' basketball uniform:

> *In my senior year at Vanderbilt, we came very close to beating Kentucky in Nashville. After that game, Coach Rupp came over to introduce himself to my father and said, "Mr. Adcock, I'd swap my whole team for your son." That humbled my father.*
>
> *I was always extremely proud to represent Vanderbilt. I am still proud to have had the opportunity. My mom and dad could not afford for me to attend Vanderbilt. Fortunately, the basketball scholarship provided me with four great years. I was fortunate to have had wonderful people around me on and off the court. I was very lucky to have played for two great basketball coaches.*

CHAPTER 8

Bob Polk Hired as First Full-Time Coach

February 27, 1947, was a date that marked the beginning of major changes in the Vanderbilt basketball program. Adolph Rupp's Kentucky Wildcats smashed the Commodores 98–29 in the SEC Tournament held that year in Louisville. Attending that humiliating game for Vanderbilt was athletic director and head football coach Red Sanders. Sanders came back to Nashville realizing he needed better players, a gymnasium and a full-time basketball coach. In the past, Vanderbilt's basketball coaches were usually former basketball players or assistant coaches in other sports.

After interviewing several candidates, a Georgia Tech assistant coach named Bob Polk was hired. Before Polk's arrival on the Vanderbilt campus, games were held at area high schools. Practices were held at the Old Gym annex located on the campus.

Polk was paid a controversial $5,000 a year in salary. He also secured a Quonset hut (the Navy Classification Center) on Thompson Lane for home games. Polk was also assured that plans would be made for a new gymnasium. Polk sold sixteen season tickets that first year and personally chalked numbers in front of the season ticket holders' seats.

Another mission for Polk was to find scholarship basketball players, which Vanderbilt had never offered in that sport. Polk dipped into his home state of basketball-crazed Indiana to sign Gene Southwood, Jack Heldman and Dave Kardokus. Sanders had secured Nashville's West End High School's Billy Joe Adcock as the Commodores' first basketball-only scholarship player before Polk's arrival.

Polk's first season resulted in an 8-14 (SEC, 4-11) record, his only losing season at Vanderbilt. The next year, his team was 14-8 (SEC, 9-5), losing to Kentucky 72–50 in Nashville and 70–37 at Kentucky.

Now that his first scholarship players were experienced, Vanderbilt gained national attention in 1949 with an overtime 65–50 victory over New York University at Madison Square Garden. The Commodores completed that 1949–50 season at 17-8 and second place (11-3) in the SEC. Vanderbilt lost twice to Kentucky that season by scores of 58–54 and 70–66. Progress had been made.

Other players to become Commodores in Polk's first few years were Bob Dudley Smith, George Kelley, Hank Duvier, Haworth Parks and Pete Robinson. Adcock graduated after the 1949–50 season and became Vanderbilt's first all-American basketball player.

With Kelley as team captain, the Commodores would finish the 1950–51 season at 19-8 and once again tied for second place (10-4) in the SEC. At this time, David Lipscomb's McQuiddy Gym was home to Vanderbilt. The Commodores also lost both of their scheduled regular-season games to Kentucky, 74–49 and 89–57. The previous year, the Commodores, with their No. 2 seed, were ousted from the SEC Tournament by Tennessee.

During the 1951 SEC Tournament in Louisville, Vanderbilt rolled by Tennessee, Georgia and Louisiana State University before playing Kentucky for the championship. The Wildcats had a super team with a great height advantage, led by seven-foot all-American center Bill Spivey. Other talented 'Cat players on the roster were Frank Ramsey, Walt Hirsch, Bobby Watson and Cliff Hagan. Kentucky entered the tournament with a record of 27-1 (SEC, 14-0) and a No. 1 national ranking. Future Vanderbilt coach C.M. Newton was a substitute on that squad.

The Wildcats jumped out to an early lead, but Vanderbilt kept it close, trailing at the half, 30–26. The Commodores trailed by 10 points in the second half before seven thousands fans who were mostly cheering for UK. But with ten minutes to play in the game, Vanderbilt cut the lead to 48–47.

The lead swapped between the teams until Kelley hit two free throws late in the game for a hard-fought 61–57 Commodore victory. It was such a huge upset that the championship trophy was already engraved with Kentucky as champion. The NCAA rule required the regular-season champion of a conference to advance to the national tournament. Polk let his team vote on whether to accept a post-season tournament if invited, but they declined. Kentucky continued on to become national champions in 1951.

Bob Polk was Vanderbilt's first full-time basketball coach, shown here with player Doug Yates. *Courtesy of Vanderbilt Athletic Communications.*

The SEC Tournament was disbanded after the next season but revived in 1979. The Commodores' 1951 SEC Tournament championship was their only crown in either era until Vanderbilt defeated No. 1–ranked Kentucky in the 2012 SEC Tournament.

The permanent home court promised Polk by the university became a reality in 1952. Memorial Gymnasium hosted its first game that year in December against the University of Virginia. Vanderbilt won, 90–83. In Polk's eight years coaching in Memorial Gym, he recorded an amazing 96-15 mark.

During a recruiting trip in the fall of 1958, Polk was in Paducah, Kentucky, when he became ill. He had a massive heart attack and spent three months in a Paducah hospital recuperating. When Polk returned to Nashville, he was bedridden. Forced to miss the 1958–59 season, his young assistant coach, Roy Skinner, became the interim head coach.

Polk was back the next season with such players as Bill Johnson, Bobby Bland, Bill Depp and Ben Rowan. They would end the season at 14-9 (SEC, 7-7), with Depp and Rowan named to the all-SEC team.

One funny but embarrassing moment came in Lubbock, Texas, at a game versus Texas Tech. From the book *Dynamite! 75 Years of Vanderbilt Basketball*, Vanderbilt radio broadcaster Larry Munson gave this account of the incident: "This one's going down to the wire, folks. Hang on. We've got Gish coming into the game. It'll be Vandy's ball out of bounds. Wait a minute. What's this? Gish has lost his pants! Bob Polk has pulled off Lance Gish's pants in front of six thousand screaming fans! The place is going crazy."

In the excitement of the game, Polk was helping Gish out of his warm-up pants and accidentally grabbed his shorts in addition. The embarrassed Gish did make a pair of crucial free throws to help the Commodores win the game by two points.

Vanderbilt basketball was now more successful than the once prominent football program. Since the 1955 Gator Bowl, Commodore football had been declining, with more and more losses. Polk had brought such prominence to basketball that every year his clubs were SEC championship contenders, and droves of fans were packing Memorial Gym.

In the summer of 1961, Polk's doctors told him he needed to give up the stress of coaching. Due to his poor health, the forty-seven-year-old Polk retired as the Commodores' basketball coach and became the personnel director at Vanderbilt Hospital. Skinner took over the head coaching duties.

The Bob Polk era at Vanderbilt was over. He retired from Vanderbilt with a 197-106 record in thirteen seasons. When Polk retired, he was easily

Bob Polk's coaching record at Vanderbilt was 197-106 in thirteen seasons, which ranks third all-time behind Roy Skinner and Kevin Stallings. *Courtesy of Vanderbilt Athletic Communications.*

Vanderbilt's all-time winningest coach. Skinner would retire in 1976 after sixteen years of coaching the Commodores to a 278-135 record. Kevin Stallings moved into second place with a 261-159 record in thirteen seasons.

Polk was out of basketball for eighteen months as his health steadily improved. In 1965, he found himself at Trinity College in San Antonio, Texas. In the dual role of head basketball coach and athletic director, he became Southland Conference Coach of the Year in 1967. He was also the NCAA National Coach of the Year for the small college division in 1968. In his three years at Trinity, Polk compiled a 69-28 record.

Polk moved to St. Louis University (1969–74) to become head basketball coach and assistant professor. In 1971, he was named Coach of the Year in the Missouri Valley Conference. Polk's overall record for the Billikens was 72-60.

Rice was his next coaching stop in 1974, but Polk retired from coaching altogether in June 1977 after a three-year record of 17-63. Polk moved to Birmingham in September to become assistant athletic director at the University of Alabama–Birmingham under Gene Bartow. He remained in that position until November 1981, when another heart attack forced his permanent retirement.

Polk passed away on March 18, 1986, at the Veterans Administration Medical Center in Murfreesboro, Tennessee, at age seventy-one. The father of modern Vanderbilt basketball was buried in Tell City, Indiana. He was inducted into the Tennessee Sports Hall of Fame in 1990.

CHAPTER 9

THE 1951 SEC TOURNAMENT CHAMPS

In 1951, more than two thousand people were waiting at the Nashville airport when the aircraft arrived carrying a group of tired but triumphant athletes. The occasion for this overwhelming greeting was the Vanderbilt basketball team returning home with the 1951 SEC Tournament championship trophy.

The original SEC Tournament began with the founding of the Southeastern Conference (thirteen members) for the 1932–33 season. The conference consisted of the current lineup minus Arkansas and South Carolina and plus Georgia Tech, Tulane and Sewanee. During a few of these years, the Commodores did not participate, since their poor record did not warrant an invitation.

Just as Kentucky is consistently one of the tournament favorites today, the Wildcats were favorites every year until the tournament's demise after the 1951–52 season (reestablished in 1979–present). Adolph Rupp's first season at the helm for the Wildcats was that inaugural SEC 1932–33 season.

In the previous seasons, the tournament champion was awarded the SEC title and invited to participate in the NCAA National Tournament. However, during the previous spring, the conference had decided to award the regular-season champ the official SEC championship. The regular-season champion 'Cats entered the 1951 tournament in Louisville having won eight consecutive tournament championships and twelve since the SEC was formed.

Coach Bob Polk took his second-place 15-8 (SEC, 10-4) Commodores into the annual event with a great deal of optimism. The last time the

This Vanderbilt basketball team won the 1951 SEC Tournament in an upset victory over Kentucky. It would be the Commodores' only tournament title until 2012. *Courtesy of Vanderbilt Athletic Communications.*

Commodores had faced the Wildcats in the tournament was 1947, when Rupp's boys embarrassed Vandy, 98–29. At the conclusion of that game, Vanderbilt's administration decided to take the game more seriously and, one year later, hired Polk as its first full-time basketball coach.

Former Vandy forward Bob Dudley Smith recalled:

> *From the beginning of the year, we seemed to develop a certain maturity, and I think we really hit our peak at the tournament. We played four good games in row, and the momentum just kept going. I believe we were a tournament-type team.*
>
> *George Kelley played for the same coach I did in high school, Emmett Strickland of West End* [Nashville]. *The both of us played on state championship teams and played in the finals three consecutive years. Dave*

Kardokus played in Indiana, and of course, the tournament fever in Indiana was sensational. Jack Heldman was the same way, and there was just something about tournament fever that you get. We played an outstanding four games.

Polk, in his fourth season as Vanderbilt's coach, led his team in the opening round against Tennessee. Commodore senior captain Kelley's hard work under the boards and scrappy play gave Vandy a 43–32 halftime lead. The Vols' poor second-half shooting enabled the Commodores to pull away for an 88–52 blasting. The balanced scoring consisted of five Commodores in double figures. Center Al Weiss led the game with 20 points, followed by Kardokus (19), Kelley (12), Gene Southwood (10) and Heldman (10). It was the worst loss Vanderbilt had ever given the Vols at that time and the Commodores' first tournament win against Tennessee.

In Vandy's second-round game against Georgia, there were fifty-one personal fouls called. Kelley, a guard-forward, collected nineteen rebounds in a 70–60 Vandy victory. Smith led Vanderbilt in scoring with 18 points, followed by Kardokus's 17. Vanderbilt hung on as Weiss, Kelley and Southwood fouled out of the game.

Vanderbilt's third game ended in a 75–63 victory against LSU. Weiss's streak shooting and Kelley's rebounding led the Commodores, who reached the tournament finals for the first time in school history.

The second game of this Vanderbilt double-header and fourth game in three days was against the seemingly invincible Kentucky Wildcats for the championship. Louisville's Jefferson Armory was packed with seven thousand partisan Wildcat fans. This edition of Rupp's powerhouse was considered his greatest at that time. Leading the Wildcats were all-American seven-foot center Bill Spivey, guard Frank Ramsey and forward Cliff Hagan—all of whom were all-SEC selections. Kentucky entered the game with only one loss on the season, a 43–42 overtime thriller against St. Louis. The No. 1 ranking in the national polls also belonged to the Wildcats. Future Vanderbilt coach C.M. Newton was a reserve for Kentucky.

Kardokus remembered:

We had a good team; we finished second in the conference two straight years, and in all honesty, we didn't think we could beat Kentucky. They beat us twice during the season pretty handily, and we just thought they were too good. We thought we could win the other games since we split with Tennessee and beat Georgia. We didn't play LSU in the regular season.

> *Kentucky was the No. 1 seed, and they had to play three games, where we played four in three days. We played Thursday, Friday, Saturday morning and later that evening. So we were tired. I just didn't think we could beat Kentucky, and I just didn't want to be embarrassed.*

Smith opened the scoring with a basket in the first minute. Four minutes later, a Spivey tip-in gave the Wildcats an 8–3 advantage. Vanderbilt hung tough, regaining the lead, 15–14, after the ten-minute mark. With five minutes to go until halftime, the Commodores struggled to a 20–19 margin.

After resting on the bench, Spivey entered the game and sparked an 11–6 Wildcat run to give his team a 30–26 halftime lead. The nervous partisan crowd began to relax with the strong finish by the "Big Blue."

Smith said:

> *When we went into the game, we had a special offense that coach designed to have three guards with me in the center. Since I could drive, I would fake and drive down the middle. We put Kelley on the wing, which moved Spivey out of the middle so he couldn't block our shots. Then we had a weave out on the front, and that was our basic offense.*
>
> *After playing that LSU game, gee whiz, we were so tired we didn't know if we could make it. We just plugged along. We were down in the dressing room at halftime when all of a sudden over the loudspeaker it was announced that Kentucky would celebrate immediately after the game in the Kentucky hotel. I was standing beside Kelley, and he turned to me and said, "My goodness, they have already counted us out."*

Five minutes into the second half, Kentucky was on the verge of blowing the game open with the scoring of Spivey and Ramsey. The duo pounded the offensive boards, extending their lead to 40–30. Kentucky began to substitute when Vanderbilt caught its second wind.

The lead was 48–39 when Kardokus hit an outside jumper that pumped up his teammates. Later, Smith connected on another jumper and a set-shot. A basket by Heldman stunned the cold-shooting Kentuckians. The score was 48–47 in favor of the Wildcats, who were scoreless in the previous four minutes.

After a Vanderbilt timeout, Kentucky's Walt Hirsch broke the scoring drought with a lay-up, but Southwood hit consecutive set-shots and the Commodores regained the lead, 51–50. Spivey tipped in a basket to give the lead back to Kentucky.

Dave Kardokus was first-team all-SEC in 1951. *Courtesy of Vanderbilt Athletic Communications.*

Kardokus and Spivey traded baskets, but Weiss fouled out of the game, sending Spivey to the free-throw line, where he made just one foul shot. Kentucky was now leading 55–53 but was about to fall due to the Commodore pressure.

Kentucky was getting one shot at the goal, and Kelley's pressure led to consecutive baskets by Kardokus and Southwood. Kelley hit two free throws. A Smith lay-up gave Vanderbilt its biggest lead, 61–55. Spivey's two fouls shots cut the lead to 61–57 with one minute and thirty-three seconds left on the clock.

Kardokus said:

> *The only time I thought we were really going to win was when we were up by two points, and George Kelley hit two free throws to put us four points ahead. That was the first time in the game I thought we could beat them. They were good. I mean good. They had Ramsey, Spivey and Hagan, who were three all-Americans. And they had Bobby Watson, who never missed.*

The rules in this era gave the player fouled the option of taking either the foul shot or possession on an inbound pass. If a player was awarded two foul shots, he could shoot the first one and waive the second shot to pass the ball into play.

Spivey was on the foul line again for two shots and missed the first attempt. He waived the second attempt, but Vanderbilt's Bob White stole Hagan's inbound pass. Kentucky fouled the Commodores three times in the final minute, but they waived each free throw and were able to run out the clock for their first SEC Tournament championship.

Smith said:

> *When we were freezing the basketball at the end of the game, Kardokus drove to the basket twice, and they wouldn't foul him because of the waiving. They knew we would just take the ball out of bounds anyway. Coach's philosophy was if they don't get the ball offensively, then how are they going to score?*
>
> *Jack Heldman did something near the end of the game that I will never forget. We raced down the court to get into defensive position, and Heldman starting screaming, "Everybody play good defense; we've got this game won. Play defense. Play defense."*

UK's Spivey led the scoring with 21. Smith led the Commodores with 15 points, followed by Southwood (14) and Kardokus (13). Kelley fouled out late

George Kelley was the Commodores' team captain for the 1950–51 season. *Courtesy of Vanderbilt Athletic Communications.*

but collected 8 points. Kentucky was awarded the SEC championship due to its regular-season accomplishment. The Wildcats continued the season by winning their third NCAA championship with a 68–58 win over Big Seven champions Kansas State.

Vanderbilt was expected to receive an at-large bid to the National NCAA Tournament or the then-prestigious NIT, but that never materialized. Newspaper reports suggest that the team was so tired from its exhausting tournament run that it voted not to accept any postseason bids.

Kardokus said:

> *That was the time that the Madison Square Garden was the Mecca, up until the year before. That was the NIT event, which was on par if not superior to the NCAA Tournament in prestige. Nobody wanted to go to the Garden anymore, and Bradley was hosting an on-campus tournament. We were invited to that, but we turned that down.*
>
> *We didn't just say we weren't going to any tournament. In those days, the NCAA was a sixteen-team tournament. You had to win the conference championship, and ironically, up until that year the tournament champion went. But they changed it that year to where the regular-season champion went. We weren't invited to that or the NIT.*

After the game, Coach Rupp entered the hospitality room where writers and coaches were gathered. Dudley Green of the *Nashville Banner* reported Rupp's remarks:

> *His opening remark to the Commodore mentor was, "Bobby, you made a grave mistake tonight. I want you to make the most of it. It is not going to happen again. You have been getting the best boys for the past three years. I haven't been recruiting but I'm starting tomorrow. I'm going out and get me some good boys."*
>
> *"How can you say something like that, Adolph," asked Harry Rabenhorst, LSU coach, "When by your own admission you have the greatest college player in the country in Cliff Hagan performing on your second team?"*
>
> *Rupp, sporting a patch over his injured right eye, wheeled to put a falcon-like glare on Rabenhorst.*
>
> *"I haven't been out of Lexington in three years to look at a boy," shot back Adolph.*

The SEC Tournament was disbanded after the next year and revived for the 1978–79 season. That 1951 SEC Tournament crown would be the only one for Vanderbilt until sixty-one years later. Coach Kevin Stallings and his Commodore squad defeated No. 1–ranked Kentucky and the SEC champs in the 2012 SEC Tournament in New Orleans. The Wildcats returned to New Orleans to win the 2012 NCAA championship.

CHAPTER 10

THE MAGIC OF MEMORIAL GYMNASIUM

The 2011–12 Vanderbilt men's basketball team played its sixtieth season in Memorial Gymnasium. When the construction of the gym was near completion in 1952, the state-of-the-art facility was one of the finest in the South. The basketball gods were so impressed that they slipped some magic dust hidden in the overhead steel rafters—or so says a myth.

Architect Edwin Keeble designed the structure with its unique interior. It looked like a huge warehouse with a raised floor. Its design was for more than just basketball, as the floor was also a stage for other activities such as plays and concerts. For basketball games, the benches are placed on the end zones near the baskets. If the benches were on the sidelines, the fans' view from the premium seats would be blocked. The gymnasium was named for the Vanderbilt men and women who served during World War II, including the 411 individuals who lost their lives during combat.

Since that first campus game on December 6, 1952, a 90–83 victory over Virginia, the magical dust has been sprinkling on Vanderbilt players from time to time. Some Commodore basketball players have been transformed into heroes, causing students to charge the floor. Evidence will show that the Magic of Memorial is not a slogan but a part of Vanderbilt basketball history. These are some of the more recent buzzer beaters and memorable moments:

January 10, 2007—With 3.7 seconds on the clock against Tennessee, Derrick Byars grabbed a Ross Neltner half-court inbound pass. Byars raced to the right side of the basket but missed a contested lay-up. Shan Foster took

A concert being held in Memorial Gymnasium in 1954. *Courtesy of Vanderbilt University Special Collections and Archives.*

the rebound from the left side for a quick put-back as the buzzer sounded. Vanderbilt beat the Vols, 82–81.

December 2, 2006—The Commodores were tied with Toledo 93–93 in overtime with the Commodores in possession of the ball and thirteen seconds left. Freshman guard Jermaine Beal drove the length of the floor, found an opening and attacked the goal. Beal's lay-up counted as the clock revealed 4.4 seconds. He was fouled on the play as Vandy hung on for the 98–93 victory.

November 30, 2005—In the game against the visiting Oregon Ducks, the Commodores were trailing 75–73 with 3.7 seconds remaining and the full length of the floor to conquer. Senior guard Mario Moore took the inbound pass, dribbled into front court and launched a running thirty-five-footer that never touched iron. The 3-pointer gave Vanderbilt a 76–75 victory.

March 24, 2005—The potency of the magic dust was evident when Vanderbilt played Wichita State during the 2005 NIT in the postseason. During a March Madness moment, the Commodores were tied with the Shockers, 63–63 with an impossible .07 seconds left. With the ESPN audience and Memorial faithful expecting overtime, Corey Smith received a Jason Holwerda full-length court pass over a Wichita defender. Smith turned around and banked in a basket, and the Shockers were shocked, 65–63.

Before Commodore legend Barry Goheen was ever born (I'll get to him later), there was Roger Schurig (1963–65). Schurig, a St. Louis, Missouri native, was known as the clutch player not only at Vanderbilt but also in the SEC. His two free throws with seven seconds left against Kentucky in 1963 gave the Commodores a rare win in Lexington.

These are some of Schurig's exploits:

January 2, 1963—Tied with Western Kentucky 69–69 with thirty seconds left, the Commodores held the ball for one final shot. Schurig took the ball to the left side of the basket and put up a one-handed shot with two seconds that swished through the basket. The Commodores won the non-conference game, 71–69. In the previous game in the Poinsettia Classic at Clemson, Schurig was the hero with a final bucket at the buzzer to win the championship over Furman, 69–68.

January 16, 1963—Vanderbilt got a break when Tennessee missed a free throw with three seconds left and a 68–68 score. In overtime, Schurig was the go-to guy when he canned a jumper with four seconds left for a 74–72 Commodore victory.

March 2, 1963—The Commodores fought such an emotional game with Georgia Tech that with two minutes left, the Vanderbilt crowd of nearly eight thousand was warned about tossing debris on the floor. A technical foul against the Commodores was threatened. The game had been tied eleven times, and neither team could build a lead of more than 4 points. Trailing 74–73, Schurig hit a jump shot at the buzzer for the 75–74 Vanderbilt win.

More Memorial Magic:

January 6, 1964—When the second-ranked Kentucky Wildcats arrived at Memorial Gymnasium, the fans were ready for a close game. The game was tied at 83–83 when John Ed Miller took an inbound pass and penetrated toward the goal with seconds remaining. Surprised that his Wildcat defender

Shan Foster graduated from Vanderbilt as its all-time scoring leader, with 2,011 points, and an all-American. *Courtesy of Vanderbilt Athletic Communications.*

didn't cover him closely, Miller pulled up at the free throw line and swished the game-winner. The Commodores upset Adolph Rupp's men, 85–83.

February 8, 1964—John Ed Miller found himself in a similar situation as in the Kentucky game one month earlier. The Commodores put on a late surge to cut into a second-half LSU Tigers' 8-point lead. With four seconds left and the score tied at 64–64, Miller tossed another shot from the foul line but missed. All-SEC center Clyde Lee was in position to grab the rebound and scored the winning basket. Vandy won, 66–64.

December 12, 1967—Third-ranked Vanderbilt managed to send the game into overtime at 75–75 when eighth-ranked Davidson came to Nashville. With the scored tied at 79–79, Vanderbilt held the ball with one minute and twenty-four seconds remaining and took a timeout with nineteen seconds left. Tom Hagan managed to get off a shot with three seconds left for the thrilling end, 81–79.

December 16, 1967—The Duke Blue Devils took a 75–74 lead over the Commodores with twenty-six seconds remaining. A timeout was called at the seventeen-second mark by Vanderbilt to draw up a play. Bo Wyenandt was the hero this time, as his jump shot with two seconds left gave the Commodores a 76–75 victory over the stunned Duke players.

January 5, 1974—In a physical game with the Tide, Vanderbilt was trailing 72–71 as guard Butch Feher missed the second of a pressurized one-and-one free-throw opportunity. An alert Terry Compton batted the missed free throw away while Feher scrambled for the loose ball. Spotting teammate Joe Ford in the open, Feher passed the ball to Ford, who was immediately covered. Feher dashed under the basket. Ford threw a bullet pass to Feher, who made a lay-up with just five seconds left. Vandy won, 73–72.

February 2, 1976—A winter snow and ice storm kept the Vanderbilt faithful to just 1,800. Ole Miss was winless in the SEC but led the Commodores with six seconds on the clock, 60–59. Dicky Keffer dribbled pass the half-court line and passed off to Jeff Fosnes. Fosnes jumped for a shot, but two Rebel defenders challenged him. While still airborne, Fosnes decided to give up the shot to Keffer. Keffer launched a thirty-five-footer that was good for the 61–60 Commodore win.

February 24, 1983—Vanderbilt was trailing arch rival Tennessee with time running out, 68–67. Phil Cox drove into the lane and collided with Vols defender Tyrone Beaman. The referee called a block on Beaman, sending Cox to the line. Cox, one of the SEC's best free-throw shooters, connected on both freebies for the 69–68 victory.

You cannot think about Memorial Miracles without Barry Goheen (1986–89) coming to mind. Goheen can be considered one of college basketball's best clutch performers of all time. Vanderbilt fans were amazed by his basketball wizardry and not only in the home gymnasium. These are Goheen's game-winners in Memorial Gymnasium:

January 15, 1986—With the Commodores trailing Tennessee 59–51 and less than a minute remaining, Goheen led his team to 9 unanswered points. He scored the last 5 points to pull out the improbable win. The guard hit a ten-footer from the left baseline with four seconds left to tie the game. On the play, Goheen was fouled, and his free throw was the game-winner, 60–59.

November 30, 1988—Denny Crum's nationally ranked Louisville Cardinals were looking to go into overtime with the score knotted at 62–62. Less than five seconds remained as the Commodores needed to run the entire court for a miracle finish. Goheen received the pass in the back court and launched a shot behind the half-court stripe. The stunned Vanderbilt fans leaped to their feet at the sudden win as the ball swished through the goal. Commodores won, 65–62.

January 14, 1989—Goheen hit a fifty-three-foot shot (by measurement) to put Vanderbilt ahead of the Georgia Bulldogs by 1 point at halftime. Georgia was winning by 2 points when the Commodores had ten seconds to bring the ball full court for the tie or win. Barry Booker collided with a Bulldog player (no call) but was able to pass the ball to Goheen. Goheen took the pass, glanced at the clock, opted to dribble behind the 3-point line and drilled the game-winning trey for the 76–75 victory.

February 11, 1989—With the game tied at 69–69, Goheen broke free for a lay-up and was fouled with two seconds left in the game against Mississippi. To the dismay of the home fans, the apparent basket was waved off. However, Goheen confidently made both ends of the one-and-one for the 71–69 win.

Even more magic:

January 26, 1991—Trailing the Georgia Bulldogs 74–72, the Commodores came down the court for a last-second game-tying or game-winning point. With the Vanderbilt shooters unable to get open for a pass, forward Steve Grant took the ball across the half-court line. Grant dribbled a few steps and launched a desperation 3-pointer. The ball went through the hoop for a 75–74 victory. It was Grant's only career 3-pointer.

December 9, 1992—With the game against Louisville tied at 88–88, Vanderbilt all-American guard Billy McCaffrey drove down the lane as only seconds remained. McCaffrey's running jumper bounced off the right side

Barry Goheen became a college basketball legend with his last-second heroics and mid-court shots. *Courtesy of Vanderbilt Athletic Communications.*

Bo Wyenandt was first-team all-SEC in 1967. *Courtesy of Vanderbilt Athletic Communications.*

of the rim, but center Chris Lawson was in position for the tip-in. Vanderbilt won the game 90–88 and went on to win the SEC title and eventually advance to the Sweet Sixteen of the NCAA Tournament.

In celebration of the sixtieth anniversary of Memorial Gymnasium, the Vanderbilt Athletic Communications staff put together a Top 60 moments in the building, including men and women. These are some of those historic games:

Vanderbilt beat Adolph Rupp and No. 1–ranked Kentucky 76–75 (1959); a jump shot by Doug Yates at the top of the circle beat Baylor at the buzzer, 61–60 (1959); No. 3 Duke fell to the Commodores in overtime (1963); Clyde Lee Day honored the senior all-American (1966); Perry Wallace broke the SEC color barrier with the first game (1967); in the late 1960s, Tennessee coach Ray Mears and his players incited Vanderbilt fans with their "walk" around the court during a UT/Vandy freshman game; Vanderbilt beat Ole Miss 130–112 for the most points scored by Vandy, still an SEC record for combined points in a game (1970).

Vanderbilt defeated Kentucky 71–69 to claim the school's second SEC championship (1974); Vanderbilt connected on thirty-five of thirty-six free-throw attempts in a win over Mississippi State, and this remains an NCAA record for percentage (.972 percent) with thirty-five or more attempts (1986); No. 2 Indiana, led by Coach Bobby Knight, lost to Vandy 79–75 but won the national championship (1986); the Commodores defeated Dean Smith and No. 1–ranked North Carolina, 78–76 (1987); Vanderbilt came from a 16-point halftime deficit to defeat the Vols 89–86 in the NIT, and the 'Dores advanced to Madison Square Garden and won the NIT championship (1990); Vanderbilt defeated No. 8 Arkansas 102–89 in a game from which Hogs coach Nolan Richardson was tossed after receiving his second technical foul early in the second half (1993).

No. 1–ranked Florida fell to the Commodores, 83–70, when Vandy coach Kevin Stallings would not give Gators' Joakim Noah the basketball after a turnover (2007); Vandy beat Kentucky by 41 points, 93–52, the fifth-largest margin of all time for the Wildcats in a loss (2008); Coach Bruce Pearl and Tennessee arrived in Memorial Gymnasium with a No. 1 ranking but fell to the Commodores 72–69 (2008); Shan Foster put on a scoring exhibition with 42 points (nine of fifteen 3-pointers) on Senior Night to tie the school record for points (2008); ESPN Game Day set up on the floor in Memorial Gymnasium for the first time, and the Commodores lost to No. 1–ranked Kentucky, 69–63 (2012).

The now sixty-one-year-old friend has seen the following renovations and additions throughout the decades: The north side balconies were added between the 1965 and 1966 seasons; the south balconies, dubbed the "Balconies That Clyde Lee Built," were completed in December 1967, raising the capacity to 11,000; in 1969, 4,500 seats were added on the east and west sides (and baselines), bringing the total number of seats to 15,581; a $25 million renovation was completed in 2002 with the addition of a practice gym, coaches' offices, a donor room and a Hall of Champions; the men's and women's locker rooms were renovated and a team meeting/video room was added prior to the start of the 2008–9 season. The current capacity is 14,316.

Since that first Commodore home game in 1952, the Vanderbilt men have a Memorial Gymnasium all-time record of 724-197 (78.6 percent). They have never recorded a losing season in the sixty-year history of the structure. Undefeated seasons came in 1955–56 (13-0), 1960–61 (13-0), 1964–65 (14-0), 1966–67 (14-0), 1992–93 (14-0) and 2007–8 (19-0).

The Vanderbilt women have an all-time record of 415-93 (81.7 percent) in Memorial Gymnasium. They have just one losing record in 1982–83 (5-6). The women have been playing basketball in the modern era since the 1977–78 season.

The magic continues!

CHAPTER 11

ROY SKINNER, VANDERBILT'S WINNINGEST COACH

This interview between Roy Skinner and Bill Traughber is from February 2007. Coach Skinner passed away in Nashville on October 25, 2010, at age eighty. Skinner is a member of the Tennessee Sports Hall of Fame and the Vanderbilt Sports Hall of Fame.

The Vanderbilt basketball program has found success over the decades dipping into the state of Kentucky for prospects. Maybe the best basketball product from the Bluegrass State to the Vanderbilt campus was Roy Skinner.

Skinner is the all-time winningest basketball coach in the university's history. Born in Paducah, Kentucky, Skinner began his collegiate coaching career at Paducah Junior College, where he had played basketball. He later played basketball and earned a degree from Presbyterian College in South Carolina.

A class at Nashville's George Peabody College changed his life. Skinner recalled:

> *I was in a coaching basketball class that Bob Polk* [Vanderbilt head basketball coach] *taught and got acquainted with him. Vanderbilt had a real good freshman team in 1956–57, and I was coaching at Paducah. Vanderbilt had a player from Heath, Kentucky, near Paducah.*
>
> *And because of that player, Polk agreed to have his freshmen play my junior college team. We beat them in Paducah, and that was the only game their freshman team lost all year. That did impress Polk. Then his assistant*

got out of coaching, and I applied for the job. Two or three months later, he hired me.

The duties that Skinner absorbed were freshman team coach, scouting and attending high school games scouring for prospects. In just his second year (1958–59) on the Commodore staff, Skinner was thrust into the title of "acting" head coach. Just weeks before the season was to begin, Skinner and Polk were in Kentucky watching a prospect in a game. Polk suffered a heart attack and was hospitalized for two months. The twenty-eight-year-old Skinner temporally replaced Polk for that season.

"Shoot no, I didn't feel any pressure," said Skinner when asked about that year. "I had confidence and some real good coaching along the way. I was ready for them."

In Skinner's lone year as acting head coach, Vanderbilt recorded a 14-10 (SEC, 8-6) season. Two years later, Polk retired from Vanderbilt, and Skinner was given the head coaching job. He said, "I was tickled to death. To have the opportunity and chance to take it over, I just couldn't wait to get started. I was so young. I didn't know what was going on. I was a fast break, more like Kentucky running-style coach. Run-and-gun and play a little defense in between. The offense was the main thing with me."

In Skinner's first three seasons his teams were 12-12, 16-7 and 19-6. Skinner said it was difficult to recruit at that time because of the tough academic requirements of Vanderbilt.

"We beat Kentucky down here in 1964," said Skinner. "That was our biggest win that year. In fact, they were ranked No. 1 in the nation when they came in here. They had just beaten Georgia Tech, and we knocked them off. That was by far the biggest win for me. We hadn't beaten them in three years."

One player whom Skinner sought locally was Nashville's David Lipscomb High School's Clyde Lee. The center entered Vanderbilt and became a basketball legend for the university. Lee holds all of the school's rebounding records. Skinner said:

It was not difficult as far as the grades to recruit Clyde. He was an excellent student and qualified. It was a little difficult because so many schools were interested in him. But I had the inside track being here close.

Of course, I worked as hard as I could at it and ended up winning. At that time it wasn't that big because he wasn't that good. He had the potential to be and certainly developed into an outstanding player.

Roy Skinner with the famed F-Troop, *left to right*: Jeff Fosnes, Joe Ford and Butch Feher. *Courtesy of Vanderbilt Athletic Communications.*

With Lee at center, Vanderbilt won its first SEC championship in 1964–65. The Commodores went 24-4 with an SEC record of 15-1. The only SEC loss was at Tennessee.

Skinner said:

> *I know I had some real good players and that was the reason for our success. One of them was Bob Grace, whose nickname was "Snake." I recruited him in 1961, and he graduated in 1965. He was from Hopkinsville, Kentucky. He wasn't that good a prospect, but he had the potential. Bob had good speed, good hands and he developed into an awful good player. He had some other good ones to play with him.*

Vanderbilt won its first game over DePaul in the first round of the 1965 NCAA Tournament. Next was a bulkier Michigan team led by all-American Cazzie Russell. With less than a minute remaining, Michigan led by 1 point. Vanderbilt's John Ed Miller drove for a basket that was disallowed due to a traveling call. The basket would have given the Commodores a 1-point lead. Michigan eventually won 87–85. If Vanderbilt had won that contest, it would have vaulted into the Final Four where UCLA became national champs.

Skinner vividly remembers one of the most controversial calls in Vanderbilt history: "The referees cheated us. He made a traveling call on John Ed Miller, and John Ed did not travel. I looked at the film probably 150 times, and there's no doubt about it. But that's all hindsight, and they beat us by 2 points in the last few seconds. If we had scored, we'd win by 1 point. I'm sure of it."

In 1966, Skinner changed the SEC with his recruitment of Perry Wallace. Wallace was a black athlete from Nashville's Pearl High School. He was the first black to play basketball in the conference. Wallace was not Skinner's first attempt to recruit black players. Skinner said:

> *I don't remember what year, but the chancellor told me that Vanderbilt was open to black athletes. I had contacted several black players before Perry and had a few to visit the campus. Because of the academics, and they were mostly from the North, they were skeptical playing in the South and the SEC with no blacks.*
>
> *I didn't come close to getting any until Perry came along. He was a straight-A student, and I practically lived with Perry. I worked awfully*

Roy Skinner with players, *left to right*: Bo Wyenandt, Gene Lockyear and Bob Warren. *Courtesy of Vanderbilt Athletic Communications.*

> *hard on him. I got some petitions, and the university got several petitions. I don't have any idea how many signatures there were, but one was from some alumni that were not in favor of us recruiting a black player. I only took that with a grain of salt. There wasn't anything they could do about that.*

Skinner led the 1973–74 Vanderbilt team to its second SEC title behind Jan van Breda Kolff. He had been coaching for twenty-five years when he suddenly retired in 1976. Skinner said he was physically and mentally worn out. He entered the insurance business after leaving Vanderbilt and retired from that line of work after twenty years. Skinner won the SEC's Coach of the Year award four different times (1965, '67, '74, '76).

The team that most Vanderbilt fans enjoy beating is the Tennessee Vols. That is a true Vanderbilt basketball rivalry. But Skinner initially looked past the Vols in his early coaching years. When asked if the Vols were the team he aimed for each year, he responded, "With me it wasn't. I was at Vanderbilt as the coach before I realized that because of our alumni I needed to concentrate more on Tennessee. But to me, beating Kentucky—that was it!"

Skinner said that his biggest and most memorable Kentucky game was in 1963, a 69–67 victory in Lexington. He said it had been years since a Vanderbilt team had achieved a win on the Wildcats' home court. Playing Kentucky meant that Skinner had to face Adolph Rupp at least twice a year. The perennial SEC champs were always tough with the discipline and tradition of the Wildcats.

Skinner said of Rupp:

> *He was extremely nice to me. I remember going up to Lexington to a baseball tournament. He was in the hospital and had gotten out of coaching. Rupp was forced out. He didn't want to leave. I think he was seventy-two at the time. I went by his hospital room, and every other word was a curse word. He was so bitter at Kentucky for firing him, which is what they did. All through the years he was extremely nice to me—except for games.*

Throughout Skinner's coaching career at Vanderbilt, he was able to recruit some of the finest shooters in the SEC. Some of these fantastic players who have donated to the Commodore tradition are Jeff Fosnes, Terry Compton, Tom Hagan, Joe Ford, Thorpe Weber, John Ed Miller and Butch Feher. When asked to single out his best pure shooter, Skinner laughed:

> *I had too many. One of the first was Keith Thomas. He was a super player. I tried to recruit a teammate of Keith's out of Louisville, Kentucky, that went to Wake Forest. Keith was real young and coming.*
>
> *I tried to get him at first for a $1,000 scholarship and then a one-year scholarship. His parents had the money, so that wasn't the biggest thing. His dad told me he wasn't interested in a one-year or partial scholarship—that he was going to DePauw University in Indiana. But I took Keith Thomas, and he turned out to be an outstanding guard.*

In his sixteen years at Vanderbilt, Skinner compiled a record of 278-135 (63.3 percent). His Memorial Gym record was an amazing 181-41 (81.5 percent). Skinner was asked about the "Magic of Memorial." He said:

The thing that got me, we won most of our home games. Somewhere along the late 1960s, early 1970s newspapers starting writing about it and coaches started complaining about us winning our home games. There were charges of referees with home cooking.

Referees bent over backward not to home cook, and I felt like we got screwed several times. They were trying to show they weren't partial to us because of the uproar. It's a super place to play basketball.

CHAPTER 12

VANDERBILT'S 1965 SEC CHAMPIONSHIP SEASON

The Vanderbilt Commodores headed into the 1964–65 basketball season with a great deal of optimism. All five starters returned from a fourth-place finish in the Southeastern Conference the previous year with a 19-6 overall record. Led by junior center all-American Clyde Lee, the Commodores were given a preseason ranking of sixth by the Associated Press.

Coach Roy Skinner's squad began the season with home wins over Rice, Southern Methodist University and Western Kentucky. The impressive margins of victory enabled Vandy to climb into the third spot in the rankings behind powerful Michigan and Wichita. The first road trip of the season would slow down the Commodores' ambition.

A 69–64 upset loss at Virginia Tech dropped Vandy to ninth in the rankings. Two days later, the Commodores traveled to North Carolina and lost, 84–78. Vanderbilt team captain John Ed Miller regrouped his teammates and won the Vanderbilt Invitational Tournament. They followed that by winning the Sugar Bowl Tournament in New Orleans, beating Texas Tech and Louisville.

"When we went on that road trip, we were third or fourth in the country," said Clyde Lee. "On that road trip all the teams ahead of us got beat, and if he had won, we would have been No. 1. It was one of those things where we were cold. We couldn't shoot well, and we played two tough teams. It did not hurt our chemistry or our attitude at all. We bounced back from it pretty well."

SEC play began with eight consecutive wins, followed by a loss at Tennessee, and Vanderbilt concluding the season with seven consecutive wins. Its 23-3 (SEC, 15-1) record gave Vanderbilt its first SEC championship ever and an automatic bid to the sixteen-team NCAA National Tournament.

"We were very optimistic about going into the regional," said John Ed Miller. "At the time, we were ranked fifth in the nation, and the competition in the SEC was beginning to pick up, which made us better. We were certainly proud of our achievements in terms of winning the conference championship. It was a great feeling. This group of folks was a team with a lot of confidence in each other."

The Commodores left for the NCAA Mideast Regional Tournament in Lexington, Kentucky, which included Dayton (21-6), DePaul (17-8) and Michigan (21-3). Vanderbilt entered its first game with a No. 5 ranking against Coach Ray Meyer's Blue Demons. Commodore starters Lee, Miller, Bob "Snake" Grace, Keith Thomas and Wayne Taylor opened the regional against DePaul, followed by No. 1 Michigan pitted against Dayton.

Kentucky's Memorial Coliseum hosted this event before a crowd of 12,000 fans, which included an estimated 2,500 from Nashville. The Commodores took a 39–32 lead at the intermission. After stretching the lead to 9 in the second half, the Demons began to use a full-court press. The press forced Vanderbilt into mistakes as a 60–52 Vanderbilt advantage was cut to 74–70.

With two minutes and six seconds left in regulation, Tom Meyer, the coach's son, stole the ball from Miller and drove to the basket, making the score 74–72. Vandy's Wayne Calvert followed with a lay-up but was called for a foul at the Demons' goal. DePaul's Jim Murphy hit both free throws, tying the game. The Demons' press forced an errant pass over Taylor's head, losing possession.

The Commodores almost won the game in regulation when Lee retrieved a pass down court. However, he was called for traveling with seven seconds. Murphy missed a long shot at the buzzer, sending the game into overtime tied at 76. With the Commodores ahead in the overtime, 78–76, Lee fouled DePaul's Errol Palmer after Palmer's field goal tied the game. This was Lee's fifth foul, and he left the game for the bench.

"I almost blew it," said Lee, who was the third pick in the 1966 NBA draft. "Right at the end of regulation, Wayne Taylor threw me a pass. I got called for traveling when a lay-up would have won the game there. Taylor got mad at me, but we went on to win it."

Palmer missed the foul shot, and two free throws by Miller gave the Commodores an 80–78 lead with one minute and thirty seconds remaining.

Clyde Lee was a Vanderbilt all-American and leads the Commodores in all rebounding records. *Courtesy of Vanderbilt Athletic Communications.*

Vandy again gained possession with the 2-point lead when Miller was once again sent to the line. He missed the foul shot, but Vandy substitute Ron Green grabbed the rebound, allowing the Commodores to keep possession.

Taylor was fouled with seven seconds as he hit the first of a one-and-one, increasing the lead to 3. Taylor's second attempt kicked off the rim back into the hands of Green. Green passed the ball to Calvert, who converted a jumper for an 83–78 win and the Commodores' first NCAA Tournament victory in history. Lee led the Commodores in scoring with 24 points. Thomas finished with 18, Miller 16 and Calvert 12.

Miller, who was twice named as a guard on the first-team all-SEC squad, said:

> *In the DePaul game, we really didn't play that well, but we won in overtime. We felt that because of the way we played, we were fortunate to win the game. In all the time that I was at Vanderbilt, there were only two games that we thought we were going to lose at any time during the game. The rest of the time we didn't think we were going to lose. We had confidence in each other, the coaching and we just knew there was going to be some way for us to win.*
>
> *If you go back and look at the record of the seniors while we were sophomores, with the close games, by and large we won. It never entered our minds that we would not beat DePaul. We had played so poorly against DePaul, and Michigan had played so well against Dayton. They were awesome. Some of our fans came around for our pregame meal, and they were telling us, "Gee, it was a great season, these guys are really good, we're proud of you, etc." After they left, we thought, "What is going on here?" They thought the season was over, but in our minds, we knew we could play with anyone.*

After the Commodores' win, they watched from the stands as Michigan devoured Dayton, 98–71. Dave Strack was the Michigan coach, with all-American Cazzie Russell his leader for the Big Ten Conference champions. The winner of the Vanderbilt-Michigan game would compete the following weekend in the Final Four in Portland, Oregon.

The underdog Commodores jumped out to a 24–17 lead in the first ten minutes with Lee, Miller and Thomas carrying the first-half burden. Russell's Wolverines took advantage of twelve Commodore turnovers, giving Vandy a slim 39–38 halftime lead.

Lee said:

Bob "Snake" Grace was a first-team all-SEC forward in 1965. *Courtesy of Vanderbilt Athletic Communications.*

> *Bob Grace and I both got four fouls early in the game. Mine came very, very quickly. Coach Skinner first sat me down, and then he decided he was going to play me one way or another. I played a large part of the first half with four fouls and the entire second half with four fouls without fouling out. I got into foul trouble that I don't fully understand today. The first two times I got the ball offensively, with my back to the basket, I made a little drop-step move and was whistled instantly for an offensive foul.*

Watching the tapes, it appeared that my elbow kind of wrapped around. I guess the official thought I was hooking the guy. Keith Thomas, who did a very good job of guarding Cazzie Russell, did foul out before the game was over. So we had to overcome the foul problems.

The Wolverines took the second-half lead, 49–47, on Larry Tregoning's basket. A Russell free throw upped the lead to 50–47, but Lee led the Commodores back, giving his team a 57–56 edge. Vanderbilt held the lead until Russell's jumper with one minute and thirty-three seconds left put Michigan ahead 81–80. Another costly Vanderbilt floor mistake gave the ball back to the Wolverines.

Michigan's Bill Buntin then hit a short jump shot, extending the lead to 83–80 with one minute and seven seconds on the clock. Vandy added a free throw. Michigan responded with a basket, and Miller answered with a 2-pointer, cutting the lead to 85–83. Michigan's Oliver Darden made it 87–83 on two foul shots with ten seconds left. Calvert hit a jumper with one second on the clock to finish the game. Michigan squeaked out an 87–85 win.

Lee said:

The Michigan people did not think very highly of us. They thought we were overrated as a team and that I was overrated as an individual, having made the all-American team. Then, after the ballgame, several Michigan fans came up to us and said they didn't realize how good we were and we did deserve the ranking. We made a few believers out of some Big Ten folks that night. They didn't know how good SEC basketball was.

Vanderbilt fouled the Wolverines on three separate occasions in the final minute, and on each occasion, Michigan missed the front end of a one-and-one. However, the Commodores did not get any of the rebounds. Then, a crucial traveling call by the officials on Miller in the last minute was also damaging.

Miller said:

Regardless of the outcome, it was a terrific game. Neither team led the other team by more than 6 or 7 points at any time in the game, which made it very exciting. We had some foul difficulty. Clyde had four fouls, while Snake had three and got his fourth within the first two minutes of the second half. Therefore, we had to play a looser defense inside than we would have otherwise, and that created some problems.

John Ed Miller was involved in a controversial official's call in the 1965 NCAA Tournament game against Michigan in the Elite Eight. *Courtesy of Vanderbilt Athletic Communications.*

> *Here we are with two minutes to go, and we are ahead in the game. We had a lot of opportunities when they missed their free throws, but we didn't get the rebounds. We were by far the best rebounding team in the SEC and one of the best in the nation. If you look at the statistics of Snake and Clyde, these guys rebounded like crazy. It was just one of those things that happened.*
>
> *The thing that always comes up about that game is what John Bibb* [the late *Tennessean* sportswriter and later editor] *put in the paper about that traveling call. He use to kid me about it and he'd say, "Now John Ed, did you really walk?" I'd say, "John, what can I say? They called it. It makes no difference." John would write about it every three or five years. He would put it in the bottom of his "AYEM" column and say, "Now I just want to ask you this, do you remember the John Ed Miller walk?"*

Lee recorded a game-high 28 points with twenty rebounds. Thomas added 21 points for VU, and Miller had 17. Russell led Michigan with 26 points. Lee was named the Mid-East Regional's Most Valuable Player, with Thomas also joining the team.

Vanderbilt's 24-4 season ranks as one of the best in the school's history.

Michigan beat Bill Bradley's Princeton in the first round of the finals but lost the championship game to UCLA, 91–80. Miller said:

> *We were forty-five seconds away from the Final Four, and the team that won was UCLA. We always thought we could beat UCLA. Our guard play would have been able to break the press better than Michigan, and that is what beat them. Michigan had Cazzie and the other big guards who couldn't get the ball down the court. If you go back and look at that particular game, that's what killed them.*

CHAPTER 13

PERRY WALLACE, FIRST BLACK PLAYER IN THE SEC

It has been very well documented that Perry Wallace (1968–70) was the first black basketball player in the SEC. Growing up in segregated Nashville, Wallace was all-state, all-city, all-region and a high school all-American from the 1965–66 Nashville Pearl High basketball team. In his senior year, Pearl was undefeated (31-0), winning the state championship in the first year of the integrated Tennessee high school tournament. Wallace was about to become a pioneer. He said:

> *I wasn't somebody who grew up saying, "I'm going to be a civil rights leader." I wanted to be a student athlete. The problems were overwhelming enough that I had to start thinking in terms of being a pioneer. Who wants to be a pioneer? Jackie Robinson didn't want to be a pioneer. He said if I'm pioneering that's good. What I want to do is be a baseball player. I was really forced to start thinking like a pioneer in terms of progress.*

The big-name college basketball schools like UCLA, Michigan and Kentucky had recruited Wallace. He looked north and made visits to Michigan, Purdue, Northwestern and Iowa. The Big Ten had already integrated its athletic programs. In the SEC, Vanderbilt and Tennessee also desired Wallace's talent. Wallace said:

> *I didn't consider the South because when I grew up, the South wasn't considering me or people like me. I didn't just decide I didn't like the South,*

> *that I'm not going to a school in the South. As I grew up in Nashville in the 1950s and into the 1960s, it was simply impossible for me to reach my dreams. I didn't have anything against the southern schools. There was a racial line drawn between us.*

At that time, Vanderbilt was experiencing some of its finest years on the basketball court. During the 1964–65 season, the Commodores won their first SEC championship with a 24-4 record. They followed that season at 22-4. These were the Clyde Lee years. Vanderbilt coach Roy Skinner had been recruiting black players but could never convince any to play in Nashville. Wallace said:

> *Here is a great magical secret on how Coach Skinner got me to Vanderbilt. He came over and said hello. He talked to my parents and me. He showed me he was a person. We were pretty down home. My parents grew up on a farm, then they came to Nashville. We liked people to sit down and look you in the eye and talk. Just tell you they're very interested and sincere in talking business with us. It's not like there was some great formula from physics; that's what Coach Skinner did.*

One week after Wallace signed his scholarship papers, Skinner signed another black player, Godfrey Dillard from Detroit. Dillard went through the same tough freshman season with Wallace, but an injury kept him from playing as a sophomore and becoming the first black basketball player in the SEC. In that era of college athletics, freshmen were ineligible for varsity play; therefore, freshman teams competed against each other. Dillard would eventually transfer out of Vanderbilt, never playing on the varsity team. There was uncertainty of what would happen if blacks played basketball in the southern states.

Wallace said:

> *That was the big question in the air. Nobody really knew the answer to it. It's not that Coach Skinner tried to do a lot of talking about that. I don't think he was trying to be deceptive. He just didn't know more than the rest of us. He was thinking like most people:* We want to get you on our team. You would be one of ours and we'd take care of you and do our best. We don't know what's going to happen.
>
> *In that freshman year, the Ole Miss freshman team game was cancelled, and that is well known by now. They claimed it was a scheduling problem,*

Vanderbilt's Perry Wallace was the first African American basketball player in the SEC. *Courtesy of Vanderbilt Athletic Communications.*

> *but they didn't want to play against blacks. There were two of us. Godfrey Dillard and I did go south to Mississippi State in Starkville, and that's where we had that baptism by fire and water.*

This was not a time when basketball was played in large arenas. Places like Mississippi State and Auburn played their basketball games in hangar-type gyms.

Wallace was a six-foot, four-inch forward, and his first ugly encounter was in Starkville. Mississippi State was forbidden by the state politicians to play in the NCAA Tournament due to the presence of black players. Wallace said:

> *This was straight racism with enthusiasm. People are enthusiastic, screaming and hollering anyway. But unfortunately, what also was part of the mix were all the name-calling and the threats. Whenever I made any mistakes, they cheered. Anything that looked like a failure. They really wanted me to fail, and they ridiculed, bullied and badgered me. They would have cheerleaders lead cheers just against me.*
>
> *This is the part that's tricky. People would have different opinions. Some people would say that the referees would allow players to rough me up. Some people would say no, that's just the game that is rigorous. In those days, a lot of the football players were also basketball players. And so that is the kind of game they played. Nobody can prove whether or not the coaches told the players to go out there and rough Wallace up because that will give us a competitive advantage. There's no proof of it.*

Wallace said that Skinner complained to the SEC administration about the abusive attention he was given during games. They felt that the referees were calling too many unnecessary goal-tending calls against Wallace. Though it was tough, Wallace kept his composure in dealing with the situation. He said:

> *I needed to be a model person. That's what a racial pioneer has to do. Everything has to be perfect and proper as best as it can. Your behavior has to be exemplary. So things like complaining, yelling back at the crowd, yelling at the players, expressing frustration was something I couldn't do. I was also smarter than that. I knew that if I expressed frustration or got into a tiff with the referees that I would spark an additional surge above and beyond the things that were going on with the crowd.*

The environment grew worse when Wallace joined the varsity. While the Mississippi schools were bad, for Wallace to play basketball at Auburn, Alabama and LSU was just as intimidating. It was believed that Florida was beginning to adapt to the racial atmosphere due to the different culture in the southern portion of the state. Kentucky coach Adolph Rupp did recruit Wallace but not personally. Wallace said:

> *Kentucky was probably the best, but not perfect. I always attribute that as maybe it was the most northern school in the South. A part if was due to their culture of sports and basketball. Coach Rupp obviously ran a tight ship. There was almost a glow about Kentucky basketball.*
>
> *The players didn't call you names. They didn't try to give you an extra elbow or push. These were excellent players, and they were coached with high standards. My lasting memory against Kentucky, home or away, other than a few scenes from people in the crowd, just wasn't the same. I think Tennessee was average. It was better than Mississippi, Alabama and Louisiana.*

Wallace's family was very supportive throughout this tumultuous ordeal. They knew most of what their son and brother was experiencing but not all. Wallace did not want his family to see the indignation he was living. He said:

> *They did not go to the road games, and I did not want them to go to the road games. They just tried to be the best parents that they could. They didn't fully know what was going on at a trip. Sometimes on the radio you could hear the catcalls from the crowd when you listened to the game. That doesn't begin to give you a flavor.*
>
> *And they got letters. From the time I agreed to sign, we had letters and phone calls from people who were threatening death and those things. They had letters that I had never seen until a few years ago. My sisters kept a lot of those threatening letters. My parents kept it from me. We kept a lot from each other because we didn't want each other to suffer.*

A bright spot for Wallace was his teammates. They supported and worked with him, trying to make a bad situation tolerable. Wallace didn't expect these young teammates who were eighteen, nineteen and twenty years old to be experts and involved in civil rights.

Wallace was an outstanding basketball player for Vanderbilt. In his three varsity seasons, the Commodores were 20-6, 15-11 and 12-14. He was

Perry Wallace (right) with teammates, *left to right*: Thorpe Weber and Rudy Thacker. *Courtesy of Vanderbilt Athletic Communications.*

named second-team all-SEC as a junior and first-team all-SEC as a senior. Wallace was also voted senior team captain by his teammates.

On the university campus, fellow students elected Wallace "Bachelor of Ugliness," the highest honor a male undergraduate could receive. Wallace ranks forty-second on the Vanderbilt career points list with 1,010. Wallace's career stats include 78 games, shooting 443 of 968 (.458) with a 12.9 scoring average. From the free-throw stripe he hit 62 percent (124 of 200). Wallace is one of the Commodores' best all-time rebounders, ranking second (894, 11.5 rpg) behind Clyde Lee.

Wallace graduated from Vanderbilt with a degree in engineering, received a law degree from Columbia University and worked in the Justice Department. In 1992, he was appointed to the Environmental Policy advisory council of the EPA. He was a professor at Howard University and the University of Baltimore. Since 1993, Wallace has been a professor of law at the American University Washington College of

Law and is tenured. Wallace specializes in environmental law, corporate law and finance.

On February 21, 2004, Wallace returned to the Vanderbilt campus and Memorial Gymnasium to receive a high honor. The university officially retired his jersey number, 25. He joined Clyde Lee as having the only men's jerseys retired. The Nashville Metro Council proclaimed it Perry Wallace Day.

Wallace said:

> *Once I got to Vanderbilt I played well, but I wasn't a super star. At the end of my career, I was the second leading rebounder in the history of the university while playing three years on the varsity instead of four years. I wasn't a great shooter or ball handler, but I grew during my years.*
>
> *That is an angle that I try to shed some light on. To be under that type pressure and have to deal with the embarrassment of not being perfect. I had to improve under that type pressure. That's one of the things I was most proud of. They didn't recruit me because they needed somebody who was black. That was the wrong formula and would not have worked.*

CHAPTER 14

COMMODORES EXPLODE FOR 130 POINTS

On December 22, 1970, Vanderbilt and the University of Mississippi got tangled up in an old-fashioned basketball shootout. The 15,400 exhausted Commodore fans got their money's worth.

At the end of the record-breaking night at Memorial Gymnasium, both schools had set one Southeastern Conference record, with sixteen school and individual scoring records. Vanderbilt won the game 130–112, a scoring record that remains today for the Commodores.

Super sophomore Johnny Neumann, who after only eight games was the nation's leading scorer, led Ole Miss in scoring. His 53 points was a game-high and stands today as a Memorial Gymnasium record for most points by an individual.

Roy Skinner's club entered the game with a mediocre 3-4 record. Coach Cob Jarvis led the Rebels at 6-1. Vanderbilt had seven players to score in double figures: Van Oliver (24), Thorpe Weber (18), Rod Freeman (16), Ray Maddux (16), Tom Arnholt (15), Rudy Thacker (15) and Jimmy Conn (10).

The Rebels led at halftime, 60–54, as Neumann went into the locker room with 26 points. Oliver, a junior, started the game at center in place of the struggling seven-foot, four-inch Steve Turner and led the Commodores to a blistering 76 second-half points.

After trailing the Rebels 71–68, the Commodores scored 19 unanswered points and coasted the rest of the game. Ole Miss was held without a field goal for seven minutes in that span.

Ray Maddux collected sixteen rebounds in the 130-point night in 1970. *Courtesy of Vanderbilt Athletic Communications.*

Vanderbilt also out-rebounded Mississippi 64–50 while winning at the foul line 26 of 30 and 16 of 30 for the Rebs. Maddux recorded a game-high 16 rebounds, joining Oliver (15) and Freeman (8) as the Vanderbilt board leaders.

The Commodores shot 51.5 percent (52 of 101) compared to Ole Miss's 50.5 percent (48 of 95). The 100 combined field goals was a then-SEC record. Only the LSU (61) and Loyola Marymount (52) game in 1990 tops the current SEC record with 113. Vanderbilt also had the edge in turnovers, 21–17.

The 242 total points is an SEC record for a pair of conference teams. Vanderbilt's 130 points is eighth best ever for an SEC team. In 1992, LSU beat Northern Arizona 159–86 for the most points scored by an SEC team. The most combined points scored involving an SEC team was in 1990 when LSU defeated Loyola Marymount 148–141 (289 points).

"This is one they will be talking about for a long time," Skinner told the *Tennessean* after the game. "It's a great feeling just to cut loose. And we cut loose tonight. Believe me, it was a great feeling to see Oliver and Maddux take charge of the boards in the last half. During that stretch when we busted it open, they just cleaned it."

Maddux was a six-foot, eight-inch sophomore who was held to just 2 points at the end of the first half. In the second half, he cleared the boards for 14 second-half points to spark Vanderbilt.

"I've been down on the third team and it's mighty dreary when you know that's exactly where you belong," said Maddux, a former all-state performer from Nashville's Stratford High School. "After I played so badly against St. John's, I realized I had lost my confidence.

"But I felt relaxed in the first half, and when Coach Skinner started me in the second half, it set me on fire. 'By golly,' I said to myself, 'if they have this much faith in me, I have to fight.' And everything felt right for me."

Maddux's son, Drew, played Vanderbilt basketball (1995–98) and ranks eighth in all-time scoring with 1,689 points.

Weber was a Commodore senior co-captain and gave all his teammates credit for the scoring barrage and all the aspects of the game. "Van [Oliver] led the way out there on the court," said Weber. "His hustling caught on, and he did a great job. Neumann is a far better all-around player than Pete Maravich ever was. He's unselfish and he's a gentleman on the court. He is also a remarkable shooter."

The tough Mississippi loss did break seven school and individual records. Neumann's scoring outburst erased the Memorial Gymnasium scoring

Van Oliver scored a Vanderbilt team-high 24 points in the Commodores' scoring-record night against Ole Miss. *Courtesy of Vanderbilt Athletic Communications.*

record of 42 points held by Kentucky's Louie Dampier and Vanderbilt's Bo Wyenandt.

"It's a heck of a game to lose, but both teams went after each other and they won," said Jarvis. "We caught this bunch on the wrong night. They wore us down on the boards and hit everything in sight. Maddux had a fine second half. We also had that long dry spell [seven minutes] without a field goal. We only compounded our troubles when we tried to catch up too quickly and made the mistakes."

Vanderbilt finished the season 13-13 (SEC, 9-9) and fourth place in the conference. Ole Miss finished that season with an 11-15 (SEC, 6-12) record.

CHAPTER 15

Vanderbilt Women's Basketball Revived in 1977

When Title IX became law in 1972, the United States government wanted women's sports in high schools and colleges to become equal to the men's competition. Colleges across the nation established basketball as an official sport for the women on campus. Basketball had been played as an intramural sport for decades, as it was with the Vanderbilt women.

Vanderbilt began competing in 1977 with Joe Pepper as the Commodores' part-time coach. One of the first players for the Vanderbilt women was Teresa Lawrence Phillips. She recalled:

> *I have always been a tough competitor because I was the only girl out there playing in our neighborhood in the 1960s. I had to be tough. That was my calling card, being physical and tough. In high school, I participated in tennis, swimming, field hockey, volleyball and basketball. It was an all-girls' school* [Girls Preparatory School in Chattanooga], *and we really didn't compete interscholastically; we mostly played intramurals.*
>
> *At that time, the girls played three-on-three half-court basketball. We wanted to play full court, and they actually hired local people to coach us in intramurals on our campus. We did travel some back in those days to Nashville to play against Harpeth Hall. We went to Atlanta to play Westminster because they would play a full-court game.*

Phillips went to Vanderbilt on an academic scholarship; collegiate sports were not on her mind. There was not an SEC for women's basketball when Phillips arrived on campus, and Vanderbilt did not field an official team. She said:

> *In 1976, they did not have a women's college basketball team; they had a club sport team. In my freshman year, I played for that club sport team. I played center at about five-foot-ten. We did not know at the time that Vanderbilt was planning on forming a women's basketball team. That was good for me because I was bored; studying didn't keep me busy enough. So I went out for the team. I thought we had some possibilities and we might have been pushing ourselves to play intercollegiate.*
>
> *Obviously, they must have been ready to do it. At that time we were AIAW* [Association for Intercollegiate Athletics for Women]. *It really wasn't NCAA; it was a different federation. Tennessee was getting big, and Tennessee Tech had really good teams. The big-name women's teams in those days were Louisiana Tech, Delta State and Old Dominion. So Vanderbilt first went intercollegiate during my sophomore year in 1977–78.*

Pepper was Vanderbilt's first women's basketball coach in a position that was part time. He came to Vanderbilt from Nashville's St. Henry's Elementary School, where he was athletic director, football coach and girls' basketball coach. This is when the modern era of Vanderbilt's women's basketball began.

Vanderbilt played a modest but challenging schedule without scholarship players with teams from the Ohio Valley Conference (OVC) and locals like David Lipscomb, Cumberland, Tennessee State, Volunteer State and Motlow State. Vanderbilt did play future SEC members Mississippi State, Mississippi, Alabama and Auburn. The very first intercollegiate game for Vanderbilt was a 73–60 victory over TSU.

Phillips said:

> *We really treaded the way, and now they are flying with state-of-the-art facilities, offices and locker rooms. Vanderbilt did not have a physical education major, but they did have PE classes. We had to dress in the same locker room as the PE folks. We drove to games in a van. We just had one uniform.*
>
> *We were playing for the love of basketball. I was talking to June Williams* [Stewart] *once—she was the former women's SID* [sports

The modern era of Vanderbilt women's basketball began in the 1977–78 season with this team that was 15-9. *Courtesy of Vanderbilt University Special Collections and Archives.*

> information director] *at Vanderbilt—and she would not take anything for those days. It was the purity of just playing, the friendships and representing your school. There is something still to be said for that.*

Vanderbilt finished that first year with a 15-9 record. The next year, the women of Vanderbilt upgraded their schedule, which produced an 11-16 record. Though the school was still not an SEC member, the schedule did include Auburn, Florida, Mississippi State, Alabama and Georgia. Phillips led that team in rebounding that season. She said:

> *I loved to rebound. I rebound now in my mind when I watch games. I did have the ability to see where the ball was coming off the rim. That helped my rebounding because I was small. I remember a girl at Tennessee Tech that blocked my shot. She was six-foot-five and I believe a second-team all-American.*

> *But there wasn't anything I could do about a girl that size. But going up a girl her size didn't really bother my rebounding. I knew where the ball was coming off. Even now after twenty years of coaching, I always know where the ball is coming off the rim.*

It was at this time that Vanderbilt began helping the program with scholarship players. "About that time, Mount Juliet High School won a state championship, and we got a couple of those girls," said Phillips. "We had Sheila Johansson and Cathy Bender. They were the first big signees we got that were 'name' players. Sheila could have gone to a lot of SEC schools. She didn't have a great career at Vandy because she tore up her knee twice."

Vanderbilt's third season resulted in a 12-14 mark. The university would not play in the SEC until it was organized for the women during the 1982–83 season. During Phillips's senior year, Vanderbilt played Tennessee for the first time under its four-year coach, Pat Head Summitt. Phillips said:

> *It was a big deal at the time to play Tennessee. Even though we got crushed by them* [77–53], *you can say you were on the floor with the Lady Vols. Even though that was in 1979–80, that is still fun to say. We set a good groundwork and built the women's basketball program with part-time coaches. We had coaches who had other full-time jobs. It was a work in progress. I am really proud how Vandy has developed their women's program over all these years. I'm pleased to say that I was there in the beginning.*

During Phillips's final season in a Commodore uniform, the addition of improved players cost her starting position held for two seasons. She seriously doubted if playing basketball was as enjoyable and almost quit the team. She recalled:

> *I was a non-scholarship basketball player, and during my senior* [year], *they began playing the new scholarship players. They wanted to play those really good girls that they had signed from high school. And I almost quit the team over Christmas break. I went home for Christmas, and my father told me that I was not a quitter. He told me not to quit the team and just do my best. That helped me later when I became a coach.*
>
> *I did go back and play on that team despite not starting, but I still played a lot. I realized they were recruiting better players and my role had changed. I really had to make that adjustment.*

Wendy Scholtens was Vanderbilt's first women's all-American in 1980, and her jersey number has been retired. *Courtesy of Vanderbilt Athletic Communications.*

Phillips was also honored with many awards at the conclusion of her athletic career at Vanderbilt. She was the first recipient of the prestigious Lady Commodore Athlete of the Year award given to the best all-around female athlete. In addition, Phillips received the Nashville Civitan's Sportsmanship Award in 1979 and 1980. She was also a student government representative in 1977–78 and was president of the Fellowship of Christian Athletes in 1980. Phillips said of the Athlete of the Year honor:

> *That was one of my proudest moments. I wasn't a great athlete. I believe at the time the award was a mixture of being a good athlete and a good citizen. I believe there were a few other things that went into that award. I like to tell that story to student athletes now about when I almost quit the team.*
>
> *I tell them not to quit and never give up, that right around the corner is a positive that can happen. But you have to persevere. I almost have tears in my eyes thinking about that time and that moment. It made me remember what my dad told me to keep on fighting and working.*

After graduating from Vanderbilt, Phillips took a job in Atlanta. Phil Lee became Vanderbilt's first full-time coach, replacing Pepper in 1980. Phillips

Chantelle Anderson was an all-American and the only SEC Player of the Year for the Commodore women. She is Vanderbilt's all-time leading scorer with 2,604 points. *Courtesy of Vanderbilt Athletic Communications.*

said that she was surprised when Lee offered her an assistant coaching position, which was part time. She had her job transferred to Nashville, and a coaching career began.

"I was able to stay at Vanderbilt for four years as an assistant coach," said Phillips. "We were getting pretty good during those four years. We won the WNIT one year while I was an assistant coach. I was getting a lot of good exposure at that time. We were in the SEC by then."

Phillips coached at Vanderbilt for four years before her reputation as a hard worker and good recruiter paid off. She was hired as the women's head basketball coach at Fisk University. At Fisk, Phillips was 62-38 with two conference championships (Women's Intercollegiate Athletic Conference) and a pair of Coach of the Year awards. Fisk did not offer athletic scholarships.

Phillips's success at Fisk gave her the opportunity to coach at Tennessee State University. In eleven seasons (1989–2000) running the women's basketball program, Phillips compiled a 150-151 record. She was asked to fill in as an interim athletic director on three separate occasions. Phillips resigned as coach to join the administrative side of athletics at TSU. She has been TSU's athletic director since 2002.

Since those humble beginnings of the Vanderbilt women's basketball team, the program has gained national prominence. In thirty-five years, the university only had four head coaches to lead the program. Joe Pepper (1977–80) was 38-39 in three seasons; Phil Lee (1981–91) was 207-126 (SEC, 32-46) in eleven seasons; Jim Foster (1992–2002) was 256-99 (SEC, 84-53) in eleven seasons, while the current head coach, Melanie Balcomb (2003–present), is 238-94 (SEC, 94-52) in ten seasons. Balcomb will enter the 2012–13 season just nineteen victories from passing Foster as the women's all-time winningest coach.

Vanderbilt has produced four all-Americans in Wendy Scholtens (1990), Heidi Gillingham (1993), Sheri Sam (1996) and Chantelle Anderson (2002 and 2003). Scholtens and Anderson are the only Commodore women to have their jersey numbers retired by the university.

Chantelle Anderson is the only SEC Player of the Year for the Commodores. First-team all-SEC members include Wendy Scholtens (1989, 1990, 1991), Heidi Gillingham (1992, 1993, 1994), Shelley Jarrard (1993), Sheri Sam (1995, 1996), Na 'Sheema Hillmon (1998), Zuzi Klimesova (2001), Chantelle Anderson (2002, 2003), Ashley Earley (2005), Dee Davis (2006, 2007), Carla Thomas (2007), Christina Wirth (2008, 2009), Jence Rhoads (2010, 2011) and Christina Foggie (2012).

Though the Commodores have not won a regular-season SEC championship, they have won six SEC Tournament titles (1993, 1995, 2002, 2004, 2007, 2009). Vanderbilt has been to the NCAA Tournament twenty-five times, reaching the Final Four in 1993 with a No. 1 ranking in the country.

CHAPTER 16

C.M. Newton Is a Two-Time Coach of the Year

When Vanderbilt athletic director Roy Kramer was in search of a head basketball coach near the end of the 1980–81 season, a chance meeting landed a veteran and proven winner. C.M. Newton was that man. Newton was one year retired as the successful Alabama head basketball coach and in his first year working in the office of the SEC commissioner. Newton said:

> *I had no thought of coaching again. When I had taken the job at the conference I was fifty years old, and I thought I had enough of coaching. I had coached for twenty-six years and thought it was time for me to do something else. I took the job in the conference office with the idea that I would be the next commissioner of the SEC. Dr.* [Boyd] *McWhorter was the commissioner and was very good about all that.*
>
> *Roy Kramer came to me at the SEC Tournament in Birmingham and said he was going to make a coaching change and wanted me to take the job. Vanderbilt was the only place that I would have left the job I had. There was something about Vanderbilt that made me say yes. At that time in the early 1980s, there were a lot of crazy things happening in intercollegiate athletics.*
>
> *Vanderbilt was the one place where I felt you could truly take the student and still win. At that time, there were a lot of places that were taking guys that had no business being in college. I just decided to roll the dice and do it. It was the best decision I made. The eight years I had there were probably the most fun years for me personally.*

Charles Martin Newton was born in Rockwood, Tennessee, in 1930 but moved to Fort Lauderdale, Florida, with his family when he was only nine months old. He grew up in the Florida city and became a star athlete, participating in basketball and baseball. Newton went to Kentucky on a basketball scholarship offered by Coach Adolph Rupp.

Newton later coached at Transylvania, a National Association of Intercollegiate Athletics (NAIA) school in Kentucky. In twelve years, Newton compiled a 169-137 record. When an opening occurred in 1968 at Alabama, Athletic Director Paul "Bear" Bryant hired Newton. Newton's overall record for the Tide is 211-123 in twelve years.

With the dismissal of Coach Richard Schmidt, who led the Commodores for two controversial seasons, Kramer persuaded Newton to leave the administrative side of basketball for the Vanderbilt campus. Vanderbilt was coming off seasons of 13-13 and 15-14 when Newton took over. Newton's first piece of business was recruiting. He said:

> *Phil Cox was the first guy we signed, and we were very fortunate to get him. I didn't have any recruiting mentality, being in the conference office that one year, and didn't pay any attention to recruiting. A good friend of mine in Kentucky told me about Phil and said he was unsigned. We signed him right away. Then from there we recruited players like* [Barry] *Goheen,* [Barry] *Booker and guys that turned out to be very good players for us.*

Cox would become Vanderbilt's all-time leading scorer with 1,724 points, surpassing the great Clyde Lee (1,691). Cox's scoring mark has been eclipsed by Matt Freije (1,891) and Shan Foster (2,011). Newton said:

> *Everybody talks about Phil being too small, but when I saw him, I thought this guy could really play. The reason he hadn't talked to any other schools was because he wanted to go to Kentucky. Phil was waiting to see if they were going to give him a scholarship. We just jumped in there and convinced him to come to Vanderbilt.*
>
> *We had Jeff Turner, Al McKinney, Jimmy Lentz, Jeff Gary and Ted Young. We had a lot of good players that Coach Schmidt had. They were young, but we had some success with them.*

The 1985–86 recruiting class would make Vanderbilt Commodore history before they graduated. Players like Goheen, Booker, Frank Kornet and Will Perdue were standouts. "They were very skilled and could shoot the ball,"

C.M. Newton was 129-115 leading the Commodores in eight seasons, which is fourth all-time in wins. *Courtesy of Vanderbilt Athletic Communications.*

said Newton. "Little Derrick Wilcox, Scott Draud, Steve Grant and Steve Reese were guys that could play. They knew how to play and shoot. We had some size when you put Kornet and Perdue in the game together, which we did. We had a good inside game."

Perdue would become the SEC Player of the Year as a senior and a first-team all-SEC selection as a junior and senior. He led Vanderbilt in scoring and rebounding both seasons. Perdue's dominance occurred after accepting a red shirt after his sophomore season.

Newton was asked about the sudden change in Perdue's playing ability from one year to the next:

> *Will grew up. It was an academic decision, not an athletic decision, to give him a red shirt after his sophomore year. That year helped him more than anything. In his junior and senior year, Will just dominated the conference. He was not only the SEC Player of the Year in basketball but also the Athlete of the Year in the SEC his senior year. That doesn't happen very often with basketball players. Of course, he had a tremendous career in the NBA. I'm very proud of Will and his continued support, concern and love for Vanderbilt. He has maintained that.*

The 1986–87 season found new rules for college basketball. The 3-point shot and shot clock were implemented. Newton had the foresight to recruit players who would benefit from the changes. He said:

> *I was chairman of the rules committee, so I certainly did see that the 3-point shot would change the college game. We experimented with it in the Sun Belt Conference and other conferences. While I was chairman of the rules committee, we put in the shot clock at forty-five seconds, the 3-point line and the coaches' box. These were three very major changes.*
>
> *Basically, we told our players that we were going to construct our offense around the 3-point shot and eliminate our mid-range jump shot. We will shoot the 3 or take the basketball inside. We eliminated that fifteen- to sixteen-foot shot. We had very good shooters. We were up there in leading the nation in attempts and 3-pointers. It became a very big part of what we were about. They had that "Bomb Squad" stuff that was kind of fun.*

Under Newton's guidance, the rebuilt Commodores were gaining national attention with their "Bomb Squad" and upset victories. During the 1986–87 season, Bobby Knight brought his No. 2–ranked Hoosiers into Memorial Gymnasium and left with a 79–75 loss. Indiana would finish that season as national champion.

The next year, Dean Smith and his confident No. 1–ranked North Carolina team rolled into Nashville with the same outcome. The Commodores squeaked past the Tar Heels 78–76 on a December evening. Newton said:

> *I was talking to Jeff Lebo* [former Tar Heel player] *about that game. The thing he remembered was we fouled him and wouldn't let him shoot the 3-point shot. If you fouled a 3-point shooter, he got two shots. That was the rule at that time. We weren't going to let him shoot the 3, so we just fouled him. He made one of his two foul shots. It was a risky thing. I'd do it again* [rather] *than let him shoot the 3.*

The 1987–88 season was memorable for Vanderbilt fans. The Commodores seemed to hit a peak with blowout wins over Kentucky (83–66), Florida (92–65), Mississippi State (82–66), Tennessee (90–62) and Mississippi (93–68). "We played about as good as a team could play," said Newton. "We were very solid defensively, and we had good board work. We handled the basketball and shot it well. We did all the things you had to do to win."

That exciting season would see the Commodores conclude the season at 20-11 with an appearance in the Sweet Sixteen of the NCAA Tournament. Vanderbilt opened with a win over Utah State that set up a match with No. 8 Pittsburgh. Goheen hit a 3-pointer to bring the Commodores within 3 points with only five seconds remaining. He hit another 3-pointer at the buzzer to send the game into overtime, where Vanderbilt won 80–74.

"When Will Perdue fouled out of that game, I told them we were going to win," Newton said. "And Will did too. When Goheen got the shot and sent it into overtime, we felt confident. Pittsburgh was the No. 1–ranked team in our region, the top seed. It was one of those few times where an 8 or 9 seed beat the No. 1 seed."

Vanderbilt lost its next game to eventual national champion Kansas with all-American Danny Manning leading the way. The Commodores lost to the Jayhawks, 77–64, to end the season. Newton said:

> *We were hoping that Manning didn't have a great night. Manning was a lot like Pete Maravich to me. He is going to get his points, and when they go to him, he creates so well. You had your choice. What we did was to let him get his points. We took the attitude that we would guard him head up and guard the heck out of the rest of them. And hope that he didn't go off. But he had such a great night on us that it didn't work.*

Goheen has become a Vanderbilt legend with his last-second heroic shots to win games. Newton remembers those Herculean nights at Memorial Gym during the 1988–89 season against Georgia:

When we came out of a timeout two points down, Kornet blocked the shot so we came back down the court with the ball. We just talked about how we didn't need a three, we just needed a two. Goheen gets the ball on the fast break with the clock winding down. He dribbles it to the corner and shoots the three and makes it. I'm thinking he doesn't know the score. I went to him and said, "Barry, what in the world were you doing? As intelligent as you are, weren't you listening during the timeout?" He said, "Coach, I knew the score. I just didn't think you could handle overtime."

In that same year, Vanderbilt was involved with one of the most controversial calls by an official that Commodore fans remember today. Vanderbilt entered the January game at Memorial Gymnasium with an SEC record of 4-2. The Florida Gators were 4-3.

The Gators' center was Dwayne Schintzius, who had been involved in some type of skirmish the previous summer that resulted in a fight with tennis rackets. In previous games, Gators' opponents' fans would toss tennis balls at Schintzius. This resulted in a warning to fans that this behavior would result in a technical foul on the home team.

With six seconds left in the game and Vanderbilt ahead 71–70, Kornet pulled down a rebound on a Florida missed field goal attempt and was fouled. Kornet hit the first of a two-shot opportunity but missed the second attempt. Florida secured the rebound and fired the ball down court and out of bounds. The clock revealed one second, and the Commodores would have had possession and an apparent 72–70 win. But as the ball sailed out of bounds, a tennis ball came flying onto the court.

Official John Clougherty charged the scorers' table to call a technical against Vanderbilt. Schintzius stepped to the free-throw line and sank both pressurized free throws. The Commodores lost in overtime, 81–78.

Newton said of the infamous tennis ball game:

It kept us from winning the conference. My gripe at that point was it puts another loss on Florida and we would have won the league. To have that happen and not have any other incidents of things being thrown on the court early without a warning or nothing was to me inexcusable. It cost us the SEC championship. There was one second on the clock, and we've got the ball getting ready to throw it in.

There was no way we were going to lose. We were going to win the game, and then all we've got to do is win no matter what Florida does and we're the champions. It was crazy to call that technical. It could have been

C.M. Newton with Phil Cox, who graduated as Vanderbilt's all-time leading scorer and currently ranks fourth. *Courtesy of the author.*

> *somebody from Florida that threw the tennis ball out there. If you had thirty tennis balls thrown on the court or barrage at Florida then that would have been different. But to have one tennis ball thrown out there and for the official John Clougherty to act that way was inexcusable.*
>
> *I think he just overreacted. Kornet fouled out, and now we've got to go through overtime with Schintzius still in the game and our center fouled out. At the time I told Clougherty, "John, I've always been a forgiving person, but I don't think I will ever forgive you for that."*

Just before that Florida game, Newton announced that he would be resigning at the end of the season to take the athletic director's position at Kentucky. Vanderbilt finished that season at 19-14 and suffered a first-round loss to Notre Dame in the NCAA Tournament. The Commodores finished in second place in the SEC, one game behind champion Florida.

Newton said:

> *I had no thought of leaving Vanderbilt. Kentucky had contacted me in early December and had offered me the athletic director's job. I turned it down. I told them I wanted to coach Vanderbilt, that I was going to retire there. I had an opportunity to meet with their president right after the first of the year on an accidental basis. He convinced me that I was not only wanted but I was needed. The "need" part really got to me.*
>
> *I decided it was my school that was in real trouble. They had all kinds of NCAA problems. It was my school that I had gone to and played for, and being wanted wasn't enough, but being needed tipped it. I talked to Roy* [Kramer] *about it, and we decided that rather than have all the speculation out there, we would go on and announce it. I told our players don't listen to this business about a lame-duck coach. I may be a duck and I may be lame, but I'm not a lame duck.*

Newton's eight-year record at Vanderbilt was 129-115. He was also SEC Coach of the Year in 1988 and 1989. Newton was the Wildcats' athletic director from 1989 to 1999. His overall record as a coach is 509-374. Newton became a member of the prestigious Naismith Memorial Basketball Hall of Fame in 2000 as a contributor to the sport.

So what does Newton think about Memorial Gymnasium?

> *It was and still is very special. It is a wonderful facility. I love the crowd being so involved. The real beauty to me at Vanderbilt is it's a university*

that puts a real emphasis on athletics but understands the true nature of the university, and that's an education.

They have never sacrificed the educational pursuits for athletics. They are one of the few places in this time of big-time athletics where the decisions made are not bottom-line dollar decisions, nor are they on the athletic side. They are academic decisions, and I have always admired Vanderbilt for that.

CHAPTER 17

EDDIE FOGLER BRINGS THIRD SEC TITLE

In December 1967, an ambitious sophomore guard was playing basketball in Vanderbilt's Memorial Gymnasium wearing the colors of North Carolina. In this era of freshman ineligibility, Eddie Fogler was playing in his third collegiate varsity game and first on the road. Nearly twenty-two years later, Fogler would reappear in Memorial Gym as the Commodores' head basketball coach. Fogler said:

> *I did play in and do remember that game. I know North Carolina got beat. When you walk into Memorial Gym for the first time, it just catches your eye because of the configuration. And like most teams when they walk into an arena, they stare around. At Vanderbilt, they stare longer than at other away arenas. But what impressed me more than anything was how good Vanderbilt's team was with the fans' interest of basketball at Vanderbilt.*

Coach Dean Smith's Tar Heels arrived in Nashville during that 1967 match-up with a No. 5 national ranking. The Commodores would surprise the men from Chapel Hill, 89–76. Vanderbilt all-American Tom Hagan, Kenny Campbell and Bob Warren each collected 18 points in the Vanderbilt upset, while Bo Wyenandt added 16. Fogler was scoreless, going 0 for 2 from the field with two rebounds and a pair of fouls.

Fogler had been a North Carolina player (1968–70) and assistant coach for fifteen seasons under Smith. He left the Tar Heels in 1986 for his first head coaching position at Wichita State, where he was 61-32 in three years.

Fogler left the Shockers to replace a departing C.M. Newton at Vanderbilt, who became Kentucky's athletic director.

Fogler said:

> *I had a great comfort zone with the academic part of Vanderbilt. I was aware of their academic reputation and their great interest for basketball. The timing was right. I was very impressed with Coach* [Roy] *Kramer* [Vanderbilt's athletic director]. *It was just time to go.*
>
> *I knew I was taking over a stable program. Of course, Coach Newton had done such a great job there. I knew that I was taking over student-athletes that were committed to being students first. I knew that there was already a good structure in place. Coach Newton did a good job in recruiting. Kevin Anglin and Willie Daunic came in that year as freshmen.*
>
> *You've got to get good players to win. I always thought personally that recruiting to Vanderbilt, most people think it is tougher than most schools. I would disagree, and I believe that Kevin Stallings has shown you can recruit to Vanderbilt. It is unique. There are enough good players out there with good academic criteria and also good enough to win in the Southeastern Conference.*

Fogler's first game as a Commodore was a 65–60 victory at SMU in 1989. Starting for Vandy were Steve Grant, Morgan Wheat, Todd Milholland, Derrick Wilcox and Scott Draud. Eric Reid was injured when the season began. Vanderbilt would finish the season at 21-14 (SEC, 7-11), including five straight victories to end the season with an NIT championship in Madison Square Garden.

"We had lost seven SEC games in a row with a bad stretch, but the gym continued to be packed," Fogler said. "Then we got on a roll and played great. Even when the team was struggling, I thought the team would get back on track. I was not surprised that we won the NIT because we were playing so well."

Fogler's next team (1990–91) was 17-13 (SEC, 11-7) and did receive a bid to the NCAA Tournament with a first-round loss to Georgetown (70–60). Charles Mayes was senior captain that season. Fogler said:

> *My second year, we were a very good, solid team. We really improved. The new players picked up the system that I brought, and the older players got better at it. I do remember we were an eight or nine seed that year and we had the dubious honor of getting Georgetown in the first round with* [Dikembe] *Mutombo and* [Alonzo] *Mourning.*

Eddie Fogler was 81-48 in four seasons at Vanderbilt and the basketball program's only National Coach of the Year. *Courtesy of Vanderbilt Athletic Communications.*

> *The chairman of the basketball committee that year was Jim Delany, my ex-roommate at North Carolina. Even to this day I blast Delany and say, "Thanks a lot, Jimbo, about getting us Mutombo and Mourning." With five or six minutes to go, we were basically tied with Georgetown. They were just too big and too good for us. And if we had won that game, we would have gotten Arizona, the No. 1 seed in the entire country that year.*

In Fogler's third season, the Commodores were 15-15 (SEC, 6-10) and lost to Rhode Island (68–63) in the first round of the NIT. Sitting out that season were transfers Chris Lawson (Indiana) and Billy McCaffrey (Duke), who were gaining a lot of attention in practice sessions. Throughout Fogler's coaching career, he was able to attract top transfers. He joked about signing transfers:

> *I probably wasn't a good enough recruiter out of high school. The North Carolina background that I have certainly was appealing to kids. I know Lawson was interested in Vanderbilt because Indiana played at Vanderbilt*

when he was at IU. So he had seen Memorial Gym and the interest in basketball from the fans, and the state of Indiana was not too far away.

Billy came to Vanderbilt because of my North Carolina background and a mutual acquaintance thought he'd be interested in Vanderbilt. I have had good luck with transfers. Even at South Carolina, I had luck with transfers. A lot of times it's geographical. Transfers are the right way to go if you get the right ones because they are mature. They understand what it takes, and they can't transfer again, so they will work hard for playing time.

Fogler's last season at Vanderbilt was magical and historical. The Commodores produced a school record 28 wins (six defeats) and won the SEC championship with a 14-2 mark. They made it to the Sweet Sixteen with wins over Boise State and Illinois but lost to Temple, 67–59. This was Vanderbilt's third and last SEC title.

Fogler said:

That team was a veteran team. The team was tough as heck; smart as a whip and could really shoot the ball. They played very unselfishly. So we had great chemistry, toughness, intelligence and shooting. We weren't very big or overly athletic, but we had everything else it took to be really good. I think the real key to that team was the senior leadership.

I can remember Kevin Anglin and Bruce Elder both coming in my office wanting to talk. They basically came in and said, "Coach, do you think you can shorten practices some?" And I said, "Nope, we got to do what we've got to do. Why are you asking? Are you guys tired? What's up?"

They thought that if I shortened practices we would be more efficient. I had so much faith and trust in their leadership, and I knew how much they wanted to win. I thought about it during that meeting, and those guys had listened to what I was saying. I did cut practices back, which went against my inclination. This is no joke, but those guys just about coached the team the rest of the year. I didn't do a whole lot. They took care of everything.

Lawson was a solid starting center, and McCaffrey became an all-American guard as a senior. Fogler was named the SEC Coach of the Year and consensus National Coach of the Year. This is the only such national honor for any Vanderbilt basketball coach. Fogler's four-year record at Vanderbilt was 81-48.

At some point in a game, Fogler would ignite the home fans when an incident would cause him to take off his jacket and fling it away. Such was the time when LSU's Dale Brown went to the scorers' table and watched as a Commodore was about to shoot free throws. So when does Fogler rip off his jacket and toss it away in a game?

"Pretty early," joked Fogler. "It is interesting that you would say that. I was just never really comfortable wearing a coat. If you watch college basketball today, you will see that coaches will coach without their coat on. I was ahead of my time. Dale and I went nose to nose after that game. He and I had a disagreement."

Incidents like with Brown are common, and Fogler just shrugs it off as part of the game:

> *I think coaches periodically have little stuff they do during a game. I think during the game, whatever goes on between coaches is really little stuff. It's not very important. It's typically forgotten. But everybody is competitive. Everyone wants to make sure they are on equal footing with what's going on in the game. More than that with coaches' problems usually occur with recruiting and not actual game situations.*

Fogler was asked about the difficulty of the benches in Memorial Gym under the goals and the difficulty of opposing teams playing in the building. He said:

> *I think initially I had problems with the benches. After a while you get used to it. You've got to learn to whistle like Kevin* [Stallings] *does. When his players hear that whistle, they turn their heads. And he stomps his foot to where he has worn out his heels. I don't think there is any doubt that a college basketball game in Memorial Gymnasium is one of the best atmospheres in college basketball in the United States. It is absolutely fabulous.*

Very soon after his fourth season ended, South Carolina made an offer to Fogler to become its new head basketball coach. Rumors were circulating that Fogler had a poor relationship with Vanderbilt's administration or was experiencing a financial situation. Fogler said:

> *I would say I loved my four years at Vanderbilt. My wife and I had a great time and are still very fond of Vanderbilt and Nashville. We have contact with more friends in Nashville than we do in Chapel Hill. No disrespect to my alma mater, but when you are the head coach at a school, it's different*

Vanderbilt won its only national tournament championship with its NIT appearance in 1990. *Courtesy of Vanderbilt Athletic Communications.*

> *than being an assistant coach. You meet so many more people when you are involved as a head coach.*
>
> *The only thing I will honestly say about it, and this is hard to believe, but it's true. I'm not sure why I left Vanderbilt. I really don't know. Now that sounds like bull, but why would I give you bull seventeen years after the fact? I honestly do not know exactly what happened. Obviously, something went awry. I just decided to go to South Carolina.*

Fogler said that he has never regretted leaving Vanderbilt for South Carolina. He coached the Gamecocks for eight seasons at a state university, which was a different challenge for him. Fogler was 123-117 in eight years at South Carolina. His best teams were in 1996–97 at 24-8 (SEC, 15-1), including the SEC championship, and 23-8 (SEC, 11-5) the following year. Fogler's last three years were 8-21, 15-17 and 15-15. Fogler's overall head coaching record at Wichita State, Vanderbilt and South Carolina was 265-197.

Fogler has been a college basketball analyst for Fox Sports in recent years. His son, Ben, was born in Nashville and was four months old when Fogler moved his family to South Carolina. In November 2010, Ben Fogler signed a National Letter of Intent to play golf for Vanderbilt's golf coach, Tom Shaw.

Fogler was asked about the most satisfactory and pleasing part of his coaching career as he looks back. His thoughts were the same as when he left South Carolina:

> *I would say this. I did say and felt like when I resigned from coaching that I was leaving with my dignity, my integrity and my sanity. And I'm proud to say that. I tried very hard to give to the student athletes and the universities that I represented what North Carolina and Coach Smith gave to me. That was very important to me.*

CHAPTER 18

KEVIN STALLINGS LEADS 'DORES INTO THE TWENTY-FIRST CENTURY

When Vanderbilt basketball coach Jan van Breda Kolff resigned at the end of the 1998–99 season, Kevin Stallings was hired as his replacement. Stallings was a successful head coach at Illinois State (1994–99) and had previously been an assistant at Kansas (1989–93) and Purdue (1983–88). He played his college basketball at Purdue (1980–82) and helped the Boilermakers to the Final Four in 1980.

While Vanderbilt sought out Stallings, he had been to Memorial Gymnasium as a basketball recruit long before his hiring. He said:

> *I played one year of junior college basketball, and I made an official visit when Ron Bargatze was an assistant coach at Vanderbilt. He recruited me. I came for a visit during a Vanderbilt/Tennessee game at which my high school teammate Steve Ray played for the Vols. I was offered a Vanderbilt scholarship but didn't take it. I ended up going to Purdue. I had been to Memorial Gym just that one time.*

Stallings is a 1978 graduate of Collinsville High School outside St. Louis. At Illinois State, Stallings was 123-63 (MVC, 75-33), including two trips to the NCAA and two appearances in the NIT. After Stallings's first season directing the Commodores, his record was 19-11 (SEC, 8-8), and the team was selected to the NIT. Vanderbilt fell to Wake Forest (83–68) in the first round. Though playing and coaching in the Big Ten was familiar, Stallings was impressed with the SEC and Vanderbilt basketball. He said:

> *I thought the league was really good when I took the job. Nothing happened to change my way of thinking after that first season. It only confirmed my thinking of how good some of these programs and players were. It was a different type of league from the Big Ten both in playing style and other things. I had been in the Big Eight (now the Big 12), where I had been an assistant at Kansas. It was confirmation for me that we had a lot of work to do, and it would be a tough task building this program where we wanted it to be.*

Leading the Commodores that first year was senior Dan Langhi, who would be named the SEC Player of the Year while averaging 22.1 points per game. Langhi was also named as an all-American. Stallings said:

> *Dan was not picked as one of the top eight guys in the preseason that year. He ended up being the Player of the Year, and Dan averaged just over 22 points a game. The next closest guy in the league was just over 16 points per game. Dan really distinguished himself, and still to this day, he is one of the best scorers and players that I have ever coached.*
>
> *He really was a shot maker and could make shots from the 3-point line and with a great mid-range game. You could post him up, and he could get you baskets and was a terrific foul shooter. Dan was a guy we could utilize in so many ways, and his skills were such that he gave me a lot of flexibility as a coach to run things. He gave us an advantage because of his ability.*

In the next three seasons, Vanderbilt was 15-15 (SEC, 4-12), 17-15 (SEC, 6-10) and 11-18 (SEC, 3-13). However, the Commodores were making progress and on the verge of consistently landing in the top portion of the conference standings. Stallings said:

> *The one thing that I completely underestimated when I took the Vanderbilt job was how long it would take to get where we wanted to be. There are no quick fixes here. You can't go out and recruit like every other team in our league and get a junior college player to fill an immediate need you have with a glaring hole in your roster. You couldn't take a lot of transfers because academically they might not be up to par. I grossly underestimated the length of time it would take to turn the program in the direction that we needed, and thus, those three years we struggled.*
>
> *Fortunately, through the determination and character of guys like Matt Freije, Russell Lakey, Scott Hundley, Jason Holwerda and Corey Smith, we were able to take that 11-18 team minus one guy who transferred and*

Kevin Stallings has seven twenty-win seasons, which is an all-time coaching record for Vanderbilt basketball. *Courtesy of Vanderbilt Athletic Communications.*

> *added Dan Cage to make a run to the Sweet Sixteen. I felt like we were making progress during that time. Obviously, 11-18 was a low point, and I'm sure that I questioned whether we were going to get it turned in the direction that I wanted. I thought we had good enough players and people to do it if it was possible.*

That Vanderbilt squad in 2003–4 had fans forgetting the disappointing 11-18 season, which is Stallings's only losing season in his career. A 23-10 (SEC, 8-8) record with a regular-season victory over No. 4 Kentucky and No. 9 Mississippi State in the SEC Tournament gave the Commodores a No. 6 seed in the NCAA Tournament. They defeated Western Michigan and North Carolina State in the first two rounds.

The Commodores made it to the Sweet Sixteen but lost to the eventual national champions, Connecticut, 73–53. Freije was named first-team all-SEC and all-American while finishing as Vanderbilt's all-time leading scorer (1,891 points). Stallings said:

I will always believe that it was Matt Freije's will, determination and selflessness that enabled our program to turn a corner. We had a lot of rough spots during that year. We had games that were absolutely must-win games. We went to Alabama for a game that we just felt like we had to win. At one point we were ahead 30–9. Matt had 21 points, and the rest of our team had 9 points. Alabama had 9 points. He just made big play after big shot that entire season to really keep us alive.

Then we got it together in the conference tournament. We had some great wins, and we got the sixth seed. We got by Western Michigan, and we ran a back-door play to get a 3-pointer to beat NC State and advance to the Sweet Sixteen. That was really the beginning of the future success that we've had those next several years.

That success enabled us to attract guys like Shan Foster that created future successes, but I look back on that '04 team of great character—a team that really bought into what we were trying to do. They were all about the team. I believe that is what paved the way for future success at Vanderbilt.

The next few years Vanderbilt were 20-14 (SEC, 8-8), 17-13 (SEC, 7-9) and, in 2006–7, 22-12 (SEC, 10-6). The Commodores made it back to the Sweet Sixteen with victories over George Washington and Washington State before losing to Georgetown. For his effort, Stallings was named the SEC Coach of the Year, and Derrick Byars was chosen as the SEC Player of the Year. Stallings said of that 2006–7 season:

In the third game of the season our starting center broke his foot. We went to a makeshift lineup. We started out that season 1-3 and got a lot of rumblings since it had been three years since our first Sweet Sixteen team. That particular team with Derrick Byars, Shan Foster, Alex Gordon, Dan Cage, Ross Neltner and Jermaine Beal probably came as close to reaching its playing potential as any team I had ever coached.

We started Cage at the power forward spot who was six-foot-four, and while that created some disadvantages for us defensively like rebounding-wise, there were some offensive advantages that we gained. We had five guys on the floor that could shoot and pass. Ted Skuchas ended up being a key player for us going down the stretch. It was a team that was difficult to guard because they could shoot and pass so well. Then they became one of the most physical teams that we had despite our lack of size. The thing that I remember so fondly about that team was we started out 1-3 with a home loss to Furman. And that team was a whisker away from the Elite

> *Eight. We probably should have been playing North Carolina to go to the Final Four.*
>
> *Derrick Byars had two unproductive years at Virginia and came in as a junior and played well but* [did] *not dominate the way he could. In his senior year, he turned the corner and began to trust us as a coaching staff. Derrick became a great player and had some of the greatest performances that we've ever had in the years I've been at Vanderbilt. Derrick Byars just became a player that maximized his enormous talent.*

During that season, the Commodores recorded one of their greatest upsets with a home victory over No. 1–ranked Florida (83–70). During the intense game, there was a moment that drew attention to Stallings and Gators' player Joakim Noah. Stallings was seen with the basketball, and Noah attempted to take possession of the ball. Stallings refused to let the ball loose. He said:

> *Somebody had started a cut back-door, stopped and we threw the pass. I happened to have been standing right in the line of the pass. Of course, I was very upset that we turned the ball over. The ball sailed out of bounds and came straight to me. I think certain players like to be in the midst of the action. He* [Noah] *just came over and tried to take the ball out of my hands for an inbound pass.*
>
> *Obviously for him to have the ball was going to be of no consequence because the official had to have the ball before play could begin because we had just turned it over. So it wasn't like he could take the ball and inbound it. I just held on to the ball and gave it to the official. He tried to take it out of my hands and at that particular time wasn't the best idea. A lot of people seemed to enjoy it. It was just one of those things that happened during a game.*
>
> *He didn't say anything to me during that exchange, but I said something to him when he tried to take the ball from me. We laughed about it after the game. That is the best game that any of my teams have ever played, that day against Florida. As far as a team performance, I can't remember any of my teams playing any better than that day. They had to play that well because Florida obviously had a great team.*

The next season, Vanderbilt had its best record in Stallings's era. The team won its first sixteen games on its way to a 26-8 (SEC, 10-6) record. After going 1-4 to begin conference play, the Commodores reeled

Kevin Stallings is known for getting his players' attention across the court by whistling or stomping his foot. *Courtesy of Vanderbilt Athletic Communications.*

off seven straight victories. One of these wins was over No. 1–ranked Tennessee in Nashville.

Vanderbilt received a No. 4 seed in the NCAA Tournament but was upset in the first round by Siena (83–62). Shan Foster became Vanderbilt's all-time leading scorer (2,011 points), an all-American and SEC Player of the Year. Stallings said:

> *That team got off to a great start in the non-conference and really played well. We had some weapons with good perimeter and inside players. That team was able to score, but at the end of the season, I think that I made a mistake. I didn't see it coming when that team developed a mindset that they could outscore anybody. Obviously, as a coach you know that defense is a priority, and our defensive numbers going down the stretch were dismal even though we were able to win games. Our games were getting tougher and tighter.*
>
> *I couldn't get that team at the end of the season to guard the way it needed to in the NCAA Tournament to be successful. And that's what*

happened in that game against Siena. We couldn't guard them. They made a bunch of shots against us, and we couldn't shut them down. During the regular season, we performed especially well offensively. That is probably one of the best offensive teams we've had and one of the leaders in the country in scoring.

Shan was a terrific player and ambassador for us on and off the court. He was a key recruit for us since a lot of high-level schools were after him. He wanted the best of basketball, academics and the best college experience. Shan was a special guy to this university and this program. His Senior Night performance against Mississippi State when he had forty-two points was absolutely the most incredible senior performance. He and Matt Freije had the most memorable Senior Nights that I have seen.

In the next three years, Vanderbilt was 19-12 (SEC, 8-8), 24-9 (SEC, 12-4) and 23-11 (SEC, 9-7). Stallings received his second SEC Coach of the Year honor after the 2009–10 season. Jermaine Beal was named first-team all-SEC after leading Vanderbilt in scoring and assists that season.

There had been a great deal of preseason hype for the 2011–12 season, with the Commodores ranked in the Top 10 of most polls. All five starters—John Jenkins, Jeffery Taylor, Brad Tinsley, Festus Ezeli and Lance Goulbourne—were returning. Added to this team was senior Steve Tchiengang, the top reserve coming off the bench. Expectations were high with Vanderbilt fans, but a slow start can be credited to Ezeli missing the first ten of twelve games due to a knee injury.

This talented squad finished the season at 25-11 (SEC, 10-6) and won the SEC Tournament in New Orleans, defeating Georgia, Ole Miss and No. 1–ranked Kentucky (71–64). This was the Commodores' first conference tournament championship since 1951. In the NCAA Tournament, the Commodores beat Harvard but lost to Wisconsin (60–57) to end their season.

Stallings said:

I think we would have handled the expectations fine had Festus's injury not occurred. Festus was never the same as he had been before at the end of the previous season when he was playing so well. The preseason hype was based on the amount of progress Festus had made in the fact that we could have had a dominant low post player, which there aren't very many in college basketball. Festus just never turned into that guy, not through any fault of his own, but I really believe he would have been that guy had he not been injured. He got injured, and that is part of the game.

That team was as talented as any that we've had for sure. I think it was a little more inconsistent than some of our better teams, which is frustrating for our fans and certainly frustrating for me. It was certainly a talented, physical and athletic group. They did things no other teams in the program's history have done. There were three NCAA Tournaments in a row and a SEC Tournament championship, the first in sixty-one years. That team performed at a high level for a long period of time, but its biggest negative was inconsistency over the course of time. You can look over the years and see that our good teams have been consistent.

The SEC Tournament win was emotional for the fans, players and Stallings. When the tournament was revived in 1979, Vanderbilt had been a disappointing participant, usually bowing out early. The emotion of surprising the Wildcats in the finals was seen when television cameras caught Stallings sitting on the bench after the game with his face buried in a towel. Stallings is not one to show those types of emotions. He remembered:

Our team had been called underachievers and a lot of things. Even when the season was over, the first article I see is that our team underachieved. I felt such a sense of gratitude and relief that they had achieved something that one other team in the program history had ever done. To do it under those circumstances to where the entire arena was decked out in [Kentucky] *blue. It was a road game for all intents and purposes and for the SEC Tournament championship against the No. 1 team in the country.*

And of course I didn't know it at the time, but they were eventual national champions. I was so happy for my players and that team to be able to experience that moment. It was emotional for me. There is a lot of hard work and a lot of time involved. Your life is consumed in trying to make moments like that happen, and to have it occur at that point, with that team in SEC Tournament on the line, was a great feeling.

It is well known that the benches at Memorial Gym are in the end zones and not on the traditional sides of the court. This has been a frustration for visiting coaches and Vanderbilt coaches. It can be entertaining to see Stallings gain the attention of his players who are on the far end of the court by stomping his foot or giving a sharp whistle. All five Commodore players will turn their heads at the same time, glaring toward their bench and coach. Stallings said:

Many years ago, I asked my staff to do an amateurish study on what we could do to get the benches moved to the sides. I brought in some former players that had been around here for long time. I told them I wanted their opinions. I went through how we would have to do this and how we would have to do that to move the benches to the sides.

They were very quiet while I was going through the things we thought would have to take place. So I asked them what they thought. There was silence for a good bit of time, and one guy finally spoke up and said, "Coach, I don't think you've won enough games here yet to do that." [Stallings laughs]

That ended any thoughts we had of moving the benches to the sides. You have to develop some communication mechanisms. I've cut down on stomping my foot since I get heel bruises. The whistle certainly comes in handy. Memorial Gym is a very loud place, and it's difficult to communicate when everybody is on the other end. But that is a good thing to happen.

In thirteen seasons at Vanderbilt, Stallings's all-time record is 261-159 (SEC, 103-105). Including his stint at Illinois State, he is 384-222 overall as a head coach. Entering the 2012–13 season, Stallings is 18 wins away from passing the late Roy Skinner (1959, 1962–76) for all-time wins in Vanderbilt basketball history. In sixteen seasons, Skinner was 278-135. Stallings was asked if passing Skinner's mark is something he's thought about and is looking forward to breaking. He replied:

Not really, and I will tell you why. My guess is it probably took me more years to win those games than it did Coach Skinner. If you stick around in one place long enough you'll set some records—wins and losses. I probably have the most losses. [Stallings laughs]

I think Coach Skinner was such a great coach and a great ambassador of Vanderbilt University, and he was a giver. He gave to people. I know the players that played here for him have a very special feeling about him. Honestly, I hope the players, at least some of them that come through here that played for me, will have a similar feeling about me when they are older and look back and reflect. I don't think it will give me any gratitude to break Coach Skinner's record. He was one of the nicest people I have ever met and truly was a guy that was deserving and worthy of being the all-time wins leader here.

CHAPTER 19

Vanderbilt's Historical Timeline

Vanderbilt became the first college to form a team for an organized basketball game on February 7, 1893. The Commodores took a Nashville trolley to the YMCA located downtown. The Commodores won that historic game 9–6.

Vanderbilt began to play basketball seriously as a university team sport with a four-game schedule in 1900–1. The first recorded win at Vanderbilt came in its second game against the Nashville YMCA, 24–9. Coach W.D. Weatherford's club was 2-2 with two wins over the Nashville YMCA and a loss each to the Nashville YMCA and the Nashville Athletic Club.

In February 1902, Vanderbilt took its first road trip. Traveling by train to Birmingham, the Commodores faced Howard College and the local athletic club. The Birmingham gym was an old warehouse where the baskets were nailed too close to the ceiling. When a shot was attempted with a long arc, the ball would hit the ceiling and fall to the floor. Vandy couldn't adapt in time and lost that game to Howard 33–23 but rebounded (pun intended) with wins over Howard and the Birmingham Athletic Club.

The 1904–5 season was cancelled by the Vanderbilt administration. It was announced that the school's gymnasium was being occupied too much by basketball, therefore interfering with gymnastics. There were no other campus facilities for the basketball team to practice. After a two-year absence, basketball at Vanderbilt resumed in 1906.

Vanderbilt had been practicing at the Old Gym that still exists on the campus today. Built in 1880, the cramped building would not allow for

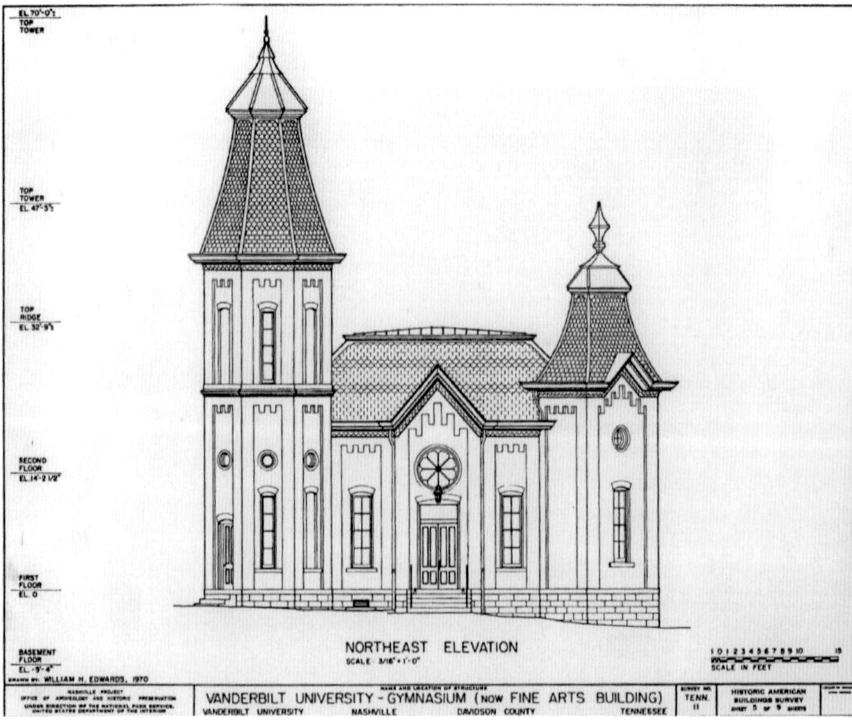

This is a drawing of the Old Gym that was built in 1880. It remains on the Vanderbilt campus today. *Courtesy of Vanderbilt Athletic Communications.*

large crowds, so an alternate site was secured. In 1908, Vanderbilt began playing at the Hippodrome, which was primarily an ice-skating rink. The Hippodrome could be transformed for basketball, indoor baseball, track, boxing and non-sporting events.

In 1907, Vanderbilt played its first intersectional games in Nashville against Columbia and Yale. The Commodores lost both games, 34–16 and 27–23. The Commodores began playing in these early years distant road games such as Mobile, New Orleans, Chicago and New York.

World War I interrupted Vanderbilt's progression in basketball as students joined the armed services to fight in Europe. When the war ended, Vanderbilt settled in and won its first championship in 1919–20 with a 14-4 record. Vanderbilt was a member of the Southern Intercollegiate Athletic Association and defeated teams like Georgia and Georgia Tech.

Vanderbilt first played the University of Tennessee during the 1921–22 season. The Commodores lost both games in Knoxville, 20–5 and 16–15.

The following year, the Commodores beat the Vols for the first time, 28–25, also in Knoxville.

During the 1920s, the SIAA was dissolved, and Vanderbilt became a member of the Southern Conference. Vanderbilt (20-4) won the 1927 Southern Conference championship with former Commodore football great Josh Cody as its coach. The Commodores swept the postseason tournament with victories over Washington and Lee, Mississippi, South Carolina and Georgia.

Vanderbilt broke away from the Southern Conference and became a charter member of the new Southeastern Conference in 1932. The Commodores finished that inaugural season 14-8 (SEC, 11-5) for third place in the league.

Vanderbilt's first star player was Brant "Pinky" Lipscomb (1938–39). The former David Lipscomb College player enrolled at Vanderbilt, bringing his left-handed running hook to the Commodores. Lipscomb was twice named to the SEC all-tournament team, setting several shooting records. Kentucky's Adolph Rupp once proclaimed that Lipscomb was one of the best players to face his Kentucky team.

During the 1943–44 years, Vanderbilt played an informal schedule due to World War II. Former Nashville vice-mayor David Scobey (1943, '45) transferred to Vanderbilt from David Lipscomb and starred for the Black and Gold.

A turning point in Vanderbilt basketball occurred during the 1947 SEC Tournament. The Commodores were shelled by powerful Kentucky, 98–29. This disaster prompted Vanderbilt athletic director Red Sanders to hire a full-time basketball-only head coach. Soon, plans were made for scholarships and a new on-campus gymnasium.

Billy Joe Adcock (1948–50) became Vanderbilt's first basketball scholarship player. Adcock was also the school's first all-American and first all-SEC player. During the 1947–48 season, Adcock was the first Commodore to lead the SEC in scoring, with a 17.1 average. Adcock ranks thirty-second on the Commodores' all-time scoring list with 1,190 points, leading the team in scoring in each of his three seasons at Vanderbilt.

Bob Polk was an assistant at Georgia Tech when he became Vanderbilt's first full-time basketball-only head coach. Polk would coach the Commodores from 1948 to 1961 with time off (1959–60) to recover from a heart attack. Polk ranks third in all-time coaching wins (197-106) in thirteen seasons. Other than Polk, one of the other applicants for that Vanderbilt coaching position was a young coach at Indiana State—John Wooden (later of UCLA fame).

Brant "Pinky" Lipscomb was Vanderbilt's first star player in SEC competition. These 1939 starters were, *left to right:* Joe Little, Ed Hunter, Bob Rymer, Lipscomb and Ross Hanna. *Courtesy of Vanderbilt Athletic Communications.*

In the early Polk era, Vanderbilt was playing home games in area high schools, the Navy Classification Center on Thompson Lane and David Lipscomb College's McQuiddy Gymnasium. Larry Munson was broadcasting Commodores' basketball games on WKDA Radio on a tape-delayed basis.

Polk's first scholarship recruiting class included Dave Kardokus, Gene Southwood, Jack Heldman and Bob Dudley Smith. These recruits played for Vanderbilt for three years from 1950 to 1952.

Under the guidance of Polk and captain George Kelley, Vanderbilt won the 1951 SEC Tournament with a 61–57 upset win over Kentucky. Legend says that the name "Kentucky" was already inscribed on the championship trophy before the Commodores' victory. This was the first SEC Tournament championship for Vanderbilt.

Memorial Gymnasium hosted its first game on the Vanderbilt campus with a 90–83 win over Virginia on December 6, 1952. Only eleven seconds into the game, Commodore Dan Finch scored the first points in the gymnasium with a pair of free throws. Moments later, Finch secured a lay-up to record the first field goal. George Nordhaus recorded a game-high 18 points for Vanderbilt.

In 1955–56, Vanderbilt recorded its home schedule with the first undefeated season at Memorial Gymnasium with a 13-0 record. Other undefeated home-game seasons came in 1960–61 (13-0), 1964–65 (14-0), 1966–67 (14-0), 1992–93 (14-0) and 2007–8 (19-0). Through the 2011–12 season, Vanderbilt has a Memorial Gymnasium all-time record of 724-197 (78.6 percent) in sixty years.

The 1961 SEC championship belonged to Mississippi State. But the Mississippi state legislature prohibited the Bulldogs from attending the NCAA Tournament due to the presence of black players participating on northern teams. Both Vanderbilt and Kentucky finished second (10-4) in the standings, so a playoff game in Knoxville was established. Kentucky won the contest, 88–67. Kentucky would be the SEC representative to the NCAA Tournament that season.

With Polk's retirement, assistant Roy Skinner became Vanderbilt's next head basketball coach in 1962. Skinner (1959, 1962–76) would go on to become Vanderbilt's all-time winningest coach. He won two SEC championships with a record of 278-135 in sixteen years and four SEC Coach of the Year honors.

In 1965, Vanderbilt won its first SEC championship, recording a 24-4 (SEC, 15-1) slate. With Skinner leading, the Commodores advanced to the NCAA Elite Eight, falling to Michigan, 87–85. Clyde Lee, John Ed Miller and Bob "Snake" Grace were part of one of Vanderbilt's most memorable and remarkable teams. Clyde Lee (1964–66), a Nashville David Lipscomb High School star, left Vanderbilt after becoming an all-American and the school's all-time leading scorer (presently ranks seventh). Lee, a two-time SEC Player of the Year, would lead the SEC in rebounding for three seasons. Lee stills holds Vanderbilt's rebounding records in three categories.

One of the first official mascots for Vanderbilt was a basset hound named George in the late 1960s and early 1970s. The dog was originally a pet of former Commodore football player Toby Wilt. It was said that George's front paws pointed in opposite directions. George received a home from an anonymous member of the Board of Trustees and was taken to all the basketball and football games.

The color barrier in the Southeastern Conference was broken with Vanderbilt's signing of Nashville Pearl High School's Perry Wallace. Wallace became the league's first black basketball scholarship player in the 1967–68 season. After enduring threats and racial slurs on the road, Wallace was voted Vanderbilt's most popular student as a senior. Wallace is currently a

Mike Rhodes was a fan favorite at Vanderbilt. Rhodes broke Clyde Lee's scoring record, totaling 1,699 points, and currently ranks fifth all-time. *Courtesy of Vanderbilt Athletic Communications.*

law professor at American University in Washington, D.C. Vanderbilt has retired his uniform number.

Vanderbilt all-American Tom Hagan (1967–69) averaged 19.9 points per game in his career. On March 8, 1969, he scored 44 points on the road against Mississippi State to set the single-game scoring record for a Commodore. The record remains today.

In the late 1960s, Tennessee coach Ray Mears incited Vanderbilt fans with his "walk." In an era of freshman ineligibility, freshman teams were formed and generally played before the varsity game. For a few times in Memorial Gymnasium, during the freshman game, Mears led his varsity team on a walk around the court to its dressing room. Vanderbilt fans were put into an uproar.

On December 22, 1970, Vanderbilt beat Mississippi in Memorial Gymnasium, 130–112. The game produced the most points in a game for the Commodores in their history. The record is also a Southeastern Conference record (two SEC teams) for total points in a game. And this was before the 3-point rule.

Vanderbilt won its second SEC championship in 1974 with SEC Player of the Year Jan van Breda Kolff leading the way. The Commodores secured a 23-5 (SEC, 15-3) record, with Skinner being awarded his third SEC Coach of the Year honor. Vanderbilt lost to Marquette, 69–61, in the first round of the NCAA Tournament.

The famed F-Troop played its final year in a Vanderbilt uniform in 1973–74. The team consisting of Joe Ford, Butch Feher and Jeff Fosnes became one of the most popular and productive classes in Vanderbilt history. Fosnes would become the university's initial first-team academic all-American.

In 1981, Charles Davis and Mike Rhodes (Town and Country) played their final season for the Commodores. Rhodes and Davis battled for the most career points in the school's history. Rhodes erased Clyde Lee's record (1,691) with a total of 1,699 points. Davis scored 1,675 career points.

Phil Cox scored 1,724 career points, becoming Vanderbilt's all-time leading scorer, in 1985. He is currently ranked fourth all-time in scoring. Cox led the Commodores in free-throw percentage in three of his four years. In 1983, Cox hit forty-three consecutive free throws, which is the third all-time record in the SEC and a Vanderbilt record.

The NCAA instigated the 3-point line for the 1986–87 season. Scott Draud hit the first 3-pointer for Vanderbilt against Virginia Commonwealth on November 28, 1986, in the Hawaiian Airlines Silversword Invitational Tournament in Wailuku, Hawaii. Since that game, the Commodores have

Billy McCaffrey was an all-American guard (1993) at Vanderbilt and a two-time first-team all-SEC performer. The transfer from Duke played two years for the Commodores. *Courtesy of Vanderbilt Athletic Communications.*

recorded at least one 3-point goal in every game through the 2011–12 season. That streak has reached 832 games. Only the University of Nevada–Las Vegas and Princeton can make the same claim of scoring at least one 3-pointer in every game.

Under the guidance of Coach C.M. Newton, the Commodores were selected to the NCAA Tournament after a fourth-place SEC finish. Will Perdue, Barry Goheen and Barry Booker led the Commodores to the Sweet Sixteen with wins over Utah State and Pittsburgh. Vanderbilt fell to eventual national champs Kansas, 77–64.

In 1990, Coach Eddie Fogler led Vanderbilt to its only NIT championship. The Commodores defeated Louisiana Tech, Tennessee, New Orleans, Penn State and St. Louis. Scott Draud was named the tournament's MVP.

Billy McCaffrey led the 1992–93 Commodores to their third SEC championship (14-2) and another appearance in the NCAA's Sweet Sixteen. Vanderbilt set a school record with 28 victories with the help of Bruce Elder, Chris Lawson, Dan Hall and Kevin Anglin. McCaffrey was named an all-American, while Eddie Fogler was consensus National Coach of the Year.

In 1995, Ronnie McMahan concluded his career at Vanderbilt just 6 points shy of Phil Cox's all-time scoring record. He did leave as the school's

Jeffery Taylor graduated from Vanderbilt after the 2012 season, finishing his career second in scoring all-time (1,897), and was first-team all-SEC as a senior. *Courtesy of Vanderbilt Athletic Communications.*

all-time 3-point shooter with 296 treys, passing Scott Draud. McMahan has dropped to third behind Shan Foster and John Jenkins.

Kevin Stallings arrived from Illinois State to become the next Vanderbilt coach in 2000. Stallings took a 1999 team that finished 14-15 to a 19-11 record and an NIT berth. Senior forward Dan Langhi was named SEC Player of the Year after averaging 22.1 points per game.

In 2004, Vanderbilt began the season with a 12-0 mark and advanced to the Sweet Sixteen of the NCAA Tournament. Matt Freije concluded his Vanderbilt career as the university's all-time leading scorer (1,891). He currently ranks third all-time.

Vanderbilt recorded its first back-to-back 20-win seasons since the 1993 and 1994 campaigns with a 20-14 mark while appearing in the NIT. The Commodores set school records for 3-pointers (322) and attempts (837); both marks are among the top five in SEC history. Vanderbilt also set a then-home record for wins with 17.

In 2007, the Commodores dropped a 66–65 decision to Georgetown in the Sweet Sixteen of the NCAA Tournament. They defeated seven nationally ranked teams that year, including No. 1 Florida, the eventual NCAA champ. Derrick Byars was named SEC Player of the Year, while Kevin Stallings was honored as SEC Coach of the Year.

In 2008, the Commodores advanced to the NCAA Tournament in consecutive seasons for the first time since 1988 and 1989. On Senior Night, Shan Foster scored 42 points and earned SEC Player of the Year honors. Vanderbilt was 19-0 in Memorial Gymnasium, which is a home record.

Vanderbilt tallied a 23-11 record in 2011. Sophomore John Jenkins led the SEC in scoring (19.5 ppg), and junior Brad Tinsley recorded the first triple-double in the school's history.

In 2012, the Commodores won the SEC Tournament for only the second time in school history. They lost in the second round to Wisconsin in the NCAA Tournament. Kevin Stallings earned a seventh 20-win season to pass the legendary Roy Skinner. Jenkins repeated as the SEC scoring champ (19.9 ppg). Other starters that season were seniors Brad Tinsley, Jeffery Taylor, Festus Ezeli and Lance Goulbourne. Steve Tchiengang was Vanderbilt's top reserve off the bench.

In the 2012 NBA draft, the following Commodores were selected—John Jenkins, twenty-third pick by Atlanta; Festus Ezeli, thirtieth pick by Golden State; and Jeffery Taylor, thirty-first pick by Charlotte. This was the first time that two Vanderbilt players were drafted in the first round (one through thirty).

APPENDIX I

Vanderbilt Men's All-Time Records

Year	Won	Lost	Coach
1900–1	2	2	W.D. Weatherford
1901–2	5	2	W.D. Weatherford
1902–3	6	0	Grinnell Jones
1903–4	6	1	E.J. Hamilton
1904–5	No Scores Recorded		
1905–6	No Scores Recorded		
1906–7	6	1	J.N. (Stein) Stone
1907–8	6	10	W.L. Throop
1908–9	11	4	E.J. Hamilton
1909–10	10	3	R.B. McGehee
1910–11	8	2	Carl (Zeke) Martin
1911–12	9	9	Carl (Zeke) Martin
1912–13	4	5	Oscar G. Nelson
1913–14	6	3	G.T. Denton
1914–15	6	6	G.T. Denton
1915–16	11	3	G.T. Denton

Appendix I

Year	Won	Lost	Coach
1916–17	3	8	G.T. Denton
1917–18	6	3	Ralph Palmer
1918–19	8	2	Ray Morrison
1919–20	14	4	Ray Morrison
1920–21	8	13	Ray Morrison
1921–22	8	8	Wallace Wade
1922–23	16	8	Wallace Wade
1923–24	7	15	Josh Cody
1924–25	12	13	Josh Cody
1925–26	8	18	Josh Cody
1926–27	20	4	Josh Cody
1927–28	5	7	Johnny (Red) Floyd
1928–29	4	13	Johnny (Red) Floyd
1929–30	6	16	Garland (Gus) Morrow
1930–31	16	8	Garland (Gus) Morrow
1931–32	8	11	Josh Cody
1932–33	14	8	Josh Cody
1933–34	11	6	Josh Cody
1934–35	9	11	Josh Cody
1935–36	9	14	Josh Cody
1936–37	6	10	Jim Buford
1937–38	9	12	Jim Buford
1938–39	14	7	Jim Buford
1939–40	10	13	Jim Buford
1940–41	8	9	Jim Buford
1941–42	7	9	Norm Cooper
1942–43	10	8	Norm Cooper
1943–44	12	3	Smokey Harper

Appendix I

Year	Won	Lost	Coach
1944–45	6	6	Garland (Gus) Morrow
1945–46	3	10	Garland (Gus) Morrow
1946–47	7	8	Norm Cooper
1947–48	8	14	Bob Polk
1948–49	14	8	Bob Polk
1949–50	17	8	Bob Polk
1950–51	19	8	Bob Polk
1951–52	18	9	Bob Polk
1952–53	10	9	Bob Polk
1953–54	12	10	Bob Polk
1954–55	16	6	Bob Polk
1955–56	19	4	Bob Polk
1956–57	17	5	Bob Polk
1957–58	14	11	Bob Polk
1958–59	14	10	Roy Skinner
1959–60	14	9	Bob Polk
1960–61	19	5	Bob Polk
1961–62	12	12	Roy Skinner
1962–63	16	7	Roy Skinner
1963–64	19	6	Roy Skinner
1964–65	24	4	Roy Skinner
1965–66	22	4	Roy Skinner
1966–67	21	5	Roy Skinner
1967–68	20	6	Roy Skinner
1968–69	15	11	Roy Skinner
1969–70	12	14	Roy Skinner
1970–71	13	13	Roy Skinner
1971–72	16	10	Roy Skinner

Year	Won	Lost	Coach
1972–73	20	6	Roy Skinner
1973–74	23	5	Roy Skinner
1974–75	15	11	Roy Skinner
1975–76	16	11	Roy Skinner
1976–77	10	16	Roy Skinner
1977–78	10	17	Wayne Dobbs
1978–79	18	9	Wayne Dobbs
1979–80	13	13	Richard Schmidt
1980–81	15	14	Richard Schmidt
1981–82	15	13	C.M. Newton
1982–83	19	14	C.M. Newton
1983–84	14	15	C.M. Newton
1984–85	11	17	C.M. Newton
1985–86	13	15	C.M. Newton
1986–87	18	16	C.M. Newton
1987–88	20	11	C.M. Newton
1988–89	19	14	C.M. Newton
1989–90	21	14	Eddie Fogler
1990–91	17	13	Eddie Fogler
1991–92	15	15	Eddie Fogler
1992–93	28	6	Eddie Fogler
1993–94	20	12	Jan van Breda Kolff
1994–95	13	15	Jan van Breda Kolff
1995–96	18	14	Jan van Breda Kolff
1996–97	19	12	Jan van Breda Kolff
1997–98	20	13	Jan van Breda Kolff
1998–99	14	15	Jan van Breda Kolff
1999–2000	19	11	Kevin Stallings

Year	Won	Lost	Coach
2000–1	15	15	Kevin Stallings
2001–2	17	15	Kevin Stallings
2002–3	11	18	Kevin Stallings
2003–4	23	10	Kevin Stallings
2004–5	20	14	Kevin Stallings
2005–6	17	13	Kevin Stallings
2006–7	22	12	Kevin Stallings
2007–8	26	8	Kevin Stallings
2008–9	19	12	Kevin Stallings
2009–10	24	9	Kevin Stallings
2010–11	23	11	Kevin Stallings
2011–12	25	11	Kevin Stallings

All-Time Head Coaching Records

Years	Head Coach	# Yrs	W	L	Pct.
1901–2	W.D. Weatherford	2	7	4	.636
1903	Grinnell Jones	1	6	0	1.000
1904, 1909	E.J. Hamilton	2	17	5	.773
1907	J.N. Stone	1	6	1	.857
1908	W.L. Throop	1	6	10	.375
1910	R.B. McGehee	1	10	3	.769
1911–12	C.T. (Zeke) Martin	2	17	11	.607
1913	Oscar G. Nelson	1	3	4	.429
1914–17	G.T. Denton	4	30	20	.400
1918	Ralph Palmer	1	6	3	.667
1919–21	Ray Morrison	3	30	19	.388
1922–23	Wallace Wade	2	24	16	.600

Years	**Head Coach**	**# Yrs**	**W**	**L**	**Pct.**
1924–27, 1932–36	Josh Cody	9	98	100	.495
1928–29	Johnny (Red) Floyd	2	9	19	.321
1930–31, 1945–46	Garland (Gus) Morrow	4	31	40	.443
1937–41	Jim Buford	5	48	49	.495
1942–43, 1947	Norm Cooper	3	24	25	.515
1944	Smokey Harper	1	12	3	.800
1948–58, 1960–61	Bob Polk	13	197	106	.650
1959, 1962–76	Roy Skinner	16	278	135	.673
1977–79	Wayne Dobbs	3	38	42	.475
1980–81	Richard Schmidt	2	28	27	.509
1982–89	C.M. Newton	8	129	115	.529
1990–93	Eddie Fogler	4	81	48	.628
1994–99	Jan van Breda Kolff	6	104	81	.562
2000–present	Kevin Stallings	13	261	159	.621
Totals			**1,500**	**1,045**	**.589**

APPENDIX II

VANDERBILT MEN'S RECORDS

POINTS SCORED (CAREER)

	PLAYER	YEARS	POINTS
1.	Shan Foster	2005–8	2,011
2.	Jeffery Taylor	2009–12	1,897
3.	Matt Freije	2001–4	1,891
4.	Phil Cox	1982–85	1,724
5.	Ronnie McMahan	1992–95	1,719
6.	Mike Rhodes	1978–81	1,699
7.	Clyde Lee	1964–66	1,691
8.	Drew Maddux	1995–98	1,689
9.	Charles Davis	1977–81	1,675
10.	John Jenkins	2010–12	1,660

CAREER (PER GAME—MIN. 50 GAMES)

	PLAYER	YEARS	G	FGM	FTM	TP	PPG
1.	Clyde Lee	1964–66	79	633	425	1,691	21.4
2.	Billy McCaffrey	1993–94	66	458	912	1,359	20.6
3.	Tom Hagan	1967–69	76	577	360	1,514	19.9
4.	Jim Henry	1957–59	68	425	348	1,198	17.6
5.	John Jenkins	2010–12	98	517	1,103	1,660	16.9

	PLAYER	YEARS	G	FGM	FTM	TP	PPG
6.	Terry Compton	1972–74	80	527	277	1,331	16.6
7.	Mike Rhodes	1978–81	103	683	333	1,699	16.5
8.	A.J. Ogilvy	2008–10	63	353	622	1,026	16.3
9.	Al Rochelle	1954–57	75	416	374	1,206	16.1
10.	Dan Finch	1952–54	65	356	333	1,045	16.1

SEASON

	PLAYER	YEAR	POINTS
1.	Billy McCaffrey	1992–93	699
2.	John Jenkins	2011–12	696
3.	Shan Foster	2007–8	691
4.	Dan Langhi	1999–2000	664
5.	Billy McCaffrey	1993–94	660
6.	Clyde Lee	1964–65	631
7.	John Jenkins	2010–11	624
8.	Tom Hagan	1968–69	608
9.	Matt Freije	2003–4	607
10.	Will Perdue	1986–87	592

SEASON (PER GAME)

	PLAYER	YEAR	G	FGM	FTM	TP	PPG
1.	Tom Hagan	1968–69	26	246	116	608	23.4
2.	Clyde Lee	1965–66	26	218	153	589	22.6
3.	Clyde Lee	1964–65	28	239	153	631	22.5
t4.	Dan Langhi	1999–2000	30	222	162	664	22.1
t4.	Jeff Fosnes	1974–75	26	238	99	575	22.1
6.	Dan Finch	1953–54	22	165	151	481	21.9
7.	Dan Finch	1952–53	18	124	124	372	20.7

	Player	Year	G	FGM	FTM	TP	PPG
8.	Billy McCaffrey	1993–94	32	217	476	660	20.6
9.	Billy McCaffrey	1992–93	34	241	134	699	20.5
10.	Jim Henry	1957–58	24	182	129	493	20.5

Single Game

	Player	Date	Points
1.	Tom Hagan v. Mississippi State	3-8-69	44
t2.	Shan Foster v. Mississippi State	3-5-08	42
t2.	Bo Wyenandt v. Alabama	2-11-67	42
4.	Clyde Lee v. Kentucky	1-2-65	41
5.	Jim Henry v. Sewanee	12-2-57	40
t6.	Jeff Fosnes v. Jacksonville	12-21-74	39
t6.	Clyde Lee v. Syracuse	12-28-65	39
t6.	John Ed Miller v. Duke	12-11-63	39
t9.	Kevin Anglin v. New Hampshire	12-21-91	38
t9.	Kenny Campbell v. Northwestern	12-21-66	38

Field Goals Made (Career)

	Player	Years	FGM	FGA	Pct.
1.	Shan Foster	2005–8	699	1,483	.471
t2.	Charles Davis	1977–81	683	1,328	.514
t2.	Mike Rhodes	1978–81	683	1,414	.483
4.	Jeffery Taylor	2009–12	665	1,378	.483
5.	Jeff Fosnes	1973–76	651	1,271	.512
6.	Phil Cox	1982–85	641	1,320	.486
7.	Clyde Lee	1964–66	633	1,383	.457
8.	Matt Freije	2001–4	632	1,412	.448
9.	Ronnie McMahan	1992–95	566	1,352	.418
10.	Tom Hagan	1967–69	577	1,114	.504

Field Goals Made (Season)

	Player	Year	FGM	FGA	Pct.
1.	Tom Hagan	1968–69	246	480	.513
2.	Shan Foster	2007–8	242	463	.523
3.	Billy McCaffrey	1992–93	241	436	.553
4.	Clyde Lee	1964–65	239	516	.463
5.	Jeff Fosnes	1974–75	238	432	.551
6.	Will Perdue	1987–88	234	369	.634
7.	Will Perdue	1986–87	233	389	.599
8.	Dan Langhi	1999–2000	222	465	.477
9.	Frank Kornet	1988–89	220	388	.567
10.	Clyde Lee	1965–66	218	457	.455

3-Point Goals Made (Career)

	Player	Years	3FGM	3FGA	Pct.
1.	Shan Foster	2005–8	367	872	.421
2.	John Jenkins	2010–12	306	699	.438
3.	Ronnie McMahan	1992–95	296	774	.382
4.	Scott Draud	1987–88, 1990–91	288	657	.438
5.	Frank Seckar	1993–96	278	675	.419
6.	Sam Howard	1998–2002	246	653	.364
7.	Barry Booker	1986–89	238	535	.460
8.	Drew Maddux	1994–98	226	641	.353
9.	Mario Moore	2003–6	197	559	.352
10.	Matt Freije	2000–4	183	515	.355

3-Point Goals Made (Season)

	Player	Year	3FGM	3FGA	Pct.
t1.	Shan Foster	2007–8	134	286	.469
t1.	John Jenkins	2011–12	134	305	.439
3.	Frank Seckar	1995–96	103	272	.379
4.	Scott Draud	1990–91	101	225	.449
5.	John Jenkins	2010–11	100	245	.408
t6.	Scott Draud	1989–90	90	208	.433
t6.	Shan Foster	2005–6	90	217	.413
t8.	Barry Booker	1988–89	87	194	.449
t8.	Ronnie McMahan	1993–94	87	228	.382
10.	Brendan Plavich	2001–2	86	195	.441

Free Throws Made (Career)

	Player	Years	FTM	FTA	Pct.
1.	A.J. Ogilvy	2007–10	471	641	.735
2.	Bobby Thym	1954–57	453	675	.671
3.	Jeffery Taylor	2009–12	452	652	.693
4.	Matt Freije	2001–4	444	565	.786
5.	Phil Cox	1982–85	442	513	.862
6.	Clyde Lee	1964–66	425	610	.697
7.	Kevin Anglin	1990–93	415	549	.756
8.	Al Rochelle	1954–57	374	498	.751
9.	Tom Hagan	1967–69	360	432	.833
t10.	Butch Feher	1973–76	349	457	.763
t10.	Barry Goheen	1986–89	349	439	.795

Free Throws Made (Season)

	Player	Year	FTM	FTA	Pct.
1.	A.J. Ogilvy	2007–8	176	229	.769
2.	Matt Freije	2003–4	175	229	.788
3.	Billy McCaffrey	1993–94	168	189	.889
4.	Dan Langhi	1999–2000	162	186	.871
5.	Billy Di Spaltro	1996–97	160	208	.769
6.	A.J. Ogilvy	2009–10	158	216	.731
7.	Kevin Anglin	1991–92	155	207	.749
t8.	Al Rochelle	1955–56	153	204	.750
t8.	Clyde Lee	1964–65	153	228	.671
t8.	Clyde Lee	1965–66	153	206	.742

Free Throw Percentage (Career, Min. 150 FTA)

	Player	Years	FTM	FTA	Pct.
1.	Billy McCaffrey	1993–94	302	343	.880
2.	Rudy Thacker	1969–71	152	173	.879
3.	Phil Cox	1982–85	442	513	.862
4.	John Jenkins	2010–12	320	374	.856
5.	Scott Draud	1987–88, 1990–91	232	276	.841
6.	Brad Tinsley	2009–12	243	290	.838
7.	Tom Hagan	1967–69	360	432	.833
8.	Dan Langhi	1996–2000	394	474	.831
9.	Tom Arnholt	1970–72	253	305	.830
10.	Mike Rhodes	1978–81	333	408	.816

Rebounds (Career)

	Player	Years	G	Reb.	RPG
1.	Clyde Lee	1964–66	79	1,223	15.5
2.	Perry Wallace	1968–70	78	894	11.5
3.	Bobby Thym	1954–57	89	872	9.8
4.	Bob "Snake" Grace	1963–65	76	837	11.0
5.	Charley Harrison	1953–56	79	802	10.2
6.	Jeffery Taylor	2009–12	134	752	5.6
7.	Bill Depp	1959–61	71	747	10.5
8.	Will Perdue	1983–88	104	708	6.8
9.	Thorpe Weber	1969–71	78	673	8.6
10.	Anthony Williams	1997–2001	110	669	6.1

Assists (Career—Kept Since 1968–69)

	Player	Years	G	A	APG
1.	Atiba Prater	1996–2000	115	517	4.50
2.	Brad Tinsley	2009–12	134	482	3.59
3.	Frank Seckar	1993–96	126	455	3.61
4.	Kevin Anglin	1990–93	129	435	3.37
5.	Jan van Breda Kolff	1972–74	80	430	5.38
6.	Derrick Wilcox	1987–90	128	423	3.30
7.	Jermaine Beal	2007–10	132	421	3.19
8.	Drew Maddux	1994–98	123	394	3.20
9.	Russell Lakey	2000–4	111	369	3.32
10.	Al McKinney	1981–84	116	351	3.03

Steals (Career—Kept Since 1979–80, Min. 50 Games)

	Player	**Years**	**G**	**S**	**SPG**
t1.	Drew Maddux	1994–98	123	214	1.74
t1.	Frank Seckar	1993–96	126	214	1.70
3.	Atiba Prater	1996–2000	115	211	1.83
4.	James Strong	1996–2000	120	209	1.74
5.	Kevin Anglin	1990–93	129	192	1.49
6.	Russell Lakey	2000–4	111	169	1.52
7.	Ronnie McMahan	1992–95	124	157	1.27
8.	Jeffery Taylor	2009–12	134	146	1.09
9.	Jason Holwerda	2002–5	128	138	1.08
10.	Jermaine Beal	2007–10	132	128	0.97

Blocks (Career—Kept Since 1979–80, Min. 50 Games)

	Player	**Years**	**G**	**BS**	**BPG**
1.	Festus Ezeli	2008–12	121	204	1.69
2.	Will Perdue	1984, 1986–88	104	157	1.51
3.	A.J. Ogilvy	2007–10	96	145	1.51
4.	Julian Terrell	2003–6	124	116	0.94
5.	Chris Woods	1992–95	121	108	0.89
6.	David Przybyszewski	2002–5	128	75	0.59
7.	Ted Skuchas	2004–7	127	72	0.57
8.	Dan Hall	1990, 1992–94	123	70	0.57
9.	Austin Bates	1994–98	111	61	0.55
10.	Malik Evans	1992, 1994–96	108	60	0.56

APPENDIX III

Vanderbilt Women's All-Time Records

Year	Won	Lost	Coach
1977–78	15	9	Joe Pepper
1978–79	11	16	Joe Pepper
1979–80	12	14	Joe Pepper
1980–81	12	16	Phil Lee
1981–82	20	14	Phil Lee
1982–83	12	14	Phil Lee
1983–84	23	9	Phil Lee
1984–85	14	13	Phil Lee
1985–86	22	9	Phil Lee
1986–87	23	10	Phil Lee
1987–88	18	10	Phil Lee
1988–89	21	8	Phil Lee
1989–90	23	11	Phil Lee
1990–91	19	12	Phil Lee
1991–92	22	9	Jim Foster
1992–93	30	3	Jim Foster

Year	Won	Lost	Coach
1993–94	25	8	Jim Foster
1994–95	28	7	Jim Foster
1995–96	23	8	Jim Foster
1996–97	20	11	Jim Foster
1997–98	20	9	Jim Foster
1998–99	13	14	Jim Foster
1999–2000	21	13	Jim Foster
2000–1	24	10	Jim Foster
2001–2	30	7	Jim Foster
2002–3	22	10	Melanie Balcomb
2003–4	26	8	Melanie Balcomb
2004–5	24	8	Melanie Balcomb
2005–6	21	11	Melanie Balcomb
2006–7	28	6	Melanie Balcomb
2007–8	25	9	Melanie Balcomb
2008–9	26	9	Melanie Balcomb
2009–10	23	11	Melanie Balcomb
2010–11	20	12	Melanie Balcomb
2011–12	23	10	Melanie Balcomb

All-Time Head Coaching Records

Years	Head Coach	# Yrs	W	L	Pct.
1978–80	Joe Pepper	3	38	39	.493
1981–91	Phil Lee	11	207	126	.622
1992–2002	Jim Foster	11	256	99	.721
2003–present	Melanie Balcomb	10	238	94	.717
Totals			**739**	**358**	**.674**

APPENDIX IV

Vanderbilt Women's Records

Points Scored (Career)

	Player	Years	Points
1.	Chantelle Anderson	2000–3	2,604
2.	Wendy Scholtens	1988–91	2,602
3.	Harriet Brumfield	1982–85	1,956
4.	Jackie Cowan	1983–86	1,875
5.	Zuzi Klimesova	1999–2002	1,867
6.	Carla Thomas	2004–7	1,774
7.	Donna Atkinson	1983–86	1,656
8.	Barbara Brackman	1982–85	1,631
9.	Christina Wirth	2006–9	1,596
10.	Heidi Gillingham	1991–94	1,593

Career (Per Game—Min. 100 Games)

	Player	Years	PPG
1.	Wendy Scholtens	1988–91	21.3
2.	Chantelle Anderson	2000–3	19.0

	Player	Years	PPG
3.	Harriet Brumfield	1982–85	16.4
4.	Jackie Cowan	1983–86	16.2
5.	Donna Atkinson	1983–86	14.3
t6.	Zuzi Klimesova	1999–2002	14.1
t6.	Barbara Brackman	1982–85	14.1
8.	Carla Thomas	2004–7	13.6
9.	Karen Booker	1984–87	12.8
10.	Sheri Sam	1992–96	12.6

Season

	Player	Year	Points
1.	Wendy Scholtens	1989–90	855
2.	Chantelle Anderson	2001–2	765
3.	Chantelle Anderson	2000–1	722
4.	Harriet Brumfield	1981–82	671
5.	Wendy Scholtens	1990–91	664
6.	Wendy Scholtens	1988–89	653
7.	Barbara Brackman	1981–82	639
8.	Jackie Cowan	1985–86	633
9.	Karen Booker	1986–87	623
10.	Sheri Sam	1995–96	612

Single Game

	Player	Date	Points
1.	Chantelle Anderson v. Mississippi State	2-8-01	41
2.	Chantelle Anderson v. Portland State	12-23-01	40
t3.	Sheri Sam v. Harvard	3-15-96	39
t3.	Wendy Scholtens v. Memphis State	1-24-90	39

	Player	Date	Points
5.	Jackie Cowan v. Cheyney State	2-9-86	37
6.	Wendy Scholtens v. David Lipscomb	1-9-90	36
t7.	Chantelle Anderson v. Tennessee	2-27-03	35
t7.	Chantelle Anderson v. Tennessee	3-25-02	35
t7.	Chantelle Anderson v. James Madison	12-2-01	35
t7.	Donna Harris v. Northern Illinois	1-3-91	35
t7.	Gayle Kinzer v. Belmont	11-21-81	35

Field Goals Made (Career)

	Player	Years	G	FGM
1.	Chantelle Anderson	2000–3	137	1,020
2.	Wendy Scholtens	1988–91	122	959
3.	Jackie Cowen	1983–86	116	800
4.	Zuzi Klimesova	1999–2000	132	779
5.	Harriet Brumfield	1982–85	119	767
6.	Donna Atkinson	1983–86	116	728
7.	Carla Thomas	2004–7	130	706
8.	Heidi Gillingham	1991–94	128	688
9.	Barbara Brackman	1982–85	116	667
10.	Sheri Sam	1992–96	122	625

Field Goals Made (Season)

	Player	Year	FGM
1.	Wendy Scholtens	1989–90	309
2.	Chantelle Anderson	2001–2	295
3.	Chantelle Anderson	2000–1	292
4.	Barbara Brackman	1981–82	277

	Player	Year	FGM
5.	Harriet Brumfield	1981–82	269
6.	Jackie Cowan	1985–86	265
7.	Wendy Scholtens	1990–91	253
8.	Sheri Sam	1995–96	244
9.	Gayle Kinzer	1980–81	242
10.	Aljeanette Bramlett	1981–82	241

3-Point Goals Made (Career)

	Player	Years	Made
1.	Merideth Marsh	2007–10	256
2.	Abi Ramsey	2002–5	252
3.	Caroline Williams	2004–7	238
4.	Christina Wirth	2006–9	235
5.	Julie Powell	1991–94	203
6.	Michelle Palmisano	1995–97	179
7.	Paige Redman	1996–99	173
8.	Rhonda Blades	1992–95	171
9.	Ashley McElhiney	2000–3	165
10.	Ginger Jared	1992–96	162

3-Point Percentage (Career—Min. 100 FGM)

	Player	Years	Made	Att.	Pct.
1.	Caroline Williams	2004–7	238	512	.465
2.	Julie Powell	1991–94	203	460	.441
3.	Hillary Hager	2001–4	142	338	.420
4.	Christina Wirth	2006–9	235	573	.410
5.	Ashley McElhiney	2000–3	165	404	.408
6.	Jillian Danker	1999–2002	158	387	.408

	Player	Years	Made	Att.	Pct.
7.	Abi Ramsey	2002–5	252	620	.406
8.	Ginger Jared	1992–96	162	410	.395
9.	Donna Harris	1990–94	145	368	.394
t10.	Michelle Palmisano	1995–97	179	456	.393
t10.	Christina Foggie	2011–12	132	336	.393

3-Point Goals Made (Season)

	Player	Year	Made
1.	Caroline Williams	2005–6	95
t2.	Christina Foggie	2011–12	91
t2.	Caroline Williams	2006–7	91
4.	Merideth Marsh	2009–10	88
5.	Abi Ramsey	2004–5	87
6.	Michelle Palmisano	1996–97	83
7.	Merideth Marsh	2007–8	81
8.	Christina Wirth	2008–9	80
9.	Shelley Jarrard	1992–93	76
t10.	Christina Wirth	2007–8	71
t10.	Abi Ramsey	2002–3	71

Free Throws Made (Career)

	Player	Years	G	FTM
1.	Wendy Scholtens	1988–91	122	681
2.	Chantelle Anderson	2000–3	137	555
3.	Harriet Brumfield	1982–85	119	422
4.	Carla Thomas	2004–7	130	360
5.	Karen Booker	1984–87	119	334
6.	Dee Davis	2004–7	126	332

	Player	Years	G	FTM
7.	Donna Harris	1990–94	129	303
8.	Ashley McElhiney	2000–3	135	298
9.	Barbara Brackman	1982–85	116	297
10.	Zuzi Klimesova	1999–2002	132	292

Free Throws Made (Season)

	Player	Year	FTM
1.	Wendy Scholtens	1989–90	236
2.	Wendy Scholtens	1988–89	197
3.	Chantelle Anderson	2001–2	170
4.	Wendy Scholtens	1990–91	156
5.	Karen Booker	1986–87	153
6.	Chantelle Anderson	2002–3	147
7.	Chantelle Anderson	2000–1	134
8.	Harriet Brumfield	1981–82	133
9.	Dee Davis	2004–5	117
10.	Merideth Marsh	2009–10	116

Free Throw Percentage (Career—Min. 160 FTA)

	Player	Years	FTM	FTA	Pct.
1.	Wendy Scholtens	1988–91	681	785	.868
2.	Merideth Marsh	2007–10	244	288	.847
3.	Ashley McElhiney	2000–3	298	370	.805
4.	Carla Thomas	2004–7	360	447	.805
5.	Dee Davis	2004–7	332	413	.804
6.	Christina Wirth	2006–9	195	246	.793
7.	Julie Powell	1991–94	195	247	.789
8.	Donna Harris	1990–94	303	393	.771

	Player	Years	FTM	FTA	Pct.
9.	Jackie Cowan	1983–86	273	359	.760
10.	Rhonda Blades	1992–95	252	332	.759

Rebounds (Career)

	Player	Years	G	Reb.	RPG
1.	Wendy Scholtens	1988–91	122	1,272	10.4
2.	Karen Booker	1984–87	119	1,096	9.2
3.	Harriet Brumfield	1982–85	119	1,067	9.0
4.	Zuzi Klimesova	1999–2002	132	964	7.3
5.	Heidi Gillingham	1991–94	128	872	6.8
6.	Jenni Benningfield	2001–4	136	851	6.3
7.	Na 'Sheema Hillmon	1995–98	125	843	6.7
8.	Barbara Brackman	1982–85	116	834	7.2
9.	Chantelle Anderson	2000–3	137	822	6.0
10.	Ashley Early	2002–5	135	811	6.0

Assists (Career)

	Player	Years	G	A	APG
1.	Dee Davis	2004–7	126	730	5.8
2.	Ashley McElhiney	2000–3	132	673	5.1
3.	Jence Rhoads	2008–11	130	547	4.2
4.	Ginger Jared	1993–96	132	516	3.9
5.	Rhonda Blades	1992–95	132	505	3.8
6.	Ashley Smith	1998–2000	90	459	5.1
7.	Deborah Denton	1986–89	117	445	3.8
8.	Allison Floyd	1978–81	102	444	4.4
9.	Cathy Bender	1979–82	105	410	3.9
10.	Jade Huntington	1989–92	119	402	3.8

Steals (Career)

	Player	Years	G	S	SPG
1.	Deborah Denton	1986–89	117	338	2.9
2.	Karen Booker	1984–87	119	293	2.5
3.	Donna Atkinson	1983–86	116	286	2.5
4.	Cathy Bender	1979–82	105	277	2.6
5.	Jade Huntington	1989–92	119	263	2.2
6.	Dee Davis	2004–7	126	241	1.9
7.	Jackie Cowan	1983–86	116	235	2.0
8.	Jennifer Risper	2006–9	120	221	1.8
9.	Rhonda Blades	1992–95	132	218	1.7
10.	Wendy Scholtens	1988–91	122	211	1.7

Blocks (Career)

	Player	Years	G	BS	BPG
1.	Heidi Gillingham	1991–94	128	413	3.2
2.	Angela Gorsica	1994–97	127	368	2.9
3.	Wendy Scholtens	1988–91	122	217	1.8
4.	Chantelle Anderson	2000–3	137	181	1.3
5.	Carolyn Peck	1985–88	117	180	1.5
6.	Carla Thomas	2004–7	130	144	1.1
7.	Mara Cunningham	1991–95	125	128	1.0
8.	Karen Booker	1984–87	119	127	1.1
9.	Harriet Brumfield	1982–85	119	112	0.9
10.	Na 'Sheema Hillmon	1995–98	125	105	0.8

About the Author

Bill Traughber is a researcher and writer of Nashville sports history. He is a graduate of Brentwood Academy and Aquinas Junior College (Nashville). The Nashville-born writer's work has appeared in *Athlon's Baseball Annual*, *Nashville Sports Weekly*, *Titans Exclusive*, *Big Orange Illustrated*, *The City Paper*, *Tennessee Titans Season Review* 2001–2, *Sports Nashville*, *Tennessee Sports Magazine* and *The National Pastime* (SABR).

His first book, *Nashville Sports History: Stories from the Stands*, was published by The History Press in March 2010, and his second book, *Brentwood Academy Football: From a Cow Pasture to a Tradition, 1970–2009* was published in September 2010 by McQuiddy Classic Printing in Nashville, Tennessee. The History Press released a third book, *Vanderbilt Football: Tales of Commodore Gridiron History*, in September 2011.

Traughber's stories have also appeared in these additional publications: Nashville Sounds 2004–12 programs, Nashville Sounds 2007–12 media guides, Brentwood Academy 2004–10 football programs, Vanderbilt University 2004–12 football game programs and Vanderbilt 2008–10 baseball media guides. His work has appeared on several websites, including nashvillesounds.com and vucommodores.com.

He has been recognized as a six-time winner in the Best Feature Writer category and a two-time Writer of the Year recipient as a member of the Tennessee Sports Writers Association. Traughber has won several other writing awards from that organization, including these in Division III as a contributor to the Vanderbilt Athletic Website (Commodore History

Corner): 2012 Writer of the Year, 2012 Best Feature Writer, 2011 Writer of the Year, 2010 Second Place Writer of the Year, 2009 Best Feature Writer, 2008 Second Place Feature Writer and 2007 Third Place Feature Writer.

Some of the author's exclusive interviews have involved Senators Fred Thompson and Lamar Alexander. Celebrities include Pat Boone, George "Goober" Lindsey, Richard Sterban (Oak Ridge Boys) and David Keith. Sports figures include Ralph Boston, Watson Brown, Bobby Johnson, Steve Sloan, Gerry DiNardo, C.M. Newton, Eddie Fogler, Roy Skinner, Kevin Stallings, Will Perdue, Perry Wallace, David Price, Pedro Alvarez, Don Orr, Bill Wade, Pat Toomay, Jeff Fisher, Steve McNair, Eddie George, Bruce Matthews and Bud Adams, among dozens of others.

His memberships include the Tennessee Sports Writers Association (TSWA), Nashville Sports Council, Society of American Baseball Researchers (SABR), United States Basketball Writers Association (USBWA), Football Writers Association of America (FWAA) and the Intercollegiate Football Researchers Association (IFRA).

Traughber's stories have taken him to Cooperstown, New York; Anchorage, Alaska; and the White House in Washington, D.C. He resides in Brentwood, Tennessee.